D0806189

SAMUEL RICHARDSON
AND THE EIGHTEENTH-CENTURY
PURITAN CHARACTER

Samuel Richardson and the Eighteenth-Century Puritan Character

by
Cynthia Griffin Wolff

Archon Books
1972

Library of Congress Cataloging in Publication Data

Wolff, Cynthia Griffin.
    Samuel Richardson and the eighteenth-century Puritan character.

    Includes bibliographical references.
    1. Richardson, Samuel, 1689-1761—Characters. I. Title.
PR3667.W6   823′.6   72-4146
ISBN 0-208-01282-6

© 1972 by Cynthia Griffin Wolff
Published 1972 as an Archon Book
by The Shoe String Press, Inc.
Hamden, Connecticut
All rights reserved
Printed in the United States of America

For Bob, who didn't

01439

Contents

Preface

This study of Richardson began with a sense of *deja vu:* specifically, when I read *Grace Abounding* for the first time, I had the unshakable conviction that its confessional, somewhat obsessive tone reminded me of something else. A re-reading of *Pamela* some years later completed the connection, and my curiosity led me to try to establish the relationship (if there was one) between Richardson's methods and those of Bunyan.

The scope of this book is deliberately narrow: I have tried to limit my consideration of Richardson's novels to an examination of his conception of 'character,' his literary devices for rendering character, and the possible sources of both. In view of this limitation several things follow. In the first place, I have tried to minimize the extent to which I refer to the work of modern critics—citing other works only when they seemed directly relevant to mine. Such a process obviously involves no negative value judgment; many important studies of Richardson are not mentioned merely because they seemed to me not to deal with the questions that I wanted to examine, and I was extremely hesitant to inflate the importance of a modest work with a multitude of footnotes.

The *Grandison* chapter posed special problems. Richardson's last novel is so much less powerful a work of art than either of his others that one might initially be tempted to slight it. On the other hand, his experimentation with the novel of manners seemed to me of very great importance in the development of the novel as a genre. Austen acknowledged it as her favorite novel, and its influence upon her work is unmistakable. This connection, however, posed a second problem: I was repeatedly inclined to define the relationship between *Grandison* and Austen's work, and the last chapter of this book on Richardson threatened to become a brief survey of Austen. I decided, finally, to all but banish Austen from the text, and such appearances as she makes are almost entirely in the footnotes. A reader might find himself more or less constantly thinking forward to Austen's work (as I did); indeed, I suspect that such a contingent view of *Grandison's* importance is inescapable.

I have a number of debts to acknowledge. Perhaps my primary literary debt is to Harry Levin. He was the finest teacher I ever had, and his own work is an admirable model to try to emulate. Moreover, he read the first version of the book with care and patience.

I am endebted to the American Association of University Women for awarding me a year's grant so that I might complete my research and write the book. The staff of Dr. Williams' Library in London was thoroughly courteous and helpful, and without their kindness, I could not have examined much of the Puritan material which is discussed in the book. Mrs. Charlotte Wolff typed the first draft of the book and patiently corrected my spelling.

My husband's ability to interest himself in a subject not entirely central to his own intellectual pursuits was of sustaining and essential importance. And I have already thanked him in an appropriate way.

NORTHAMPTON, MASSACHUSETTS
1972

CHAPTER I

Richardson's Methods of Characterization

When a new form of literature appears or a new literary technique is invented, scholars often tend to discuss it in terms of its antecedents. Perhaps because Richardson was an acknowledged innovator, much of the writing about his novels has followed this pattern: we can find studies which link his work to the French Romance, to earlier epistolary fiction, to the sentimental drama of his day, and to religious literature of the period. Such an approach has obvious value. For one thing, by providing an appropriate historical perspective, it enables the modern reader to examine a work with a knowledge of the literary traditions which would have informed the sensibilities of the original audience. What is more, a study of literary indebtedness can sometimes explain elements of a work which might otherwise puzzle a twentieth century reader.

There is, however, an alternative to this method: instead of asking what existing literary traditions an author drew on, we might ask instead why he ever felt the need to go beyond these traditions. To put it another way, what problem did he encounter that required him to devise new forms or new techniques? If the particular innovative work was a popular success (as Richardson's novels were), we might ask the further question, what needs of the reading public were uniquely served by these literary developments? Certainly we do not dismiss the importance of specific literary indebtedness when we examine innovation in these terms; however, we do somewhat alter our consideration of it. Thus we would tend to ask *why* an author had drawn on one or another of the literary forms in his background (to the exclusion of others that he might have used). What function did this borrowing serve in the solution of his artistic problem?

This study will examine Richardson as a psychological novelist, focusing primarily on his methods of depicting character. And in this capacity Richardson must be seen as doubly inventive. In the first two novels and especially in *Clarissa,* Richardson devised a method of characterization which has justly won him two centuries of acclaim. It is not enough to say that Richardson was capable of exposing hidden motivation and self-deception in these works; earlier writers of fiction—Defoe and even Aphra Behn—had done as much, though less well. Richardson's particular genius lay in his ability to capture the dynamics of character under stress: he anatomizes identity by detailing its disintegration. Thus in *Clarissa,* he investigates the dilemma of a woman who is systematically deprived of the opportunity to engage in those roles which comprise and sustain her identity; and he chronicles in minute detail the crisis of identity which inevitably follows.

Our just admiration at this achievement, coupled with the relative clumsiness of his last novel, has led many critics to overlook the fact that Richardson was equally inventive in *Grandison:* for if *Clarrisa* is the first psychological novel, *Sir Charles Grandison* is the first novel of manners. The most cursory examination will reveal the differences in characterization. Clarissa is isolated, racked with self-doubt, driven to relentless self-examination, and consigned to an apparently endless rehearsal of detail in an attempt to recapture a coherent sense of self. Grandison and those who populate his world are indefatigably sociable. They seem to take positive joy in the many successful human interactions which serve to confirm their confident sense of self-esteem. The problems which they do encounter are almost uniformly external ones: how best to do one's duty, how to spend one's emotion most beneficially, how to accept possible defeat most gracefully. Thus one might say that in *Grandison* Richardson deals with those problems which Clarissa was not fortunate enough to face—problems which can arise only in the lives of people who are offered the opportunity to engage in a variety of well-defined, morally consistent social roles.

These two methods of characterization, so widely different, seem an unlikely combination to have been formulated by the same author. Their dissimilarity, however, masks the underlying relationship between them; for as we shall see in much greater detail, both were responses to the social dilemmas of the day. Richardson's novels were extremely topical, focussing on the skein of problems attending the new, upwardly mobile middle-class—and most particularly on the relationship between social stability and individual character. Massive social change produced a threat to the coherence of personal identity, and the analytical approach to character in *Pamela* and *Clarissa* was Richardson's artistic rendering of this identity crisis. The portrayals in *Grandison,* employing a different mode of characterization, are designed to demonstrate the results of a reestablishment of social order. As the agonized psychological probing of *Pamela* and *Clarissa* is an appropriate way to depict identity in crisis, so the confident social articulation of personality in *Grandison* is appropriate to the assertion of a unified, coherent sense of self.

Finally, if when we consider the question of literary indebtedness we bear in mind the problems that Richardson was attempting to solve, it becomes clear that several different aspects of the novels draw heavily on elements in the Puritan tradition.[1] The upheaval which affected his generation was that social revolution by which diligent Puritans and Puritanical Anglicans were transformed into prosperous businessmen. In their different ways, Richardson's characters are all attempting to adjust to this revolution. Their personalities can clearly be shown to have grown out of the alternatives offered in the Puritan tradition; their solutions are permutations of this tradition. As we shall show later, Richardson's most important literary antecedent, at least in the matter of depicting character, is Puritan devotional literature. The delineation of identity in crisis finds literary expression in the Puritan diary; the portrait of the socially confident and effective personality may be found in the *Saint's Life.* Thus, just as Pamela's, Clarissa's, and Grandison's personal problems develop from the Puritan character, so Richardson's literary innovations grow out of traditional Puritan modes of portraying character.

Although the problems that interested Richardson had to do with personality, we cannot comprehend these problems fully unless we know something about the social conditions which produced them. Recent historians have punctured the myth of "Augustan Peace": England's era of civil disorders had ended, but a period of great social adjustment followed in its wake. To oversimplify (as Richardson, in fact, does), an industrious, highly moral class of Puritanical businessmen were attempting to infiltrate the ranks of an entrenched upper class. All of Richardson's major characters are engaged in secularizing an essentially Puritan attitude, and their difficulties are those which typified one or more generations during the early eighteenth century.

When we speak of Puritanism in the eighteenth century, we are referring not to the religious movement of the sixteenth and seventeenth centuries—nor even solely to the dissenters who were the descendants of that tradition. We are identifying the social system, the family patterns, the attitudes toward oneself that were fostered by the religious ethic and which persisted after its death. By 1700 these patterns were typical not only of dissenters but of many Anglicans as well, especially lower-class Anglicans; as Weber has suggested, they were patterns that shaped the lives of the upwardly mobile businessman. Tawney asserts: "Straitened to no single sect, and represented in the Anglican Church hardly, if at all, less fully than in those which afterwards separated from it, [Puritanism] determined not only conceptions of theology and church government, but political aspirations, business relations, family life and the *minutiae* of personal behavior."[2] When men whose lives embodied the dicta of Puritan morality found increasing prosperity in the expansion of a mercantile economy during the early eighteenth century, their new wealth thrust them into a way of life unlike the one with which they were familiar and in many ways antipathetic to it. Every man who made good suffered at least some personal dislocation; many must have experienced great discomfort.

This social phenomenon might not have captured Richardson's attention had it not been so widespread. However, far from being limited to isolated cases, the disruption took on nationwide proportions. Below the level of the great merchant princes there was "a stratum of businessmen of every kind in every town in the land: country bankers, wholesale dealers, shipowners, shopkeepers and all those other members of the distributing trade who supplied the demands of a population growing in size and wealth. It was a layer that thickened as the pace of economic life accelerated, as the towns grew, as tastes became more sophisticated and pockets fuller. Sir Dudley Ryder, the Attorney General who was created Baron Ryder of Harrowby on the day of his death, came from such a family. His father, the son of a Dissenting parson, was a linendraper, whose shop, at the sign of the Plough and Harrow, was in Cheapside, at the corner of Ironmonger Lane."[3] Such a man as Ryder offers vivid illustration of the hodgepodge of cultures that were lumped together, and he moved from Ironmonger Lane to the palaces of the landed families carrying with him the habits and ways of mind that he had learned in his youth. He appears to have been industrious, conscious of the value of money; true to the Puritan tradition of self-examination and moral bookkeeping, he kept a diary. He was, in this combination of interests and activities, typical of the first and second generations of the mercantile middle class. "They were hardworking, adventurous, abstemious, ingenious and tough. They were frontiersmen breaking new ground, whether it was in adapting machinery, organizing labour, or exploiting new markets with new products. Often from Puritan backgrounds, they were hard on their workers, though not so harsh as they have been made out; . . . they were equally exacting with themselves. And they had boundless ambition."[4]

The result of this social upheaval was a generation of people who were uncertain about how to deal with some of the most commonplace details of their lives. To look at the situation from a printer's or an author's point of view, what emerged was a large reading public that bought books which eased the transition by giving practical advice. For the businessmen (at various levels) there were such works as Defoe's *A Tour thro' the Whole Island of Great Britain*, Richardson's *The Apprentice's Vade Mecum*, and Lillo's play *The London Merchant*. The new journalism—*The Spectator Papers* and *Defoe's Review*, to mention only two of many periodicals—appealed to both husband and wife, as did Richardson's *Familiar Letters* and a number of similarly secretarial books. For the children there was an outpouring of righteous, conservative, lecturing manuals on behavior. Devotional literature, which had tended to focus upon the adult, was now increasingly directed at children. Little catechisms for children, collections of children's prayers, sermons and devotional works designed specifically for the adolescent audience became almost as common as their adult counterparts had been earlier.[5]

Such books deal only with the surface problems. Clearly Richardson was interested in the problems of transition, even at this superficial level; he did write *Familiar Letters* and the *Vade Mecum*. Yet his later work shows that he perceived an even deeper failure of adjustment which the novels are designed to explore; and the best way to understand the personality problems that interested Richardson is to study his historical era in the light of certain modern discoveries in ego psychology.[6] Increasingly, such men as Erik Erikson have investigated the relationship between social environment and personality, and their work has yielded several interesting conclusions.

Although the tendency to form an identity may be innate, identity or character is not. The new-born baby has no character or personality—not even an awareness of the extent and limitations of his own body. The sense of self is born only as the infant begins to become aware of his environment and to distinguish himself from it. Character develops slowly, the product of multiple interactions between the child and his surroundings. His own sense of coherence, his perception of himself as a distinct, individual self, is likewise a product of social interaction. Just as a human is unable to develop a coherent personality unless he has a relatively consistent environment; so once he has developed identity, he continues to need that relatively consistent environment in order to sustain and reconfirm his sense of self. His psychological well-being is thus dependent upon the ability to find external confirmation for the personality he has developed.

Recently, psychologists have begun to wonder what effect rapid historical change would have on individual personality. They have found that because of the intimate relationships between environment and personality formation (and confirmation), instability in the outer world tends to threaten the inner world of identity. The reason is simple. If personality is developed by internalizing certain relationships *as they are defined within the society of which one is a part,* and if a sense of well-being is maintained only when these internalized relationships can be repeatedly confirmed by interaction between an individual and his environment, then any major disruption of that environment will affect the stability of the individual personality. As Erikson observes: "We cannot seperate personal growth and communal change, nor can we separate . . . the identity crisis in individual life and contemporary crises in historical development because the two help to define each other and are truly relative to each other."[7] When an individual is deprived of the opportunity to engage in the roles by which he has come to define himself, his personality is denied rather than reaffirmed. Thus identity crises may have their roots in "the tensions of rapid historical change:"[8] and the sense of dislocation and disruption, the sense even of desolating isolation that frequently afflicts those who are in the throes of an apparently exuberant period of progress and change is nothing more than a reflection of the attendant identity crisis.

What effect will this identity crisis have upon an individual? We might say that the *absence* of acute self-awareness is a sign of well-being. Erikson says: "An optimal sense of identity . . . is experienced merely as a sense of psychological well-being. Its most obvious concomitants are a feeling of being at home in one's body, a sense of knowing where one is going, and an inner assuredness of anticipated recognition from those who count." (Surely, this is an apt description of Charles Grandison.) Conversely, a morbid self-consciousness indicates that something is wrong. We are most aware of our identity "when we are just about to enter a crisis and feel the encroachment of identity confusion."[10] Prolonged introspection, a tendency urgently and repeatedly to question behavior and motives, to doubt the success of one's actions or of relationships with others, to examine the coherence that informs both moral behavior and simple daydreams—these are symptoms of unrest within the personality itself. Sometimes there is the tendency to formulate an objective embodiment of the self—in a diary or a journal, for example[11]—as a hedge against disintegration. Always, there is a dissatisfaction with the present *self* and a desire to regain the happy unself-consciousness that attends the healthy personality.

When an identity crisis has been occasioned by rapid historical change, the individual can find several different ways of resolving his difficulties. Perhaps the most effective is to try to discover roles in the emergent society which correspond to relationships in the individual's past experience—even if these were not previously important or dominant—and by a permutation and alteration of already existing elements within his personality to effect an adjustment to his new environment. Alternatively, he might have to restructure his personality around new roles which have been created to meet the demands of an altered environment. Finally, the individual may resist any change in himself, seeking instead to find a social environment which, like the one that he has lost, will confirm his present personality and not require him to change.

We have seen that rapid social change in the early eighteenth century affected the public lives of those involved in it; as the effects of social transition passed into the family life, as role patterns become uncertain, these historical changes also produced problems of personality. The most complete evidence of this effect can, of course, be found in Richardson's novels. We can, however, get some preliminary insight into the relationship between social change and character if we examine two manuals dealing with familial problems: Defoe's *The Family Instructor* (1715) and *Religious Courtship* (1722).[12] *The Family Instructor* is a series of moral lessons set in the form of dialogues between members of a family. The work focuses on the condition of a person who assumes a conscious definition of self which is contradicted by his behavior; in religious terms, this dilemma is seen as the avowing of pious attitudes by someone whose way of life reveals contempt for religion. Surprisingly, what Defoe portrays here is not so much conscious hypocrisy as the confused state of someone acting "unlike himself"—or at least unlike the person he believes himself to be. In the introduction, Defoe alludes to this state of confusion by saying: "But we are, I say, arrived at a time in which men will frankly own a thing to be their duty which at the same time they dare omit the practice of and in numerable arts, shifts, and turns, they find out to make that omission easy to themselves, and excusable to others. One part of this work is pointed at such, if possible, to make them blush at their unaccountable rashness, and to shame them out of such a sordid inconsistent course, as that of living in the allowed omission of what they acknowledge to be their duty."[13]

The problem which lies at the root of all the difficulties discussed in the manual is that erosion of values which causes the members of a family to be uncertain about their roles: the father and mother are no longer capable of assuming a position of authority; the child perceives discrepancies between his parents' statements and their behavior, and he reverses the traditional relationship by undertaking to catechize them. The small child asks his father: "Do the fathers teach their children [about God]?"[14] The father answers that assuredly they do; and the child counters, "Dear father, you say, the fathers are to teach their children, and are ministers to their families, and you are a minister, and yet I was never taught. I wonder what all this is."[15] The child asks whether he must go to church and pray; the father assures him that he must, and the child answers: "Why, father, you seldom go yourself. It is only for little boys to learn then, is it?"[16] The cause of his moral confusion is, as Defoe clearly indicates, the family's economic success. The older children of the family "had run a great length; they had been indulged in all possible folly and levity, such as plays, gaming, looseness of life, and irreligious behaviour, not immodest nor dishonest: these they were not yet arrived to: but they were bred up in gaiety and gallantry, as being of good fortunes and fashion; but nothing of religion, more than just the common course of going to church, which they did, because it was the custom and fashion, rather than with any other view."[17]

Religious Courtship, the second of Defoe's conduct manuals, deals with more intimate effects of social disruption. The book consists of a series of dialogues between parents and children, sisters and brothers, and couples who are courting—all principally concerned with the problems attendant upon intermarriage. The theme which links all these dialogues is the confusion encountered when an individual's private life becomes bound up with people whose beliefs and practices are unlike his own.

The specific cases which the manual considers ring many changes on the basic problem: what will happen when a man marries a woman of different faith; what problems will arise when a woman marries a man who professes to be religious but who lives as a libertine; what kind of a union will result when two religious people from different faiths marry; what will be the effect upon children when their parents differ about modes of religious worship and proprieties of social conduct; what will happen to a religious servant in an irreligious house; what will happen to a servant in a house whose religion is different from her own; and so forth and so on. Some of the actual problems which Defoe chooses to discuss might well have suggested the plot of either *Pamela* or *Clarissa*.

Even more important, both Defoe and Richardson investigate conflicts about fundamental duties. "Suppose the Husband and Wife . . . have Children, what Foundation of Eternal Schism is there in the Family! Some of the Children adhere to the Father, some to the Mother; some worship *in this Mount;* and some no where *but at Jerusalem;* some go with the Father, some with the Mother; some kneel down with the Father, some with the Mother; 'till as they grow up, they really learn not to kneel down at all; Family-Education, united Instruction, Caution, Example, they are all dreadfully mangled and divided 'till in the End they come to nothing; and the Children grow out of Government, past Instruction, and are all lost." [18] To the extent that the roles which are governed by this confusion of duties form an essential element of the self, then to that extent will personality disorders emerge. Defoe's principal concern in both of these manuals is, of course, religious; only in the novels does he address himself to the psychological dilemmas which are implied here. And it remained for Richardson to explore these dilemmas in depth and detail.

There is, then, a complex skein of essentially social problems which served as the starting point for all of Richardson's novels: defining the duties of a child and the limits of parental authority; adjusting the changing relationship of women and men; interpreting the woman's role—both in the family and in society generally; assessing the value and "power" of money; and defining the boundary between one's obligations to society and one's own moral integrity. Had Richardson's temperament been more given to system-building, his works might have been "problem novels," focusing on the issues themselves and treating them with the specifically philosophical intentions of a Hardy or Huxley. However, he saw the breakdown of social order as important principally insofar as it affected character. Ironically, nowhere in any of the novels does Richardson portray an identity crisis which is, by modern standards, successfully resolved (save, perhaps, in the elusive portrait of Clementina). Clarissa never does attain a new personality which could enable her to resume successful relationships with others. Her suicidal refusal to do so contains, perhaps, an implicit condemnation of the society which she would have had to enter (though Richardson never makes such condemnation explicit). She is true to her own vision and apparently happy to move on to a higher realm of reality, although her friends and Richardson's own audience were less than pleased with her choice. Indeed, taken together, the three novels describe a completed cycle: Richardson begins, with *Pamela,* in social disruption; he moves on in *Clarissa* to explore the devastating effects of that disruption on individual identity; and in *Grandison,* he concludes with the portrayal of a new social order and a new kind of man and woman.

CHAPTER II

Richardson's Sources

Every social system has its own set of idealized character types which help an individual to define himself and others within that system. These ideals change from society to society and within a society from one historical period to another; to list merely a few—the Courtier, the Patriot, the Hero, the Good Worker, the Elder, the Warrior, the Tycoon—is to summon a rich variety of times and places before the imagination. Sometimes these ideals are specifically limited with regard to age, sex, or station: the Courtier is clearly a man (not a woman) of refined birth; an Elder cannot be young. Others can include both men and women, and even children, from many stations: anybody can be a Patriot, and anybody who works can be a Good Worker. These images are almost always evaluative, and simply to classify an individual in terms of one is to make some assessment of his moral stature, of his duties, or of his value to the community; the Good Worker, for instance, is usually a positive image, the Fop a negative, somewhat foolish one. The historian who studies an era and the man who lives within that era both employ these ideals as a way of placing people.

These images of the self play an important psychological role to the individual when he comes to define his own identity. We might aptly term them "ego ideals," images which (as Erikson states) "could be said to represent a set of to-be-striven-for but forever not-quite-attainable ideal goals for the Self."[1] They provide a shorthand way of thinking about oneself and of describing one's relationship to society: for a man to say "I am a Warrior" is, in some groups, to say everything about him that is of general significance. Yet they are, after all, inaccurate ways of defining the self: no man is ever truly and completely a Warrior, though he may spend much of his conscious life in striving to become one. Ego ideals are not single roles or single relationships; rather, one might speak of them as attitudes, manners, sets of expectations that can play a part in many relationships. The man who thinks of himself as a Courtier can manifest this self-image in several aspects of his life (Castiglione has shown us how many); the Tycoon's vision of himself may affect the way he treats his wife, his children, or his employees—it may be reflected in the way he dresses or in the way he spends money.

We have noted that the disappearance of certain key roles in an individual's life can bring about identity crisis; however, the severity of this identity crisis may be lessened by the fact that ego ideals change more slowly and with greater continuity than specific real-life relationships. For example, a woman's image of herself as a Mother is supported in the first instance by her relationship with her own children; when the children grow up, her mothering relationship to them may be completely lost. She can retain her image of herself as Mother, however, by interpreting this ego ideal in a more metaphorical, less literal manner: *Mother* might be transformed into *Motherly Person,* and the woman could sustain this new self-image by adopting a Motherly attitude or manner in any number of roles and relationships still open to her. Such adaptations occur regularly to meet normal changes within the life of each person; and similar alteration of ego ideals can help an individual—or a society—to meet historical change. The Warrior may have great dignity in a society whose primary occupations are hunting and fighting. When the roles that sustain such a society cease to exist, the ego ideal of Warrior (with all the many implications it may have in the numerous roles a man may play) will be lost unless it can be transformed. Hence the Warrior becomes a Sportsman; the Happy Warrior becomes a politican; and the General with no wars to fight becomes an Old Soldier. The specific relationships that initially accompanied the ego ideal are lost; many of the manners and expectations, however, have been retained and applied to new roles through an adaptation of the ego-ideal.

One of the purposes of this study is to demonstrate that Richardson is heavily indebted to English Puritanism, both in his manner of defining character and in the literary methods that he has chosen to portray individuals; and we can clarify the nature of his indebtedness by employing this concept of ego ideal.[2] Thus we would say that he derives his notion of identity or character principally from Puritanism because the ego ideals by which the seventeenth-century Puritan judged himself are the same as those by which the characters of Richardson's novel are defined. The identity crises recorded by all the novels in some measure are occasioned by the loss of the real-life roles which originally sustained these ego ideals; and the resolution of the identity crises is made possible by a modification of Puritan ego ideals, by their redefinition into secular rather than religious terms. Finally, Richardson's methods of characterization are fictional adaptations of those traditional ways of depicting the Puritan character that may be found in the religious literature of private devotion.

There were three ego ideals that dominated the Puritan's image of himself: Puritan as Self-Examiner, Puritan as Virtuous Example, and Puritan as Saint.[3] Each was related to a specific stage of man's religious life. Present-day notions of the "typical" Puritan are most closely related to the ideal of the Self-Examiner, probably because this role was intended to dominate throughout most of a man's life on earth.

Puritanism had carried the isolating movement of the Reformation to its natural conclusion. Both the denial of the minister's role as bearer of God's grace on earth and the espousal of a Calvinist creed, which made the question of salvation foreordained and unique for each man, led to a concentration on the individual soul to the exclusion of all else. It was each man's lonely duty to recognize the occasions of sin in his life (so that they might be avoided), to discover the inclinations to sin within his nature (so that they might be eradicated or at least suppressed), and most important, to prove the existence of a pattern of salvation in his own life (so that he might be comforted in his thoughts of the hereafter). This series of religious tasks was enjoined upon every man, woman, and child from the moment of birth until death; it could be neither evaded nor suspended. Literally hundreds of spiritual manuals were written during the seventeenth century to urge the necessity of lonely self-examination, and when the religious Puritan returned to Anglicanism, he did not cease to use these manuals for guidance. Baxter's works were reprinted throughout the eighteenth century, as were Bunyan's. Foxe's *Book of Martyrs,* the Bible, and Bunyan's works were given to almost every child to assist the early reader in his informal schooling.[4] Lewis Bayly's work, *The Practice of Piety* (given to Clarissa by her family along with *The Whole Duty of Man* so that she might improve her behavior) went into its seventy-first edition in 1792; and Thomas Gouge's *Christian Directions* was reissued in 1733 and again in 1742 (two years after *Pamela*).

The tone of these manuals is universally severe. "Let no day pass thee wherein thou dost not call thyself to a strict account," the spiritual advisors warned. "This task I must confess is somewhat hard to set upon . . . but assuredly the constant use of it shall make a man see better and more comfortable days."[5] Nor was the dilemma of salvation one which could ever be completely resolved during a lifetime; all were cautioned not to seek easy comfort but to "fix both our eyes upon our own unworthiness, vileness, and insufficiency,"[6] since "a holy despair in ourselves is the ground of true hope."[7]

The characteristics or attitudes of the ego ideal associated with this task are those which define the image of the Puritan as Self-Examiner. First there is an inclination to direct one's attention inward toward an inspection of the workings of the mind rather than outward to the events of the world. This tendency might be termed introspectiveness, but it is a rather narrowly defined sort of introspectiveness, specifically preoccupied with the problem of motivation. Thus the potential sinner would be obsessed with asking whether an apparently harmless act had been tainted by hidden desires or by the indirect expression of sinful intentions. Puritan Divines wrote eloquently on the subject of the "secret sin"—that particular weakness which, if undiscovered and unchecked, would destroy man's soul.

The cardinal duty of each Christian therefore, was to discover through extensive self-examination his own secret sins and then to keep watch over them. In *The Practice of Piety* (probably the most popular of all Puritan manuals), Lewis Bayly suggests that each man begin the day with a repentant, self-searching prayer: "Here thou mayest confess unto God thy secret sins which do most burthen thy conscience, with their circumstances of the time, place, person, and manner—how they were committed, saying 'But more especially, O Lord, I do here with grief of heart confess unto thee &c.' "[8] Discovery of the secret sin—or, as we would call it, self-knowledge—was called "Heart Knowledge"[9] and the difficulty of obtaining this Heart Knowledge, even with prolonged and unremitting self-examination, was a major theme of the Puritan manual. "The working of the devil in men's souls (being an invisible spirit) is with such inconceivable sleight and crafty connivance that men in the estate of nature cannot possibly feel it or perceive it."[10] "As in every man there is one element, one humour, and ordinarily one passion predominant, so also one work of darkness and way of death . . . And it is that which his corrupt and original crookedness by a secret sensual inclination and bewitching infusion of Satan singles out and makes special choice of to follow and feeds upon with greatest delight and predominant sweetness."[11]

Now it is impossible to deny that Richardson's novels suffer from a degree of emotionalism, and this is especially true of *Grandison*. However, it is equally true that Pamela and Clarissa are interesting to us because they are so driven to search out hidden motivation, both in themselves and in their lovers. We see them in a time of stress, a period during which their one compelling task is to discover some ultimate truth about themselves. Pamela's ability to know herself is limited (we shall see this more precisely when

we examine the novel later); but even Pamela views herself and those about her as creatures whose hidden motives must be accounted for. The letter-journal is filled
with questioning: why does she stay; what are her feelings toward Mr. B.; why does he give her clothes and
money; what are Colbrand's intentions. One could go on
at length. Clarissa is more sophisticatedly aware of her
own unexpressed desires, and conceives the uncovering of
them to be her single most important task. She repeatedly
urges Miss Howe to read the letters and act as a conscience
to point out weaknesses; and she questions her own motives unendingly. Such passages as the following are
typical: "But let me examine myself: Is not Vanity, or
secret Love of praise, a principal motive with me at the bottom?—Ought I not to suspect my own Heart?" (I, 134).[12]
"But oh, my dear! my calamities have humbled me enough
to make me turn my gaudy eye inward; to make me look
into myself. —And what have I discovered there?—Why,
my dear friend, more *secret* pride and vanity than I could
have thought had lain in my unexamined heart" (II, 264).
"I hope, my dear, I do not deceive myself, and, instead of
setting about rectifying what is amiss in my heart, endeav-
or to find excuses for habits and peculiarities, which I am
unwilling to cast off or overcome. The heart is very deceitful" (IV, 103). A modern reader might miss the significance of Clarissa's remarks, but few eighteenth-century
readers could misinterpret Clarissa's need to "examine
myself," her fear of "secret Love of praise" and "*secret*
pride," and her acknowledgement that "the heart is very
deceitful."[13]

A second characteristic of this Puritan ego ideal is a preoccupation with minutiae, and this trait, too, has theological significance. William Perkins, an early Puritan
Divine, explains the passion for detail. "The smallest sins
are entitled with the same names [as] that sin is which is

expressly forbidden in that commandment to which they
appertain. . . . Hatred is named murther, and to look
after a woman with a lusting eye is adultery."[14] The
Puritan had no church to assure him that he might win
salvation by obeying its rules; he had to discover a pattern
of salvation in his own life, and the proof of such a pattern
could be denied by the most trivial offense. One could
afford to overlook nothing. A general indictment of the
flesh is really an attack upon every element of normal
human life, and there is no ready way to limit the object
of one's watchfulness: any of a man's acts could, by this
logic, condemn him to damnation—eating, breathing,
sleeping, exercising, working, even uttering a prayer
(without *exactly* the proper sentiments).

A third characteristic, closely related to the second, is a
preoccupation with sexuality. Obviously this interest is
merely a refinement of the more general need to monitor
all bodily activities; however, it assumes an importance
which surpasses the others because the Puritan saw this
sensual sin as the most tempting and most dangerous.
Ironically, his fascination with sex makes him seem pruri-
ent (perhaps it was even the case that he fooled himself
and *was* in fact seeking covert gratification of "sinful"
desires). However, the conscious intention was precisely
the opposite: the intention was, by incessant watchfulness,
to prevent sexual sinning.

No one was free from the need to notice and control his
every sexual inclination. As Haller says, "Matrimony,
needless to say, also brought its trials to the spirit. . . .
The man had his part, to provide, to teach, to catechize,
but naturally his wife and her part also invaded his mind,
often without his leave. 'Wandringe thoughtes against my
will' runs one entry in Richard Rogers' diary 'with some
likeing of them about b.' "[15] These thoughts of his wife
even interfered with Rogers' prayers: "I began to wax cold,

the which grew upon me by reason of lingering after Ba[rbara]."[16] Rogers was not alone in his predicament. Owen Stockton's diary is filled with his anxiety concerning lustful thoughts and desires, for he too seems to have been inappropriately fond of his wife. He devises several stratagems to overcome the sin: "In pursuance of those means for mortifying the lust of the flesh, I determined with my wife to say the Promises of God more frequently. . . . I determined also when I should feel the working of any lust presently to look up to Jesus."[17] Elias Pledger, who was not married, confesses his temptations to commit "indecent actions";[18] and he piously extends his desire for purity to the problems of a young female cousin. "On Thursday night I had some discussion with a near relation concerning the many temptations to uncleanness which were offered her from a Beastly Sodomite in the country where she was two or three weeks. But her chastity, by the providence and special grace of God . . . stood invincible, notwithstanding all his solicitations."[19] Some of these accounts, like Pledger's, are amusing; others, like Stockton's, are pathetic. All share, however, the conviction that an unremitting attention to the dangers of sexual feelings— in oneself and others—is a necessary prerequisite for salvation.

Both Pamela and Clarissa demonstrate their preoccupation with minutiae; we see it primarily in their manner of narration. It is a peculiar idiosyncrasy of both, for example, that they almost never draw conclusions or make generalizations about their experiences. Instead, the reader is assaulted by a barrage of words, gestures, descriptions; and long before the heroine herself has pieced these bits of information together, the reader may have surmised explanations that the narrator is apparently incapable of seeing. There is, of course, an advantage to this mode of narration: much of the evocative power in Richardson's novels comes from the immediacy with which we experience the events—an immediacy which would be violated by a narrator sufficiently self-possessed to make moral judgments and evaluations for us. Still, this way of presenting the world, in a flood of curtseys and clothes, pen and ink, compliments and threats—mountains upon mountains of unsifted detail—makes the narrator/heroines seem strangely different from their audience. Most people *do* engage in some kind of subordination when they reflect upon their experience, and especially when they write about it; and this preoccupation with minutiae is a character trait which wants some explanation.

When the heroines carry this attitude even into their descriptions of the attempted seductions, our charge of "peculiarity" may well become an accusation of vulgarity. And yet both charges proceed from an insufficient understanding of the character-ideals which inform the novels. The experiences narrated in the letter-journals have an inescapable religious significance for both Pamela and Clarissa. All of life was, in some sense, a religious trial (as Bunyan had demonstrated); hence the heroines, like their Puritan forerunners, tended to dwell upon the particulars of any given event. The anxiety which attaches particularly to the seductions is a perfectly standard response to what was generally viewed as the most dangerous temptation man had to confront; it was important to record each such temptation because each was a possible occasion of sin. Thus Pamela's conscientious record of Mr. B.'s enticements and Clarissa's agonizingly meticulous chronicle of Lovelace's schemes were not so much salacious in intent as they were moral. These were the temptations to lust. The more frequently they came, the greater the danger; the more consistently they were resisted, the greater the triumph and reassurance of salvation. There may be hypocrisy involved, of course; but it is the hypocrisy of a religious movement, not of any single member. So Pamela seemed, to most of her readers, a woman caught in the throes of trial and uncertainty. It took a critic of rare perspicacity to condemn not the woman but the tradition which had produced her, and Fielding in *Joseph Andrews* seems to have been uniquely qualified.

Finally, there is a fourth characteristic which was an accepted element in the Puritan stereotype of Self-Examiner, and this was the tendency to take conscious account of all virtuous behavior. After all, the tendency to relentless introspection originated in the desire to discover God's preordained pattern in an individual life. Seeking sin and eradicating it fulfilled only half the task; the other half was seeking reassurance. Ideally, this reassurance took the form of a spiritual sense of God's blessing—typically, the Puritan would feel "enlargement" while praying. Often, however, God's blessing was felt in more material terms. Seventeenth- and eighteenth-century manuals encouraged the tendency to translate the theological struggle into more wordly terms; it seemed only natural that the labors of this life should be leavened with detailed descriptions of the reward that awaited the Elect (spiritual hardships to be compensated tangibly). Thus no picture of earthly suffering failed to be accompanied by a glowing portrait of the sanctified Elect. "They shall be all kings and priests: spiritual kings to reign with Christ and to triumph over Satan, the world and reprobates . . . Oh what a comfort is this to poor parents that have many children, if they breed them up in the fear of God and to be true Christians! Then are they parents to so many kings and priests."[20] The equation had an insidious appeal: heavenly riches could be described only by comparing them to the riches of this earth, and (as the theologian might caution) such a view of God's reward was only a metaphor; man cannot really equate God's grace with temporal wealth. However, the subtlety of this distinction was all too often lost, and the Puritan who looked for evidence of God's grace often did so by literally measuring his monetary security. Prosperity could be viewed as proof of God's approval and adversity as a sign of displeasure. A popular seventeenth-century commentary on the Book of Ruth makes this money/virtue equation very clear. "Afflictions are commonly the Lord's witnesses against us for something amiss in us. . . . In affliction let us search out our ways and repent of our sins. . . . The reason why Boaz yieldeth to take her to wife; her portion was her virtues, for which she was generally commended of all. . . . Hence may arise many lessons; . . . virtue maketh even the poor and strangers too to become famous. . . . A godly man will take a wife for her virtues, as Boaz doth here Ruth. . . . Good report for virtue in a woman is a good portion and a means of preferment. . . . Let parents hence learn to bring up their daughters virtuously, it is a good portion and means of preferment. This may comfort poor maidens which be virtuous, and want friends and goods, by a good report yet may they match well; let them strive, therefore, though they want goods, yet to get grace and good conditions, as piety and religion in heart and modesty in countenance, apparel, and gesture; let them preserve chastity. . . . If thus they be beatified and enriched, they have a better portion than many pounds."[21]

It is not a long step from "Ruth Recompense" to "Virtue Rewarded." And both merely reflect the general Puritan tendency to measure virtue according to money. The tendency as seen in Richardson's novels emerges most clearly in the characters of Pamela and Mr. B.: *Clarissa* is a great novel partly because it manages to rise above this rather disagreeable side to the soul-searching Puritan, and when *Grandison* deals with the relationship between money and virtue (Sir Charles would claim such a link), it expands and justifies the simple Puritan equation. Yet in the first novel, Richardson seems to have adopted these offensive expectations almost completely; the striking similarity between Mr. B.'s address to Pamela on the eve of their marriage and the passage quoted above will demonstrate just how thoroughly the attitudes of Richardson's characters echo those of their Puritan forerunners. "To all that know your Story and your Merit, it will appear, that I cannot recompense you for what I have made you suffer. . . . I have Possessions ample enough for us both; and you deserve to share them with me; and you shall do it, with as little Reserve, as if you had brought me what the World reckons an Equivalent: For, as to my own Opinion, you bring me what is infinitely more valuable, an experienced Truth, a well-try'd Virtue, and a Wit and Behaviour more than equal to the Station you will be placed in: To say nothing of this sweet Person, that itself might captivate a Monarch" (II, 132-133). For both Pamela and Ruth, "good report for virtue in a woman is a good portion and a means of preferment."

There is a secondary characteristic associated with this recognition of personal virtue, and that is the tendency to find fault in others. The Puritan presumably spent a good deal of his conscious thought attempting to discover the qualities of the elected Saint in himself. When he received some reassurance about his own doubtful state, it was all too easy to transfer this search from himself to his neighbors. Such a practice was, within limits, condoned and even encouraged by the standard Puritan Divines. For example, in his manual *Christian Directions*, Thomas Gouge has the traditional section concerning watchfulness over one's own soul, and he provides fifty pages of minute instructions for the appropriate execution of this duty. When, however, Gouge comes to discuss behavior in company, the treatise takes a subtle turning. The Puritan, now no longer the subject of his own scrutiny, begins to assume the very qualities of righteousness and virtue which have been the object of his introspection; having assumed them, he transfers his moral energy to the conduct of others. Gouge counsels, "Grieve and mourn for the sins thou discernest amongst bad men. It is noted oft, and commended as a special grace in sundry of God's Saints that they have been greatly troubled in themselves at the dishonor done to God by the sins of others. When thou observest any wickedness committed by thy neighbor reprove him for the same. . . . He who doth not reprove his brother when he seeth him do amiss doth indeed hate him and not love him; for there is no love like the love of reproof, when proper and prudent."[22]

Both Pamela and Clarissa seem to have been impressed with the necessity of such a duty. Pamela's apparent smugness tends to take the form of self-congratulation: she is obsessed to record every compliment she receives, every sign of virtue that has been noted by others. However, her attempts at reformation—reclamation of a rake, as Richardson was ruefully to term it—are limited to Mr. B. Much more of Clarissa's character reflects this aspect of the Self-Examining ideal. From the very beginning of the novel, Clarissa defines herself in terms of conscious moral superiority (she is struggling with the sin of Pride, as we shall see later). Thus the captious behavior which flowers in her relationship with Lovelace has already been well-established in the relationship with her family. She taunts her brothers and sister with their weaknesses; and when they retaliate, she defines the situation in a way that further enhances her own merit. "Indeed, my dearest love [Permit me to be *very* serious] I am afraid I am singled out (either for my own faults, or for the faults of my family, or perhaps for the faults of both) to be a very unhappy

creature!—*signally* unhappy! . . . *Strange*, I may well
call it; for don't you see, my dear, that we seem all to be
impelled, as it were, by a perverse fate, which none of us
are able to resist? —And yet all arising (with a strong appearance of self-punishment) from ourselves? Do not my
Parents see the hopeful children, from whom they expected a perpetuity of worldly happiness to their branch-
ing family, now grown up to answer the till now distant
hope, setting their angry faces against each other, pulling
up by the roots, as I may say, that hope which was ready to
be carried into a probable certainty? (II, 263-264). Early in
the novel, Miss Howe warns her of this too-conscious
virtue. "Why should you, by the nobleness of your mind,
throw reproaches upon the rest of the world? Particularly,
upon your own family—and upon ours too?" (II, 182).
And Lovelace is also aware of the significance of her
remonstrating posture. "Her whole air . . . expressed a
majestic kind of indignation, which implied a believed
superiority of talents over the person to whom she spoke"
(III, 54). There is no doubt that Clarissa carries this common Puritan tendency to its limits—adapting the characteristic to meet the needs of her own very complex nature—
just as Pamela's brand of self-esteem is unique. Yet their
similiarity to those self-righteous, witch-burning men of
God in the seventeenth century is not accidental.

   What is striking about these characterizations is not that
they exhibit isolated resemblances to elements in the Puritan character; rather the complex set of attitudes and expectations that dominate them—concern with motivation;
preoccupation with minutia, especially the minutia of
sexual temptation; and conscious recognition of "good"
behavior—were the very tendencies that defined the Puritan ego ideal of Self-Examiner. The modern reader might
well miss the connection (Richardson's reader probably
would not) because the specifically religious element has

been dropped. That is, this was an ego ideal that had originally been sustained by a series of well-defined spiritual
tasks; the drama was almost entirely internal. When
Richardson adopts this ego ideal, the theological roles
which had sustained it were, for the most part, gone;
worldly ambition had replaced religious fanaticism in the
life of the Puritan-turned-merchant. Hence the drama
tends to move outward: Pamela has her way to make in
the world, and the coupling of her "Virtue" with this
heightened attention to worldly success makes the girl
and the novel both seem shoddy. *Clarissa* surpasses *Pamela*
because it returns to the inner life: the novel really *is* about
temptation and self-examination; and when Clarissa dies,
she moves on to the traditional reward of the Puritan Saint
(as described by Miss Howe in her long concluding letter).

When Richardson chooses a method of characterization
appropriate to these essentially Puritan prototypes, he
uses literary modes which had been devised earlier by Puritan writers. Yet his audience was not the theologically
concerned audience of the seventeenth-century dissenters;
Richardson's public was impatient with excessive moralizing and eager for diversion. Thus his novels, aiming to
give instruction in the guise of entertainment, fuse two
quite different traditions. In form they grow out of the
epistolary genre; in content and technique, however, they
are indebted to the Puritan tradition.

This appears a very odd combination. Richardson found
all novels morally suspect—remember the lesson of Polly
Horton, seduced into wicked ways by a mother who indulged her fancy for "Romance and Novels, Songs and
Plays, and those without distinction, moral or immoral"
(*Clarissa*, VIII, 294)—and in Richardson's day, the epistolary novel had been put to rather scandalous use by such
authors as Mrs. Manley, who wrote *New Atalantis*, and
Hughes, whose popular "translation" of the Heloise-Abe-

lard correspondence was notable chiefly for its interpolated amorous detail. Richardson took pains to distinguish his own work from the common run of epistolary fiction. In the preface to *Clarissa* he warns "considerate readers" not to "enter upon the perusal of the Piece before them as if it were designed *only* to divert and amuse. It will probably be thought tedious to all such as dip into it, expecting a *light Novel*, or *transitory Romance*; and look upon Story in it . . . as its *sole end*, rather than as a vehicle to the Instruction" (I, XV). Yet an epistolary novel could be expected to attract a wide (if initially unsuspecting) audience; Richardson, a life-long trader in books, would have been aware of this. The shrewd little businessman made it a positive moral good to become a bestseller, thereby conveying his moral lesson to as wide an audience as possible.

Richardson's technique of combining genres did not begin with his novels. Katherine Hornbeak offers a penetrating insight into the general influence of Puritanism on Richardson's style. Discussing *Familiar Letters,* she observes that "although in *form* Richardson's book is a *letter-writer*, in *spirit* and *content* it is very closely allied to the *domestic conduct books.*"[23] She accounts for the literary marriage in the following way: "If we wish to orient Richardson's work, if we wish to make a genetic study of the letter-writer and the novels, we must approach them by way of the books which were most widespread among the middle class, the social stratum to which Richardson and his readers belonged. . . . Devout dissenters and Anglicans in the sixteenth and seventeenth centuries eschewed fiction and read books of edification, such as . . . Jeremy Taylor's *Holy Living* and *Holy Dying,* Foxe's *Book of Martyrs,* etc. In these books Richardson and his readers had their roots."[24] Certainly one implication of Hornbeak's work is that in *Familiar Letters* Richardson responded to the Puritan-Cavalier conflict by trying to effect a literary synthesis of the two traditions. The novels simply continue this effort.

Richardson, himself, frequently confirms such an interpretation—as, for example, in the following excerpt from a letter to Lady Bradshaigh.

> Read my Story through and you will see that in the Example Clarissa sets, Meekness of Heart is intirely consistent with that Dignity of Mind, which on all proper Occasions she exerts with so much distinguishing Excellence, as carries her above the irascible Passions. . . .
>
> You will before now have the whole work courting your *Acceptance* and *Perusal*. If it may not have the Honour of the Latter, you must not however deny it that of the former— Be pleased in this Case to honour the Volumes with a Place with your Taylor's Living and Dying, with your Practice of Piety, and Nelson's Fasts and Festivals not as being worthy of such Company, but that they may have a *Chance* of being dipt into Thirty Years hence. For I persuade myself, they will not be found utterly unworthy of such a Chance, since they appear in the humble Guise of a *Novel* only by way of Accomodation to the Manners and Taste of an Age overwhelmed with a Torrent of Luxury, and abandoned to Sound and senselessness.[25]

The epistolary elements of the novels are those which seem most evident to the modern reader; evidently it was the Puritan elements which most interested Richardson.

Capturing the character of the Self-Examining Puritan posed literary difficulties for seventeenth-century dissenters, and they devised a number of techniques specifically designed to solve the problem. The principal difficulty originated in the fact that the Puritan's most important psychological and spiritual task—that of continuously doubting and questioning the very nature of his own identity—permitted him to arrive at no stable or coherent definition of self. If he fulfilled his religious duties rigorously, he was in a state of perpetual crisis. One way in which the Puritan pursued a definition of self was by the keeping of a diary. The journal thus conceived would not be the record of *events* in the individual's life, certainly not one of events in the public world; it was to be a chronicle of his inner life, a record of the complex workings of his mind and an account of God's dealings with him. The diary became for its author a kind of *alter ego*. Regular entries were to be made spontaneously and honestly, with no form or order imposed upon them save the chronological order of a daily record and the unifying viewpoint of the single individual to whom everything had happened. Yet, of course, order did eventually emerge. Form and characterization merged. Recurrent events became important *because* they were recurrent; their very frequency indicated something about the narrator's life just as his reactions to them gradually revealed the inner self. For instance, the man who was concerned about his tendency to laziness would voice that concern, perhaps not every day, but often. Over a period of time, this voiced concern appeared and reappeared, just as the concern itself did in his life. In this way the Puritan diary genuinely became an accurate mirror of its author's inner life. "I will rise in moderate time, neither excessively early nor remarkably late; I suppose generally about six o'clock. . . . I began my good resolutions with rising at five this morning, and if I can go on to do so every morning, it will be a considerable step gained. . . . I will never be in bed, if I can well help it after five o'clock. . . . Since my return home, I have most shamefully trifled away my time by lying in bed far too late. . . . I lamented the misspending of my time, especially by lying in bed."[26] In this way of portraying character, it is the emergent *pattern* of events and emotions (rather than, say, their placement in a structured chain of events) that determines their importance. Needless to say, such a method of characterization is not economical: it requires repetition, verbosity, redundancy; and only by patiently accepting these qualities can the diary's reader discover the identity embodied in the work. To *impose* order (thereby, perhaps, making the personality of the diarist more readily accessible) would be to violate the very function that this form of characterization was designed to serve.

There is a breathless quality to many of these diaries—entries made in haste before the significance of an important happening could be distorted by the selective process of memory. "This afternoon I felt a strong desire to enjoy more liberty in thinking upon some vain thing which I had lately weaned myself from. . . . If I had not either written this immediately or by some other means met with it, I had almost been gone from this course and become plainly minded and idle as before."[27] The very act of writing could help protect one from sinful inclinations; certainly the act of writing on the moment could protect the diarist from his own tendency to self-deception. "Enter resolutions in your note books," a diarist warns. "The truth is [that a] Christian's note books more faithfully register than their hearts; and [it is] easier for the devil to blot out a good resolution out of our minds than out of our books."[28]

Because the process of writing itself became a comfort and served a vital function in the diarist's sense of spiritual well-being, most diarists express their sense of relief at the help a diary could give them in fulfilling the virtually impossible standards for self-knowledge that their creed set. One diarist begins: "What follows I intend for the help of my memory concerning the work of God on my soul, which I desire thankfully to commemorate."[29] Another diarist writes, "This was the first year in which I began to keep an account of my time in this method. If the Lord bless me I mean to hold on, and I hope use will make me more and more perfect in it; 'tis a pleasing, profitable, heavenly art."[30] The diary provided an objective embodiment of the author's personality—one which revealed a certain coherence, one which could be studied and understood—and any threatened loss of the manuscript was a source of anxiety. As one diarist observes: "Mr. St. . . . going for London was stopped and searched. The warrant was for me also. [This occurred during the period of the persecution of nonconformists.] His diary was taken from him; the Lord prevent any prejudice from it either to himself or any other. I have found a great deal of good by this way of review daily and am loth to give it over."[31]

There is no doubt that the process of externalizing the self so that it might be examined was a significant act of piety and one which was urged by many Puritan theologians: in 1656 a devotional manual entitled *The Journal or Diary of a Thankful Christian* was published by John Beadle, a preacher who wished to set out methodical instructions for the keeping of a diary; and as late as 1728, the noted dissenting Divine Isaac Watts wrote, "And do Thou instruct me how to write down my sins and Thy mercies, that I may not forget what Thou hast done for me, and what I have done against Thee."[32] However, the fact that the diary was an external, coherent embodiment of personality was even more important to the psychological well-being of its author. The occupation of watching over the body invited the Puritan to define himself largely in terms of the righteous will, obsessed to eradicate any vestige of human weakness and fleshly corruption. Such a definition of self is dangerous; for the iron will is undeniably a punishing rod, and as it grows stronger, the distinction between the "Self" that controls and examines and the "Self" that conceals and sins may break down. Both selves necessarily inhabit the same sinful flesh; the damning will and the sinful humanity of the individual Puritan insensibly merge, and as the power to condemn is refined, it may lead to an inescapable, diffused anxiety.

In large numbers of these diaries, one discovers a pathetic expression of despair, a sense of unworthiness, of sin, of impending doom and disaster which has no identifiable link with any specific or correctible sin. Henry Newcome reflects, "I should never think I have no need to pray to God. . . . We are *always in danger.* Evils may arise of nothing."[33] "I was in great distress, being under the power of slavish, causeless fear," another diarist confesses;[34] and still another complains, "To be afraid where no fear is, is sometimes the sin of God's people, and oftentimes the punishment of wicked me."[35] Children brought up in such a tradition quite naturally absorbed this sense of fear, often before they were at all able to comprehend any reason for it. It was accompanied by a view of the world as an essentially inimical place; and by a kind of perverse logic, which is, of course, quite consistent with the Puritan's general condemnation of the body, the child came to see these dangers in the world as the result of his own essential unworthiness. Oliver Heywood reports an example of such behavior. "My John, on Lord's day sennight being Nov. 4, I being from home and my maid out of the house, at her return found him weeping bitterly, sore bleared, having begun it as he was reading a chapter [of the Bible]. She of a long time could not get from him the cause; he still sobbed and took on very heavily. At last he told her it was because he had sinned against God and had offended Him."[36] The child was only seven at the time, and Heywood's comment on the incident is: "Blessed be God for this beginning of God's work upon his heart."[37]

Sometimes, then, a diary is not so much the embodiment of personality as the pathetic chronicle of the struggle to preserve sanity and identity. This objectified self, formless as it might appear, reveals coherence to the eye of its

examiner. It records God's blessing as well as man's transgressions. And most important, it offers a way of obtaining psychological distance between the persecuting conscience and the despicable sinner. That is, a man who read
his own diary might judge its contents (and thereby himself) harshly; yet there is a real and psychologically reassuring distinction between himself in the role of reader (and
judge) and himself as subject (and sinner). This distance
then provides a means of controlling (limiting, if you will)
the destructive scope of his condemnation. The impulse to
suicide might be transformed into the resolution to reform.

These qualities, then—the merging of characterization
and form by the use of repetition, wordiness and redundancy; the technique of writing to the moment; the objective embodying of the narrator so that he might examine
himself; and even the use of the diary-*alter ego* as a way of
maintaining sanity—can all be found in Richardson's
novels. Perhaps the most revealing way to demonstrate
their presence is to look at his idiosyncratic use of the letter.
One might suppose that the fundamental criterion for a
letter is that it be a means of exchanging information; a
letter presupposes the existence of a relationship, and this
simple fact is the implicit basis for the traditional letter-
books, which describe the appropriate attitudes and
rhetorics for different relationships. Certainly the letters
of Richardson's characters are written with some desire to
inform their recipient, but in *Pamela* and *Clarissa* this
motivation is surprisingly weak.[38] For one thing, though
these heroines may want to tell what is happening to them,
they rarely listen to their correspondents' advice or comments on that experience. Pamela consistently fails to heed
her parents' advice to come home, and Clarissa just as
consistently ignores all the practical advice that her pleas
elicit from Miss Howe. The letters are irregularly answered;
and, most surprising of all, they continue to be written

even when the heroine sees no opportunity for sending them to their correct recipient or for receiving an answer. Pamela writes letters and hides them under rocks in the garden; Clarissa writes letters and sews them into her clothing.

The obsessive need to write—the frantic hiding of pen and paper and the even more hysterical concealment of the letters themselves—is entirely disproportionate to the heroines' desire to communicate with the specific person addressed. It is the writing of the letter, not its sending or receipt, on which all emotional energy is focused. As Clarissa confesses:

> And indeed, my dear, I know not how to *forbear* writing. I have now no other employment or diversion. And I must write on, altho' I were not to send it to any-body. You have often heard me own the advantages I have found from writing down everything of moment that befalls me; and of all I *think*, and of all I *do*, that may be of future use to me: for . . . every one will find, that many a good thought evaporates in thinking; many a good resolution goes off, driven out of memory perhaps by some other not so good. But when I set down what I *will* do, or what I *have* done, on this or that occasion; the resolution or action is before me either to be adhered to, withdrawn, or amended; and I have entered into *compact* with myself, as I may say; having given it under my own hand to *improve*, rather than to go *backwards*, as I live longer. (III, 221).

Furthermore, the qualities of repetitiveness and verbosity which mark all of Richardson's novels seem to proceed from this source: the heroine's need, not necessarily to be heard or read, but to *write*.

The most reasonable conclusion is that the letters are primarily important as records for the writer herself, and both Pamela and Clarissa give ample support to such a view. Both repeatedly enjoin the intended recipients to keep the letters so that their authors may reread them. "As I may not have Opportunity to send again soon," Pamela tells her parents, "and, yet, as I know you keep my Letters, and read them over and over. . . . and as it may be some little Pleasure to me, may-hap, to read them myself, when I am come to you, to remind me of what I have gone thro', and how great God's Goodness has been to me (which, I hope, will further strengthen my good Resolutions, that I may not hereafter, from my bad Conduct, have Reason to condemn myself from my own Hand, as it were): For all these Reasons, I say, I will write as I have Time, and as Matters happen" (I, 49). When it becomes impossible to post the letters, both girls do keep them to reread themselves.

The letters serve their writers in much the same way that the spiritual diary had served their Puritan ancestors. They are the record of a trial—overfull of detail so that no morally incorrect interpretation might be imposed on them. They are written on the moment, a practice which seems demented if we judge it in terms of the sexual drama that is taking place but which becomes understandable if we focus instead on the spiritual dilemma that each girl believed herself to be facing. And they are written for the express purpose of self-examination. Indeed, Clarissa's language is a ghostly echo of some of the Puritan diaries we have cited. "Every one will find that many a good Thought evaporates in thinking; many a good Resolution goes off, driven out of Memory perhaps by some other not so good," she writes. Two generations earlier Henry Newcome observed: "Enter resolutions in your note books. The truth is [that a] Christian's note books more faithfully register than their hearts." Even her use of the notion of a compact (saying, "I have entered into *compact* with myself, as I may say; having given it under my own hand to *improve* rather than to go *backward,* as I live longer") is a specially Puritan usage of that theological term.

What emerges most clearly is that for both Clarissa and Pamela their letters are of use principally to the authors, treasured because they reflect the mind of the writer and preserved because they serve as record both of past conduct and of resolutions concerning the future. They are evidences of self-expression at least as much as they are attempts at communication. (Indeed, the most important instances of communication—between the girls and their lovers—is always verbal.) And they are objective embodiments of the self—*alter egos*—which can be examined and judged dispassionately.

The letters as *alter ego* serve their authors primarily as a mirror in which the hidden self may be revealed and judged; but the fact that the letters are a concrete embodiment of personality serves other functions in the novel as well. Pamela and Clarissa want to keep the letters and examine them; their lovers make stealing the letters an intrinsic part of the attempted rape. And if the heroines are frantic to write and then hide the product of their labor, Mr. B. and Lovelace are obsessed to possess their written work— both men seeming to see the epistles (as the girls themselves do) as a part of the writer's personality. There is something indelicate, something almost hilarious, in Mr. B.'s pursuit of Pamela's letter-journal; however, in terms of the development of plot, this pursuit is entirely necessary. His acquisition of her letters and journals is the turning point of the novel: after he has seen her character thus unself-consciously revealed, his genuine affection cannot be stifled. He sends her away to save her virtue, and then recalls her to make her his legal wife. " 'Your Papers shall be faithfully return'd you; and I have paid so dear for my Curiosity in the Affection they have rivetted upon

me for you, that you would look upon yourself amply
reveng'd if you knew what they have cost me.' " (II, 7). In
this case, "heart knowledge" has led to love.

In *Clarissa* Lovelace's greed for the letters takes a more
ominous tone. Here as in *Pamela* , possession of her letters
is bound up with the violent rape of her body, and the
strategems used by Lovelace (involving elaborate decep-
tions) are in accord with his more vicious nature. Here,
too, his perusal of the letters that reveal her character so
unreservedly convinces him finally of his love for her. Yet
in *Clarissa* the heroine herself employs the letters not
merely as a mirror in which she may see her own image
honestly reflected, but as a means of fending off suicidal
depression. As we have seen in discussing the Puritan
diary, conscience must find some way of separating the
object of condemnation from the individual character who
judges; otherwise, castigating conscience is turned inward, and the sinner who would eradicate sin may find
himself obliged to condemn his whole nature, his entire
life. As Clarissa's trial forces her to acknowledge the extent
of her own pride, even of her own sexuality, she finds it
increasingly difficult to fend off thoughts of self-destruction as a way of releasing herself from an apparent prison
of sinfulness. As we shall see in much greater detail later,
her ability to find value and virtue in the objective record
of her trials is the crucial factor in turning her away from
thoughts of suicide. Thus for Clarissa the letters are not
only a convenient mirror of identity; they are ultimately a
device for retaining identity.[39]

Though Richardson makes most extensive psychological
use of the Puritan ideal of Self-Examiner and most skillful
literary use of the characterizing elements of the confessional diary, these are not the only reflections of Puritan
self-definition that we can find in his novels. For example,
he also employs the ego ideal of Puritan as Virtuous
Example. This was a simpler and less pervasive ideal of

character; it was meant to apply to only a limited period in any adult's life.

If every Christian spent his religious life searching for proofs of God's mercy to him—that is, proof of a pattern of virtue in his own life which might qualify him for Sainthood after death—then occasionally, at least, some men discovered cause for reassurance. When this occurred, an individual Puritan came momentarily to define his life as a manifestation of the virtue that God had blessed him with. (As we shall see shortly, this view of identity was common at the moment when a dissenter felt qualified to join a congregation). As one blessed by God, he might serve as a model for others. Transgressions, though undeniably still present, were absorbed into the larger pattern of grace: thus he might take the attitude "I have sinned in these many ways, and *still* God has blessed me with proofs of redemption."

If we compare this way of defining identity with the first that we discussed, we can see that it is a much more limited, much more highly stylized view of personality; it was not a "realistic" view, nor was it intended to be so. Any description of character which reduces the complexity of personality to a model of virtue will be necessarily selective; and the defining quality of this second prototype was its deliberate idealizing. The Puritan, when he thought of himself as an example of virtue, did not dwell on his sinfulness unless it heightened the drama of his conversion. He emphasized his own lack of faith only to make God's mercy towards him more remarkable. His trials were not genuine threats because his knowledge of the inevitable outcome would take the uncertainty from them. And the pervading attitude was a moralizing one: the clear implication of every act—"others can profitably learn from my example."[40]

This image of personality as Virtuous Example cropped up in a number of different literary forms. It appeared in sermons and in Biblical commentaries, where familiar religious figures were admired as models of a particular virtue: Job for his patient acceptance; Ruth for her loyalty and chastity. In the literature of personal devotion, it appeared in the spiritual autobiography. Individuals wrote autobiographies for a number of reasons. A man who kept a diary for himself with instructions that it be destroyed when he died, might write an autobiography for the enlightenment of his children or one meant to be left for the instruction of his relatives and friends—or even for the public at large—after his death. Both Henry Newcome and Oliver Heywood, whose diaries we have already cited, wrote autobiographies for the use of their children; Benjamin Franklin's *Autobiography* was written for the instruction of his son, William. In their diaries, Newcome and Heywood are casuistical, self-criticizing, and doubtful about the ultimate meaning of their experience; in the autobiographies they adopt a pious, lecturing tone and offer wise generalities about the meaning of their experience. The diaries are unstructured, repetitious daily accounts; the autobiographies are more highly structured and selective, aiming to distill a lesson of virtue from individual experience.

The most famous of all Puritan autobiographies, Bunyan's *Grace Abounding,* belongs to another class, the autobiography written as a set exercise to be submitted as part of the requirements for entrance into the congregation of a dissenting church. Relatively few of these survive because they were seldom put into print and bound, although they were made public at the time of their composition, presented to both minister and congregation, perhaps written out to be read aloud.[41] In these autobiographies the applicant would relate God's dealings with him in such a way as to justify his acceptance into the covenant of faith. His description of his life would be his

proof of worthiness to be numbered among those tentatively assured of Election.

The techniques of characterization in all of these exemplary forms are similar. We have already observed some
of them. There is an explicit assertion that the individual
life portrayed has instructional value for the lives of others;
thus the individual who is seen as a model of virtue is in
no permanent way isolated by his experience. The tone of
the account is pious, even canting; there is an unstated
assumption of superiority. When the narration is first
person, the struggles and trials that are reported have lost
some of the intensity that might be found in similar situations in a diary. After all, the audience and narrator both
know that there will be a successful end to the struggles.
The torment may be wracking, but it will lead inevitably
to the moment of grace. What was lonely self-discovery
for the diarist becomes in the autobiography a general
illustration of God's grace and a specific proof of the narrator's worth.

Obviously, the most explicit use Richardson makes of
this ego ideal and the modes of characterization associated
with it is in *Pamela*.[42] The clear indication of her position as virtuous example is the subtitle, "Virtue Rewarded." From the outset, then, the reader knows that
Pamela's trials are to prove a vindication of her chastity,
and though her struggles are reported in an apparently
ingenuous and artless manner, the conflict has a sham
quality: it is difficult to feel that she is really open to temptation. Certainly one source of this problem in the novel
is Richardson's ambiguous tone in his treatment of the
heroine. She cannot be both Self-Examining Sinner and
Exemplar of Virtue—at least not in the same novel; the
tone of the first would be unsure and self-condemnatory
while the tone of the second would presume success and a
degree of superiority. When Richardson permits his novel

to become an exemplum, with Pamela the embodiment of successful virtue, the tension created by her efforts at self-examination are destroyed.

Unfortunately, there is ample evidence that both Pamela and her creator perceived her ordeal in the light of an exemplum for others—even before it has been made explicitly clear to the reader that she will not yield. Thus she says to Mr. B. " 'But to what End, Sir, am I to stay? . . . And to what Purpose? And in what Light must I appear to the World? Would not *that* censure me, altho' I might be innocent? And you will allow, Sir, that if there be any thing valuable or exemplary in a good Name, or fair Reputation, one must not despise the World's Censure, if one can avoid it.' " (I, 283). Pamela thinks of her experience in terms of her moral reputation, and she is clearly not about to shun her role as exemplar. She conceives of herself in appropriately Biblical terms, spending part of her captivity rewriting Psalm 137 with herself and her "captivity" as the central theme.

Just before the wedding her father remarks that the Book of Ruth would offer a fine parallel to the honor done her. After her marriage, the entire county seems glad to accept her as a model of virtue. The words "example" and "exemplar" run through the narrative as a recurrent theme. Pamela reports, for instance, "Lady *Darnford,* at whose Right hand I sat, kissed me with a kind of Rapture; and called me, a sweet Exemplar for all my Sex. Mr. *Peters* said very handsome Things; so did Mr. *Perry*; and Sir *Simon,* with Tears in his Eyes, said to my Master, 'Why, Neighbour, Neighbour, this is excellent, by my Troth. I believe there is something in Virtue, that we had not well consider'd.' " (II, 52).

There is a rather tasteless merging of public and private events in the novel which originates in Richardson's aim of presenting Pamela as an Example of Virtue. If she is to

fulfill that public religious function, then the details of the
struggles which describe her virtue must be made generally
available. What is by its nature a private, even intimate,
series of occurrences must be brought rather boldly to the
general view. Thus the letters and Pamela's journal are
passed freely among her friends and relations since the
documents serve as proof of her virtue, assuring both her
right to be rewarded and her worthiness to be imitated.
Lady Davers puts the matter rather explicitly: " 'Except
one had known these things, one should not have been
able to judge of the Merit of your Resistance. . . . It was
necessary, Child, on Twenty Accounts, that we, your
and his Wellwishers and Relations, should know, that he
had try'd every Stratagem, and made use of every Contri-
vance, to subdue you to his Purpose, before he marry'd
you' " (III, 44). And once *completely* informed, Lady Davers exults: " 'Happy, thrice happy Mrs. B.! May you long
live the Ornament of your Sex, and a Credit to all your
Acquaintance! Such Examples as you set, how are they
wanted in an Age so depraved!' " (IV, 79).

Richardson clearly indicates his intentions for *Pamela*
in the Preface to *Grandison,* where he asserts that it was
designed to exhibit "the beauty and superiority of Virtue
in an innocent and unpolished mind." What Richardson failed to understand fully, failed even to see consciously, perhaps, is that the ego ideal of Self-Examiner and
that of Virtuous Exemplar are not compatible and that
the techniques used to depict them are discordant. His
failure to sort out this mixture of aims and techniques lies
at the heart of the novel's failure.

In his adaptation of both the Puritan prototypes we
have discussed, Richardson has made secular rather than
strict religious use of them. In his work with the ideal of
Self-Examiner he remains closest to the Puritan image;
Clarissa, especially, seeks self-knowledge as a means of

purification. Even here, however, there is a hint that she might do well by being "good" (this is especially evident in Miss Howe's and Bedford's remarks at the end of the novel). In *Pamela* the identification of goodness with improvement in social and economic station is grossly obvious. As we have seen, the link between the two spheres was implicit even in very early Puritan thought, and Richardson has chosen to focus on this traditional association of spiritual and wordly success and to elaborate and expand the connection. Unfortunately, neither ideal is particularly suited to this approach: the Self-Examiner was traditionally isolated in his moral task; the exemplar supposedly dealt in intangibles, and when he failed to limit his aims, he seemed hypocritical even when portrayed by seventeenth-century Puritans. Yet Richardson was not writing in a theocracy. His audience sought the answers to material rather than spiritual questions, and their problems of adjustment had more to do with social position than with eventual acceptance into a divine community of the Elect. Richardson was consciously aware of the difficulties of the new bourgeoisie, and in his use of a third Puritan model for personality he finally found a vehicle appropriate to his essentially secular purpose.

The ideal of the Puritan Saint was the image of man who had achieved as much perfection on earth as an imperfect being is capable of. The Saint, as conceived in this theological tradition, differed greatly from the medieval Catholic notion; Catholicism tended to emphasize the miraculous, and the legends of the Church of Rome hint at a struggle between good and evil so dark and mysterious that man can only fear and marvel. There was nothing miraculous at all about the Puritan Saint, for dissenters believed that all were Saints who could find God's grace manifested through their worldly actions and through the conduct of their everyday lives.

This belief led to a focus on social value and on the importance of community. Election for each individual meant eventual participation in the Community of the Elect in Heaven. Ironically, the tortured isolation of the Puritan diarist on earth was designed to enable him ultimately to join that joyful community which lay beyond his reach, like the beatific vision of some Old Testament saint. The hope of belonging to the Community was never long absent, and a desire for ideal brotherhood pervades all Puritan thought. In the theological terms of *Pilgrim's Progress* it is Christian's poignant vision of Paradise: "Then I heard in my Dream, that all the Bells in the City rang again for joy; . . . Now just as the Gates were opened to let in the men, I looked in after them; and behold, the City shone like the Sun, the Streets also were paved with Gold, and in them walked many men, with Crowns on their heads, Palms in their hands, and golden Harps to sing praises withal . . . And after that, they shut up the Gates: which when I had seen, I wished myself among them."[43] In political terms it is Milton's lyric vision of "a free commonwealth . . . the manliest, the equallest, the justest government";[44] for the iron man of New England it is "a city upon a hill [where] the eyes of all people are upon us."[45]

All who had been preordained for heaven (that is, all of the Elect) were, by definition, Saints. No man could be *assured* of his condition while he was alive, yet all men avidly studied their own lives and those of others so that they might recognize the attributes that marked the Saint and set him apart from those not of the Elect. Earthly communities were rough imitations of the ultimate community in heaven; and, fittingly, a man's claim to become a citizen in the latter was supposedly revealed by his performance as a citizen in the former. Goodness, thus defined, was an essential *social* virtue.[45]

The manners or attitudes which dominate this ego ideal of Saint were proficiency and a certain air of busyness: the Saint would engage in many life roles, and he would perform them well. A noted Divine remarks that "such as are real saints show it in their several capacities."[47] The Saint thus defined would be notable because of his capacity to live profitably and harmoniously with all other righteous men. His holiness would be manifested in his activity in innumerable daily duties—his skill as a preacher, his efficacy as a writer, his dutifulness as a husband, his tenderness and authority as a father, even his devotion to his secular calling (that is, to his job). Presumably, the Saint would be a success, well-adjusted and respected by his neighbors.

Since no one could be certain of Sainthood while he was still alive, all the literary portraits of the Saint are posthumous. The earliest accounts of Puritan Saints are found in Foxe's *Book of Martyrs,* first published in 1559, and these are virtually all accounts of the lives of historically important people. Yet even in this early work we can see an insistence on placing the Saint in an everyday communal setting. In the seventeenth century Samuel Clarke took up the task left by Foxe, and his work continues to insist that God's chosen people led exemplary but not miraculous lives. In Foxe the lives of kings and famous men were told; next, ministers were added; and in Clarke's later publications the lives of exemplary laity, even of women, came to be included. Gradually, the genre of the *Saint's Life* gained wide representation in funeral sermons. A good man or woman would die, and an inspiring, short account of his life—depicting him as a Saint now called to rest with God—would be included in the sermon preached at his burial. Sometimes the sermon was later printed and sold, and the person whose life was recounted would join the ranks of the celebrated Elect. Thus by mid-

seventeenth century, even the simplest people might have
their lives perpetuated to serve as models for succeeding
generations.

The literary form of the *Saint's Life* moves even further
than the autobiography from the form of the diary. There
is little emphasis on temptation and sin and correspondingly much more on virtue and good works. For one thing,
the point of view has shifted. Both the diary and the autobiography are first-person accounts, and for that reason
a moderate, even critical attitude is usually maintained
toward the subject in order to preserve the appropriate
mien of humility. Even when the author of an autobiography is recording his virtues with what seems to us
evident satisfaction, the self-praise is seldom overt; there
is at least the superficial gloss of modesty or self-depreca-
tion. In the *Life*, however, the subject is seen through the
frankly admiring eyes of the eulogizing minister or
author. Moreover, because the entire purpose of the *Life*
is to present the complete and final exemplum of the virtuous life, there is no need, no occasion, to dwell on the
subject's imperfections. What is perhaps of even more
importance, however, is the change in the way personality
is defined. The subject has left the lonely struggle of his
earthly journey forever behind him to dwell in eternal
fellowship with God's Elect in heaven; thus the anguished
isolation of the diary is abandoned, and the *Saint's Life*
turns to characterize the subject almost entirely in terms
of the meaningful relationships he has had with others,
showing him as a successful and productive member of
God's community on earth.

This shift, is, of course, partly a matter of expedience.
No outsider could have firsthand knowledge of another's
soul-struggles. Yet there is abundant evidence that the
authors of many of these *Saints' Lives* read the diaries of
their subjects; thus they could have, had they so desired,

focused their delineation of character on the internal struggle. Their failure to do so seems clearly to indicate that they intended a more social portrait of their subject, intended it because in this manner they might emphasize the fact of the individual's acceptance into the Great Community that all hoped eventually to join.

To illustrate the striking differences between the two conceptions of character, we might compare Henry Newcome's personality as it is reflected in his diary and as it is delineated in the *Saint's Life* which was his funeral sermon. Newcome was subject to severe fits of anger, and his efforts to repress this passion were often associated with violent nightmares. He seems to have regarded this failing as his chief sin, and notations concerning it appear in approximately one out of every five entries in his diary. In the *Life*, this same tendency to anger or passion, as it was called, is discussed, but there is a remarkable difference in emphasis. The author begins by viewing Newcome as one of a long line of ministers who labored for the good of God's people and who then moved on to a blessed reward after death. He catalogues Newcome's virtues—his "good natural parts" and "genius"[48]—and asserts that these, enriched by his industry, brought forth many good works, most notably his theological publications. The author continues: "His temper was sincere, candid, and generous to and beyond his power. His discourse was ingenious, innocent, pleasant, and profitable to a high degree. His deportment was grave, yet sweet and obliging. These virtues were lodged in a soul truly Christian."[49] Such a characterization may seem incongruous to one who has known Newcome through his diary; yet the author does not distort even in eulogy, and Newcome's quick temper is acknowledged. "He was but a candidate for the state of perfection, and *was a man subject to like passions as we are,* which he hath now put off, together

with mortality." [50] However, the infirmities are of little
interest and the author moves on to discuss Newcome's
virtues. "But certainly this notwithstanding, he had a
truly Christian spirit and did abound in choice experience
of God's dealings with himself and others. His life was
filled up with a uniform series of faithful services to God
and to his generation."[51]

Ironically, then, while Newcome himself struggled to
focus his own attention on his daily temptation to anger
and formed his notion of his own character out of his
sense of isolated despair (it was, after all, he who exclaimed,
"I should never think I have no need to pray to God . . .
We are *always in danger*. Evils may rise of nothing."),[52]
this notion of personality is no longer of interest to the
biographer of Newcome as Saint. What is important now
is Newcome's role as the agent of God on earth, a role
which is proven by the effect that he might have on those
around him through his writing, through the "uniform
series of faithful services to God and to his generation,"
and through his skill as a preacher (elaborately described
in the latter portion of the *Life*). Once the Puritan is pre-
sumed to have achieved irrevocable membership in the
society of Saints, he is characterized in social terms. His
importance is delineated by his significant contributions
to the earthly community in which he has lived, and his
character is defined in each of his numerous interactions
with other people, not in the solitude of self-examination.

Such was always the case in these *Lives* of the Puritan
Saints. In Clarke's *Lives*, for instance, a minister's skill
in preaching or in otherwise moving good Christians
toward God is always noted. When the subject is an author
as well, a complete list of his books, frequently with sum-
maries of the more important ones, is appended to the
Life. All ecclesiastical offices or academic positions held
by the individual are described, together with commenda-

tion for the effective execution of the duties of those offices. Rarely did the nonconformist hold public office; but when he did, the fact is noted as well. Nor is the account limited to these "official" roles, for even the minor, everyday social interactions of the Puritans could be proof of sanctification. Clarke says of Elizabeth Wilkinson, "Never was a wife more full of sincere love and respect to an husband, whom she loved entirely and was as entirely loved by him. Her affection to her children was very tender."[53] Every social role was important in these *Lives*, for any one of them could reveal the character of the Puritan as one of the Elect.

The ego ideal of Puritan Saint appears in all three of Richardson's novels; however, his use of it in *Clarissa* most closely approximates the traditional religious portrait. Indeed, unless we understand the spiritual relationship between Self-Examiner and Saint, the literary relevance of the ending of *Clarissa* is liable to escape us. Clarissa dies several hundred pages before the end of the novel. Why, we might wonder, does Richardson prolong the obsequies to such apparently tasteless lengths?[54] The response to this question would have been obvious to a member of Richardson's audience: Clarissa's private anguish had ended, and her private ordeal has fitted her for the posthumous role of Saint. Complete rendering of her character requires both the private and the public image; thus the long novel concludes with an account of her in the modes traditionally appropriate to her final role as Saint. Miss Howe's long letter to Belford (Thursday, October 12) might be viewed as Clarissa's funeral oration. It is an almost classic delineation of a member of the Elect. Here we have an unabashedly admiring third-person description of the heroine's daily activities and habits; and Clarissa is portrayed as possessing all of the typically Puritan virtues appropriate to her sex and station—among them, diligence, domestic efficiency, abstemiousness, charity, and filial piety. The intimacy of the ordeal has led to this final retrospective view: Clarissa's life has community value as a pattern of grace. And if Miss Howe's evaluation seems pale by comparison to Clarissa's own anguish, at least it has the virtue of being traditionally "correct."

In *Pamela* and *Grandison* Richardson modifies the Puritan ideal: for one thing, his characters achieve "Sainthood" *before* they die, a useful if sometimes unattractive achievement. Their social virtue, then, is spelled out at some length and in undeniably worldly terms. When Pamela's trials end, for instance, she assumes a public life in which goodness is defined by her contributions to the community; and her significance as part of the community in which she lives is especially evident in *Pamela II*. Mr. B.'s fortune grows to have moral potential when it is put at her disposal. So Pamela writes to her parents: "Look among your poor Acquaintance and Neighbours, and let me have a List of such honest, industrious Poor, as may be true Objects of Charity, and have no other Assistance; . . . And I will chose as well as I can; for I long to be making a Beginning, with the kind quarterly Benevolence my dear good Benefactor has bestowed upon me for such good Purposes" (II, 323). We shall see the extent and nature of Grandison's Sainthood later, but we can say here that he carries the notion of secular Sainthood to its logical extreme. Richardson shifts our vantage in this last novel so that we see Grandison almost entirely through the eyes of a frankly praising group of family and friends. His principal virtues are efficiency and that unmistakable Puritan busyness; and having achieved virtual perfection on earth, he moves calmly and effectively through all of life's vicissitudes—the unchanging, equanimous public man.

Once we have seen the models of character and characterization that inform Richardson's novels, we might return to the vexing question of indebtedness. Strictly speaking, what we have demonstrated is merely a *prima facie* case: there is no proof that Richardson ever read a diary—or any of the other literature mentioned here. His eyesight was very poor, and in his later years he seems to have done little reading. Still, it would be very surprising if Richardson did not know this Puritan literature. Certainly he knew the devotional manuals. Hornbeak has shown his use of them in *Familiar Letters*. Miss Howe describes Clarissa as having kept a religious diary before her trials began,[55] so Richardson was evidently familiar with that genre. He expresses his admiration for Bunyan, claiming that "Bunyan may be of greater Use to the Multitude . . . than Mr. Pope's writings."[56] It would be extraordinary had Richardson not known of the funeral literature depicting the Puritan Saint. A man of fifty, Richardson's age when he first began *Pamela*, would have attended funerals. Alas, the eighteenth century was an age in which people died young; he lost his first wife, and of his twelve children, only four grew to maturity. The picture of a Saint given in the funeral sermon was by way of being a set piece, and a man of Richardson's melancholy experience must surely have heard many examples. Finally, G. A. Starr has recently demonstrated the extent to which Defoe employed the structure and characterization of the Puritan autobiography in the construction of his novels.[57] Richardson, who had printed and revised several of Defoe's pieces might well have recognized this debt. Clearly there seems to have been contemporary recognition of Richardson's debt. Though *Shamela* is the best known of the imitations of *Pamela*, it is not typical of the response, for there were several continuations which began with Pamela's marriage and extended Richardson's flattering portrait into her later life. Of these there were three major examples;[58] and of these three, one took the form of a journal. It began with daily entries and lapsed into less frequent ones, finally concluding with Pamela's exemplary death—all quite clearly in the Puritan tradition.

Still, we can never single out a given Puritan work and, through close textual examination, prove Richardson's direct or deliberate indebtedness. The debt, if there is one, is of a more general sort. These images of character dominated the Puritan culture of the seventeenth century. Many of them persisted into the eighteenth century, increasingly secularized to meet the demands of a new monied society (Weber and Tawney suggest some of the common variants). Richardson had been reared in a culture heavily influenced by these notions of identity; perhaps even in his own life, the categories and attitudes of Puritanism were those which most readily come to mind. Most important, however, the Puritan ego ideals that we have discussed were perfectly suited for a discussion of the problems that Richardson wanted to consider.

The new middle-class of the eighteenth century faced problems of rapid social and historical change which made it liable to personality disruption. All three of Richardson's novels deal with some aspect of this identity crisis. Now the religious Puritan of the seventeenth century also found himself in a situation which produced identity crisis. To be sure, the causes of the dislocation were different: the Merchant found himself insecure in a newly monied society; the Puritan was insecure because his wished-for identity as Saint could never be confirmed until after death. Yet the psychological state was the same for both. And more important, the same ways of defining character would be appropriate to both. Thus the ideal of Self-Examiner is the means by which the Puritan hopes to discover a solution to his spiritual problem; and in Richardson's novels, the same ideal is employed to seek a solution to personality problems which are essentially secular in origin. What is more, there was available to Richardson an entire, well-established literary tradition created for the express purpose of capturing character in the throes of identity crisis. Under the circumstances, it would have been surprising if he had not availed himself of this tradition. The ideal of the Saint is even more obviously relevant to the problems of Richardson's age. If the Puritan's goal of membership in the Heavenly community was reflected in his desire to see himself as a successful member of an earthly community, very little alteration is needed to transform this spiritual quest into a purely secular one where adjustment to society and worldly success are pursued as ends in themselves. In his novels, Richardson postulates a solution to the endemic personality disruption of his age through his characterization of Grandison, the perfectly adjusted public man (perhaps the principal difference between Grandison and his predecessors is that Grandison can live to enjoy his success). And here again, the literary modes for depicting the successful citizen had already been created for Richardson's use by a flourishing body of Puritan material.

In speaking of Richardson's debt to Puritanism, we have been talking in rather general terms about character and characterization, speaking of ideal images or cultural norms. Despite the influence of these ideals, Richardson's novels are about specific people and particular problems. The historical changes that prompted the secularization of these images of character brought immediate and painful dilemmas to those who made up his reading public, and it is to these dilemmas that he addresses himself in the novels. It is certainly to be hoped that an understanding of Richardson's debt to Puritanism will clarify his apparently unique literary methods; however, for a complete understanding of his work, we must examine the novels in detail, identifying the loss of roles which leads to personality disruption and tracing the slow and painful solutions which Richardson postulates.

CHAPTER III

Pamela

Despite its enormous and immediate popularity in the eighteenth century, most critics today regard Richardson's first work as a novel with major deficiencies. Too often we read it or teach it for the wrong reasons: it is a social document; its length (by comparison with *Clarissa*) makes it relatively accessible; we can read it without having to resort to an abridgment. Certainly it is an easy novel to ridicule, and many modern critics and teachers indulge in facile condescension. Yet even its most vehement detractors find the book strangely compelling; it may not be a great novel, but it is fascinating. Because we have limited the present study to an investigation of characterization, some of the more interesting aspects of the book do not fall within our purview. What is more, many of the experiments with characterization that Richardson began in *Pamela* were brought to fruition in *Clarissa,* and to deal with them here would be only to anticipate the fuller discussion in the sections on *Clarissa.*

Perhaps, then, we can most profitably explore this novel by raising two questions: why do we still feel *Pamela's* force, why do we expect it to be a great work; and seccondly, why are these expectations disappointed, why do we reject the novel as a betrayal of its own potentiality? As we shall see, these are both questions answered only by an examination of Richardson's techniques of characterization.

The novel and Pamela herself assault us with an immediate and almost embarrassing familiarity. There is no "setting of scene," no background, no attempt to place the heroine in a wider context; from the beginning, reader and heroine are closeted alone to face whatever ordeal awaits.[1] Such a narrative method has several implications. For one thing, there is almost no opportunity to gain distance and perspective; there is, to put it another way, no narrator to pull back dispassionately and comment on Pamela's world (as Flaubert does in *Madame Bovary*). Moreover, though Richardson portrays Pamela as innocent and vulnerable, he would never have us believe that she is morally uncertain. She is not a Tom Jones or an Evelina, confronting an unfamiliar, complex world and unable to recognize the machinations of evil. Quite the contrary. She is preternaturally suspicious, as the very first letter demonstrates; and in intelligence, moral fortitude, and quick-wittedness, Pamela is the equal of both her adversaries and the members of her audience. Nothing in the novel suggests that there is need for an alternative view to Pamela's—either in the form of an omniscient narrator or as irony—to explain the moral framework to the reader. We are meant to identify with Pamela in her Odyssey, not to judge her.

Given this set of assumptions, what significance can we

attach to the incidents of the novel? If we see the work as a moral and essentially Christian document (as Richardson did), the encounters with Mr. B. are those temptations which test the virtue of the heroine: she can perceive good and evil accurately enough; what she does not know is her ability to withstand evil. Thus Pamela's trial should do two things. It ought to reveal her own weaknesses to her; the story would have little meaning if Pamela knew with perfect certainty that she was invulnerable to attack. By definition, every human has weaknesses (even Christ was subject to temptation), and it is his moral duty to know them. Furthermore, by withstanding the force of sin, Pamela can demonstrate herself worthy of reward.

Insofar as Pamela's task is one of self-discovery, we can make the following observations concerning her. First, her aim is identical with that of the reader who comes to know her in the course of the narrative even as she comes to know herself. There is no barrier between reader and narrator— not even the overt assumption that this is fiction, since it has the artless air of a genuine account[2]—and we become implicated in Pamela's existence merely by eavesdropping on her letter-journal. Second, her method of narrating the events which comprise her trial is precisely suited to this aim of self-examination. Here Richardson's adaptation of the Puritan diary form becomes especially significant. The Puritan kept a record of his trials in order to discover the hidden components of his personality. His creed had taught him that temptation inheres in the sinful inclinations of the human body; and his diary was often a detailed, obsessive catalogue of the dangers he encountered, along with a careful record of his success or failure in resisting them.

We learn about Pamela slowly, through her spontaneous and unstructured account of the contest with Mr. B. Whether or not we know the specifically religious significance of Pamela's narrative method, we sense that the prolixity and self-indulgent repetitiveness of her account can be justified *only* on the condition that Pamela's task is similar to our own—that is, only if she employs this technique as a means of discovering character.

The intimacy with which the novel accosts us seems to confirm this expectation; and yet, as the story moves slowly on, we come to realize that Pamela is really a morally static creature. Only her station changes. *We* glimpse the hidden recesses of her nature while *she* remains divinely ignorant of them; and oddly enough, though we may find her a singularly salacious or greedy young woman, it is not these "vices" for which we condemn her. (Other heroines, Moll Flanders or Sister Carrie, are scarcely better.) What we cannot forgive Pamela is her self-deception and dishonesty: she has enticed us to follow her and then wantonly betrayed our concern for her and our confidence in the felicity of her account. The very fact that her narrative is compelling now turns against her. The more we have become entangled in her story, the more we resent her wrongheadedness, her (apparently) willful blindness. The only excuse for such a proliferation of detail, such repetitious lingering over each and every temptation, is the assumption that *only* by such repetition may character be inferred or Pamela come to understand herself better. Such is the justification for these qualities in the Puritan diary. Yet Pamela slips away from the moral task of self-discovery, and the reader who recognizes her delinquency must find other—perhaps less complimentary—explanations for Pamela's narrative method. Thus, ironically, the very power of Richardson's method leads us to anticipate a kind of ultimate truth which the novel fails to give; Richardson's potential for greatness is undercut by his failure to satisfy the expectations he has aroused.

The uncertainty with which Richardson defines Pam-

ela's character eventually infects the entire novel. One of
the earliest things we learn about Pamela is her fearfulness;
the first letter to her parents concludes with a hasty post-
script: "I have been scared out of my Sense; for just now,
as I was folding up this letter, in my late Lady's Dressing-
room, in comes my young Master! Good Sirs! how was I
frighten'd! I went to hide the letter in my Bosom, and he,
seeing me tremble, said, smiling, 'To whom have you been
writeing [sic] Pamela?'—I said, in my Confusion, 'Pray
your Honour forgive me!—Only to my Father and Mother.'
He said, 'Well then, let me see how you are come on in
your Writing!' Oh how asham'd I was!" (I, 3). Pamela's
extraordinary caution is justified (or so it would seem)
by Mr. B.'s subsequent behavior, and thus this first letter
defines the terms of her ordeal. Her resolute virginity is
repeatedly tried until the force with which she rejects the
temptation finally converts even the tempter.

Yet the reader who endures Pamela's trials to their triumphant conclusion may not accept this definition at
face value. Seen with some perspective, the girl's confusion
is totally inexplicable. Mr. B. has offered no insult; she
was doing nothing wrong. What kind of hysterical infla-
tion, we might wonder, has led to these emotional excesses,
these gasped phrases, and this profusion of exclamation
marks? The only way to make sense of the passage is to
see it not as a report (since its highly colored tone would
scarcely make it accurate) but as a revelation of Pamela's
expectations. She anticipates misbehavior on Mr. B.'s part;
she looks for violence where none might reasonably be
expected; she reacts not to Mr. B.'s behavior, but to her
own anticipations. From Mr. B.'s point of view (a vantage
which is unfortunately absent from the novel), Pamela's
conduct could be nothing short of provocative. Thus the
role which he plays in the attempted seduction is not altogether clear. Pamela reacts to her expectations that he

will assault her before he has offered the slightest indelicacy. If, after several such incidents, his actions finally do confirm these expectations, can we conclude, as Pamela does, that she was correct all along? Or should we infer that her initially groundless fears have finally enticed him to action?

We cannot be certain that Pamela is the culprit either. Richardson may have lost the opportunity to reveal hidden depths in Pamela by failing to examine her behavior and motivation (certainly we tend to impute artfulness to her); it is at least possible, however, that her expressions of anxiety are justified, and the ambiguity of this first scene develops as the novel unfolds. We never know enough about Pamela to be able to judge whether in a given instance her evaluation is reliable or whether the world we see through her eyes is nothing more than a distortion.

For example, the related themes of violence and sexuality are repeatedly articulated: Pamela is fascinated with a bull that has gored one of the cook-maids; and the animal becomes synonymous with the threat of sexual violation. The bloody accident insinuates itself into her thoughts, and the bull as symbol becomes part of her vocabulary. Thus she describes Colbrand: "He is a Giant of a Man, for Stature; taller, by a good deal, than *Harry Mawlidge*. . . . He has great staring Eyes, like the Bull's that frighten'd me so; vast Jaw-bones sticking out; Eyebrows hanging over his Eyes; Two great Scars upon his Forehead, and One on his left Cheek; and Two huge Whiskers and a monstrous wide Mouth; blubber Lips; long yellow Teeth, and a hideous Grin" (I, 225). The danger associated with the bull is equated with the seduction offered by Mr. B., and both are absorbed into her more general view of the world as essentially inimical. "Let Bulls, and Bears, and Lions, and Tygers, and, what is worse, false, treacherous, deceitful Men, stand in my Way, I cannot be in more Danger than I am" (I, 227). Much of the time Pamela seems to see this kind of antagonism or deliberate sadism as an essential ingredient in all man/woman relationships.

Because she narrates her own story, this vocabulary becomes the sole vehicle through which we perceive her world. Yet the very words, as extensions of her incompletely defined nature, play us false. She is deterred from leaving the B. house for fear of crossing a meadow in which the bull is grazing. "I looked, and saw the Bull, as I thought, between me and the Door; and another Bull coming towards me the other Way: Well, thought I, here is double Witchcraft, to be sure! Here is the Spirit of my Master in one Bull, and Mrs. *Jewkes's* in the other. And now I am gone, to be sure!" (I, 205). When she reaches the safety of the house she "saw they were only two poor Cows, a grazing in distant Places, that my Fears had made all the Rout about (I, 205).

We can draw no clear moral inference from this confused set of impressions; and Richardson has merely added to the confusion by impugning the reliability of Pamela's reporting without in any way defining the limits of her distortions. We cannot know whether her fearfulness about the world has led to error or whether the isolated incident is intended merely to show her reluctance to leave Mr. B. And if this episode is ambiguous, what are we to make of Colbrand, Mrs. Jewkes, or Lady Davers? Richardson's failure to dissect Pamela's nature, then, belies the method of characterization he has chosen and ultimately taints the validity of the narrative itself.

One reason for this shortcoming may be Richardson's desire to deal with the social implication of Pamela's story. Personal disruption and social change are often linked; and while Richardson merely hints at the first—teasing his readers with glimpses of a complex and uncertain identity without allowing either reader or heroine a complete view—he attempts to deal explicitly with the second. His intention is announced in the subtitle, "Virtue Rewarded"; and one view of the novel might well define Pamela's ordeal as a kind of *rite de passage* from which she earns her new title. This way of reading the work would have the advantage of accommodating Pamela's static moral position: she does not become a lady; she already *is* a natural-born noblewoman, and the progress to her "rightful" social position need involve no alteration, either of moral character or of personality.

At least one critic[3] has suggested that much of the power of *Pamela* derives from a retelling of the Cinderella myth, the story of a young girl (who might be any one of the readers) elevated to social heights that had seemed unattainable. Yet there is an important difference between *Pamela* and *Cinderella*. The latter is a fantasy—Cinderella has a fairy godmother who conveniently provides her ward with all the accoutrements which society has denied her; the reader may dream of being like Cinderella, but unless she has taken leave of her senses, the kind of transformation postulated by the children's story is not fixed upon as a real-life option. Richardson's novel, on the other hand, is relentlessly realistic; he does not claim to be feeding the fantasies of his readers. Quite the contrary. He claims to be offering them a genuine model for their own lives: Pamela's reward in the rapidly expanding world of the eighteenth-century merchant might come to any girl with Pamela's persistent virtue.

In terms of the religious models on which Richardson drew, we might say that one motive in depicting Pamela was to show her as the figure in a religious autobiography might be shown—as a moral exemplum.[4] We have already noted the extent to which Richardson apparently wanted his readers to perceive Pamela as a model for virtuous behavior, and the subtitle clearly points to this intention, should we otherwise miss it. Yet if Pamela *is* to be seen as exemplary, the manner of her narrative becomes puzzling, indeed indefensible. After all, the events which comprised an autobiography were fittingly narrated after the event had been resolved; they were, moreover, carefully selected so that the moral of the story should not be lost. The reader knew from the beginning that neither suspense nor lengthy exploration of character were aims of the autobiographer, who had obviously survived his ordeal precisely because he was there to tell about it. In an autobiography, then, the reader could understand clearly that both narrator (as principal character) and his story were important primarily as vehicles for the lesson they taught. And such a moral aim conflicts uncomfortably with the breathless and apparently spontaneous quality of Pamela's tale.

Clearly Richardson has not sorted out his intentions in this first novel. Those qualities which strengthen the portrait of Pamela as exemplum—the tiresome reiteration of her good qualities, her own avowals of virtuous intention, ultimately the tendency to organize the revelation of her character and experience to show "the Beauty and Superiority of Virtue in an innocent and unpolished Mind, with the Reward which often, even in this Life, a protecting Providence bestows on Goodness" (*Grandison*, Preface)— all undercut the more "realistic" element which makes the novel seem so promising. The reader, who responds to both elements in the novel, may not comprehend Pamela's character and may even resent her for not being what he has anticipated.

Even if we disregard those elements of the novel which lead us to expect psychological analysis, and focus instead on Richardson's "social" intention, his failure to perceive the complexity of the problem he has posed makes the novel a failure. Pamela's search is not unlike the Puritan's. She acts on the implicit assumption that there ought to be a correspondence between virtue and rank and that society should tender some official and general recognition of individual merit. The sense of community pervaded all Puritan thought; individual struggles and trials were endured precisely because they might lead to membership in one of those communities which were the earthly counterparts of the community of Saints in heaven, and self-examination was pursued with the hope that the identity which it revealed might merit election. Pamela wishes to join a secular, not a religious group; but there is the same belief that trial and temptation are the means by which identity is discovered and the same hope that personal virtue can determine one's place in society. Richardson fails to understand that while personal virtue might well be a feasible means of determining rank in a theocracy, it is substantially less "valuable" in a society whose distinctions are based on inherited position or acquired money.

In a society which does not regularly reward virtue with social recognition, it is not enough that isolated individuals should receive a public reward commensurate with private merit. In order for this correlation to become established, a new system of social roles must develop which permits the typical individual to expect that he will receive a return proportionate to his private virtue. This is a problem which Richardson eventually does acknowledge and deal with in *Grandison*; however, in *Pamela* he seems oblivious to it. As a result Pamela inevitably appears vulgar and greedy. The girl Richardson apparently wanted to depict—the simple girl who cares more for goodness and chastity than for wealth and position—literally cannot exist in the upper classes as he describes them for the simple reason that there are no social roles which can adequately define such an identity. Distinctions in "high life" (as Richardson shows it) are made according to income and rank; when the simple girl is justly elevated, her excellence is *necessarily* rendered in terms of the class she has joined. In the world of Richardson's novel, the moral worth in a servant has to be expressed by wealth and prestige among the gentry. He "solves" the problem of social change by simple-mindedly equating their values, a transposition with unfortunate consequences for the coherence of the novel.

For example, Pamela's reward—the very identity she has won with such ardor—depends on maintaining existing social distinctions; without these distinctions, there could be no reward (as Richardson has defined it). Thus Pamela clings in a most unbecoming manner to the notion of a rigid and highly stratified society, seeing her own case as merely "a happy Exception to the Rule" (III, 324). Ultimately, the very process by which Pamela has won her own prize becomes threatening to her; and once she has attained position, it is in her interest to enhance her own role by preventing others from emulating her. The harshness, the intolerance and downright vulgarity of her attitude is even more objectionable than the method of her initial climb. When she catches an errant serving girl in a flirtation with Mr. B.'s nephew, she inveighs, "Little did I expect, *Polly*, that you would have shewn so much Imprudence. . . . You are under my Protection. I was once in as dangerous a Situation as you can be in: And I did not escape it, Child, by the Language and Conduct I heard from you. . . . Do you think, if I had sat me down in my Lady's Bedchamber, and sung a Song, and hem'd twice, and Mr. B. had come to me, upon that signal (for such I doubt it was), and I had kept my Place, and suffer'd myself to be rumpled, and only, in a soft Voice and with an encouraging Laugh cry'd, How can you do so? that I should have been what I am" (III, 363-365). Pamela needs reputation, approval, acceptance, and praise to maintain her position. Even one successful Polly would take away from her achievement, and hundreds of Pollys would make her new status meaningless.

Pamela's moral position in maintaining such an attitude is untenable: her world is demonstrated to be inadequate precisely because it does not offer an appropriate place to the virtuous low-born; Pamela's own ordeal is a direct result of this injustice. Richardson seems to present his novel as a lesson of virtue rewarded, yet it is difficult to imagine that such a series of trials could be institutionalized as the preliminary to passing into the upper classes. Not every young lady can be so "fortunate" as to meet with the temptations of a Pamela, and yet nowhere in the novel is an acceptable alternative offered. Pamela must be correct in seeing her marriage as a "happy Exception to the Rule"; and yet if she is, if virtue must languish for want of recognition or reward, then the very society whose mores she so enthusiastically embraces must be condemned—and Pamela with it.

This inherent incongruity undermines the entire moral structure of the novel. Mr. B. must be "immoral" at the outset; if he were not, Pamela would never have the opportunity to display her assets. His behavior is described initially in terms of Puritan stereotypes that were to become bourgeois cliches—the wicked, rich man preying on the poor but honest soul. Pamela rejoices in her lot, and the apparently irreconcilable conflict between rich and poor literally becomes the theme of her captivity.

> For, Oh! we *pity* should the Great
> Instead of *envying* their Estate;
> Temptation always on 'em wait,
>   Exempt from which are such as we.

> Their Riches, gay deceitful Snares,
> Inlarge their Fears, increase their Cares:
> Their Servants' Joy surpasses theirs;
>   At least so judges *PAMELA*.
>   (I, 118)

Yet when riches come, Pamela unconcernedly forgets the value of poverty and accepts the standards of her adopted class, while Mr. B. is revealed as intrinsically virtuous for no other apparant reason than that a moral heart beats under every *gentleman's* waistcoat.

Throughout the struggle, Pamela maintains an active interest in sustaining social order. She clearly does not want to triumph over Mr. B., begging him repeatedly to play the part of a master and treat her with even minimal respect. After the marriage he is expected to assume the traditional male role of moral instructor, as if he had never in any way violated the trust implicit in his authority. Similar apparent conflicts between prescribed authority and moral duty are also glossed over; so Pamela ignores her parents and Mrs. Jervis when their advice is inconvenient, but she never questions their right to give it or her own duty to obey. She simply suspends the rules of the game—just long enough to win—and then feverishly sets out to reaffirm them.

Ironically, it is the very complexity of Richardson's vision of the world that produced many of the novel's imperfections. Had he been content merely to write a little, pious, semireligious tale, had his ambitions led him no further than the homiletic truths of his earlier works, the gross mistakes of *Pamela* would never have been born to offend us: it is his potential for greatness that so insidiously undermines his first novel.

Richardson falters just where he should be most strong—in the rendition of character. At the outset of the novel we are beguiled into thinking that we can find Pamela's character transcribed into the letter-journal; she is, we believe, rattling on unself-consciously, telling us everything, making her story a mirror of the identity she has determined to discover. On these terms we are willing to accept her, willing to listen endlessly to the details of her temptations, willing to allow her three or four words where one might suffice, willing even to credit her with the compliments she so dutifully records. As soon as her trials seem over (and that may be well before Mr. B. ceases his threats, for we become gradually aware of the fact that Pamela's virtue is so secured that none of these sallies represents any real menace to her at all), we begin to perceive another kind of girl, characterized in literary terms which seem stylized and controlled. What had begun as spontaneous confession concludes as a series of domestic scenes interspersed with familiar essays. Pamela voices her opinions about current drama, her views on Locke's *Treatise on Education,* her solutions to the problem of an unfaithful husband. And she assumes this intrusively instructive air without ever having come one step along the way to understanding herself. The frightened fifteen-year-old girl becomes a boring, lecturing maiden aunt. Perhaps (the suspicion insinuates itself into our minds) she was *really* this way all along; perhaps she never intended moral discovery. But if such is the case, then the details of her "temptations" (since they could no longer have validity as the only means for discovering her true self) were never anything more than salacious, lip-smacking vulgarity.

Assuredly we cannot condemn Richardson for not doing something that he never intended to do in the first place. To be specific, we cannot accuse him of failing to write *Clarissa* when he wrote *Pamela.* However, we can remark on his failure to use a method of characterization which was appropriate to his intention: it was, conceivably, a lapse on Richardson's part to employ the technique of "writing to the moment" in a situation where the outcome was a foregone conclusion. And if he cannot be faulted for creating a Pamela instead of a Clarissa in his first novel, surely Richardson *can* be taken to task for having employed those narrative techniques which would have been appropriate to a Clarissa—and which were not appropriate to a Pamela.

The transformation from serving girl to lady is no more satisfying than the techniques used to render Pamela's character. Certainly the "Cinderella" quality of Pamela's transformation is appealing; it is the very substance of Romance. But Richardson did not see himself writing Romance: "In my Scheme I have generally taken Human Nature *as it is*; for it is to no purpose to suppose it Angelic, or to endeavor to make it so."[5] Yet his heroine adapts to her new life, is accepted by her former adversaries, with an ease and grace that belie the anguish of her trial. Richardson never inquires about a possible conflict between what she has learned as a girl and what is demanded of her as Mrs. B. In short, the very real difficulties which would have attended such an alteration of status are denied.

Even more serious, perhaps, is Richardson's failure to answer the more general questions which his narrative raises. What exactly is the nature of a child's duty to his parents and to other figures of rightful authority; is a child ever justified in violating his obligations of obedience; and what can a child do when different authority figures demand contradictory things? What is the nature of the relationship between men and women; are men, by temperament, violent and cruel, and do they willfully prey upon the helplessness of women, or is the sadistic man an abnormality; must women always submit to the authority of men; what are they to do if a man misuses that authority; if the woman is superior in virtue and intellect, what role ought she to assume? What is the significance of money: are the poor automatically virtuous, simply because they are poor; are the poor and the rich always and implacably hostile to each other; does money automatically corrupt those who possess it, or may money sometimes be a force for moral good—and if so, under what conditions?

The superficial ethic that emerges from the novel—that the resolutely virginal will get money—is as simple-minded as it is offensive. Presumably it was acceptable to at least some of Richardson's audience, perhaps because it embodied so clearly the cant of Puritanism turned commercial. English Puritanism had always shown a dangerous tendency to concretize the benefits of virtue; and Richardson, with the caution of a man new to the business of novel writing, backs away from any attempt to deal with the serious, real problems that his work raises, choosing instead to reinforce the prejudices of his audience.

The modern reader who has been so irresistibly compelled by the talkative girl at the beginning of the novel feels himself betrayed. There is just enough of a seemingly unself-conscious Pamela to pique curiosity, but never enough to satisfy. The "virtuous" Pamela, the Pamela who has become Mrs. B., and the exemplary Pamela all seem to get in the way; the narrative that began so urgently and with such apparent spontaneity has become a pirouetting, grotesque, and decidedly inferior comedy of manners. Real problems have been buried in layer upon layer of vapid conversation. By the end of the novel, Pamela appears to have satisfied herself, at least, in the acquisition of an appropriate identity; but she has, despite all the testimony she gathers, failed to appease us.

CHAPTER IV

Clarissa and Her Family

It is difficult to know how completely Richardson recognized the faults of *Pamela* and sought to correct them in *Clarissa*. He was evidently disturbed by the romantic response to Mr. B.'s villainy, and the characterization of Lovelace was intended as a warning to "children against preferring a man of pleasure to a man of Probity upon that dangerous but too commonly received notion, *that a re-formed rake makes the best husband*" (Preface).[1] The introduction of several points of view in *Clarissa* may well indicate Richardson's awareness of the difficulties resulting from the first-person narrative used in *Pamela*; and whatever his conscious intention, certainly this change permits an unambiguous understanding of the work and of its moral implications. However, the most important improvement lies in the very conception of the problem of the novel. As the failures of *Pamela* resulted from an inadequately detailed analysis of character in crisis and a superficial conception of the nature of social change, so the greatness of *Clarissa* can be attributed to Richardson's success in facing the literary problem of exploring transformations of character in a changing society.

The role of women as defined by the traditional, religious society of Richardson's day was relatively unambiguous; and the attribute which best defines woman's place might well be "dependent." Girls were not educated in the same manner as their brothers—not necessarily because anyone thought them less gifted, but simply because they had no need for "masculine" learning. Even the charity schools perpetuated this tradition; as M. G. Jones says, few of the women teachers "were required to teach writing; fewer still arithmetic. Knitting and " ' plane needlework' " were expected in their stead."[2] Woman's sphere was in the home; she did not work, and if she had any brothers, she did not even inherit. The money which was settled on her by her father at marriage was handled by her husband, who gave her an allowance (the size of which was usually determined by the amount of her dowry). Even if she was widowed, the bulk of her husband's estate would be left to their oldest son. Because women knew so little of the world, their decisions would naturally be made for them, by their parents when they were children and by their husbands after marriage.

In such a system the cardinal virtue of the woman would, of course, be obedience (and we might well remember that the Puritan Milton conceived of nothing less than the loss of Paradise itself as a result of woman's insubordination). *The Whole Duty of Man*, perhaps the most popular of all seventeenth- and eighteenth-century devotional manuals, describes the wife's role this way. The wife "owes obedience. . . . In all things which do not cross some command of God's, this precept is of force, and will serve to condemn the peevish stubborness of many wives."[3] Thomas Gouge, whose *Christian Directions* was reissued in both 1733 and 1742, is even more explicit. "The main duty of the wife's part is subjection. . . . The subjection of the wife to the husband implieth two things. 1. That she acknowledge a superiority in her husband. 2. That she put in practice such duties as do issue and flow from the acknowledgment of that superiority. The former is not only a duty, but the ground of all other duties whatsoever."[4]

The position of children is equally clear. No child could have the right of self-determination, even in those areas where his personal inclinations might move him to want to assert his own preferences. Indeed, "of all the acts of disobedience, that of marrying against the consent of the parent, is one of the highest. Children are so much the goods, the possessions of their parent, that they cannot without a kind of theft, give away themselves without the allowance of those that have the right in them."[5] "Children ought not to take unto themselves wives or husbands *without*, especially not *against* their parents' consent. And therefore such children shall adventure to join themselves in marriage in opposition to their parents, how can they expect a blessing from God upon them? Yea they have rather cause to fear the curse of God upon them, and their posterity."[6] Such views may seem stringent or unrealistically severe to us, but it is certain that Richardson and many like him took them in deadly earnest. His letters are filled with affirmations of the duty of a girl to obey her parents in the matter of marriage and of the equally binding duty of a wife's obedience to her husband.[7] As he writes to Lady Bradshaigh, "I am sorry to say it, but I have too often observed, that fear, as well as love, is necessary, on the lady's part, to make wedlock happy; and it will generally do it, if the man sets out with asserting his power and her dependence."[8]

This series of duties imposed upon women was balanced by a matching system of mutual duties and obligations of the husband and parents. Thus if the wife owed her husband obedience, he in turn was obliged to treat her "with mildness and respect."[9] If the child be compelled to absolute obedience, his parents in turn were enjoined to have the welfare—and especially the moral welfare—of the children be their only concern. "Parents must take heed, that they use their power over their children with equity and moderation, not to oppress them with unreasonable commands, only to exercise their own authority, but in all things of weight to consider the real good of their children, and to press them to nothing, which may not consist with that. This is a rule whereof parents may often have use, but in none greater than in the business of marrying their children."[10] The ideal result was, of course, not (as is so often pictured) a system of tyranny and misery, but a series of complimentary duties and obligations which, if honorably and well performed, protected the welfare of all. Within such a system the differing roles of husband and wife, parent and child, could never be in doubt.

Clarissa's position when we first encounter her can be understood only if we view her character in terms of the society just described, for both she and her parents conceive her primary obligation to be obedience—to them before she is married and to her husband afterwards. Indeed, the word duty runs like a recurrent *motif* throughout the painful and protracted family struggle. " 'If you *can* comply, remember it is your *duty* to comply.' . . . 'It is your *duty* to acquiesce, if you *can* acquiesce.' " (I, 286-287), her mother counsels; and her sister exults when the mother agrees to see her only " 'if you can be dutiful at last' " (I, 331). Her father, her uncles, her aunts and all the family unite in this rallying call; even the chambermaid observes " 'Nothing will do but duty, Miss!—Your Papa said, Let her tell me of *deeds*!—I'll receive no *words* from her' " (II, 93). Clarissa herself never rejects this standard for judging behavior, and her problem arises not in deciding whether or not to do her duty but in trying to determine just what that duty is. The obligations of subjection can never be suspended. "Is the want of reward, or the want even of a grateful acknowledgement, a reason for us to dispense with what we think our duty?" (I, 194), she asks Miss Howe. "I should not know how to square it to my own principles, to dispense with the duty I owe to my Father, where-ever it shall be his Will to place me . . . For I do assure you, I would sooner beg my bread, than litigate for my right with my Father: Since I am convinced, that whether the Parent do his duty by the Child or not, the Child cannot be excused from doing hers to him" (II, 177, 60). These views seem to represent Richardson's own, for he too declares, "The want of duty on one part justifies not the non-performance of it on the other, where there is a reciprocal duty. There can be no merit, strictly speaking, in performing a duty; but the performance of it on one side, when it is not performed on the other, gives something so like a merit, that I am ready almost to worship the good mind that can do it."[11]

The force of this obligation to obedience or duty can be traced throughout the novel, and it is the motivating factor in much of Clarissa's behavior subsequent to the moment when she leaves her father's house. Her endless delays in arranging matters with Lovelace must be attributed in part to the tenacious desire for parental approval of her marriage, and even her acceptance of the ridiculous farce with Tomlinson is testament to the urgency of her need for reconciliation. Obligation and duty are almost always held superior to personal preference; even her acknowledgement of a genuine love or passion for Lovelace could,

therefore, never dissuade her from seeking to reestablish
her relationship with her family. Moreover, the obsessive
terror over the reaction of her father—the visions and fantasies of returning to him on her knees—and her inex-
pressible horror at the thought of a parental curse must
be attributed at least in part to this traditional notion of
the child's obligation to duty. As Gouge and so many
theologians like him were wont to remind one, the child
who defies his parents in the matter of marriage can expect
no blessing; "yea they have rather cause to fear the curse
of God upon them, and their posterity."[12]

If the characteristic virtue of the woman in this dependent position was obedience, the appropriate act of piety
was humility and the personal attribute most likely to accompany it was passivity; the three joined to form a set of
mutually reinforcing supports on which to structure a definition of the feminine nature. It should not surprise us
then to discover that the trait which seems to dominate
Clarissa's nature, recurring again and again throughout
the course of the novel, is the tendency to apparent submissiveness or passivity in her relationships with others.
She was, after all, the product of a system which had taught
her this mien as appropriate and the daughter of a mother
whose own unwillingness to act provided a clear model
for the child. Early in her trials Clarissa recognizes this
element in her nature; "They have begun so cruelly with
me, that I have not spirit enough to assert my own Negative" (I, 48), and (not unpredictably) she looks to her friend
for sufficient support to rally her. But even the faithful
Miss Howe does not delude herself as to the nature of
Clarissa's character. "You ask me to help you to a little of
my spirit. Are you in earnest? But it will not now I doubt
do you service.—It will not sit naturally upon you. You
are your Mother's girl, think what you will" (I, 59). Ironically, even this ostensible search for the strength to act

becomes for Clarissa merely a covert method for reaffirming passivity. Miss Howe urges her to take lawful control of the estate she has given into her father's hands. Clarissa meditates the action and then rejects it, capable only of seeing her own weakness and the terrible possibility of error which is latent in any overt action. "All young creatures, thought I, more or less, covet independency; but those who wish most for it, are seldom the fittest to be trusted either with the government of themselves, or with power over others. This is certainly a very high and unusual devise to so young a creature. We should not aim at *all* we have power to do" (I, 134). Still she asks for advice, and still Miss Howe urges action. Again the advice is rejected, but the attitude of expectant dependency is never altered.— "Give me, my dearest Miss Howe, your opinion, what I *can*, what I *ought* to do" (II, 51)—so that the suppliant refrain ritualistically seeking advice which will never be followed ceases to have any value as communication and becomes instead simply a method by which Clarissa confirms her own image of a submissive self.

Indeed, the reader, with Miss Howe, grows impatient with Clarissa as she clings to this attitude beyond all reason, beyond any hope of happiness. Why does she never leave Lovelace? Certainly she could were she sufficiently determined to do so; even Lovelace himself admits, " 'Tis certain I can have no pretence for holding her, if she will go" (III, 79), when he first takes her from her parents, seeing her as one "whom I had no good pretence to *hold*, if she *would* go; and who could so easily, if I had given her cause to doubt, have thrown herself into other protection, or have returned to Harlowe-Place and Solmes" (III, 82). We know from her own letters that she has perpetual doubts about him, and yet she stays on. She rejects Anna Howe's money, forbids her to journey to London and help, disdains even to quit the infamous house where she is lodged despite her growing apprehension about Mrs. Sinclair and her girls. Of course, escape becomes increasingly difficult the longer she hesitates, but there is no doubt that escape is possible—at first by perfectly ordinary means and even later by the exertion of a certain amount of ingenuity and courage.

One explanation for this behavior lies in Clarissa's definition of herself. In a letter addressed to the Reverend Mr. Stinstra, Richardson makes the following observation. "Men and women are brothers and sisters; they are not of different species; and what need be obtained to know both, but to allow for different modes of education, for situation and constitution, or perhaps I should say, for habits, whether good or bad."[13] He is engaged in explaining his remarkable knowledge of the woman's mind, but the statement is even more valuable as an insight into his definition of the feminine identity. If men and women are not essentially different, then their definitions of themselves *as* men or *as* women must be learned. Furthermore, insofar as the role of being a man or of being a woman becomes important in an individual's definition of himself, society's interpretation of the differences between men and women will necessarily become incorporated into an individual's own identity.

In the case of Clarissa, society saw obedience, humility, and passivity as necessary attributes of the woman's role; and consistently throughout Richardson's novels, women who behave otherwise are viewed scornfully—even by such a lively personality as Anna Howe, who declares, "Indeed, my dear, I do not think a *Man-woman* a pretty character at all" (III, 207). If these characteristics are really, as Richardson intimates, those which serve to distinguish men from women (and, to a lesser degree, women from each other), then in a meaningful sense part of Clarissa's identity consists precisely in her passivity; for it ordinarily makes very little sense to speak of a person's behaving in one way and yet being another. Thus Clarissa's apparently irrational adherence to a submissive or passive mode of behavior is merely an anxious attempt to cling to the role of woman as it had been traditionally defined and an even more desperate desire to preserve the nature of her own identity. A different attitude would necessarily presuppose an alternative definition of self; and another conception of her identity would, in turn, necessitate some other alternative interpretation of woman's role. (We might remember, parenthetically, that the much more lively Anna Howe had lost her father and therefore lived in a home where the mother had assumed a certain degree of dominance and control.)

In the light of this notion we can understand more clearly, perhaps, the severity implied by the Lady Davers' notion of Pamela as a "sauce-box" or a "Miss Pert"— epithets whose insult lies in the imputation of unseemly pride (unconsciously ironic insults from one whose own manner was unbecomingly harsh). In like manner, only Pamela's apparently excessive humility, the counterpart of Clarissa's passivity, can correct the mistaken impression.

Certainly much in Clarissa's nature can be traced to the attitudes of her society; but she is much more than a stereotype, and the true complexity of her nature lies beyond these purely social determinations. For instance, the reader becomes quickly aware of the fact that Clarissa has a nice appreciation of her own value, despite the very elaborate attitude of humility and passivity that she strikes. She quotes the preamble of her grandfather's will to Miss Howe, a document which states that "Clarissa hath been from her infancy a matchless young creature in her duty to me, and admired by all who knew her, as a very extraordinary child" (I, 30); and when Miss Howe remarks, "You see what you draw upon yourself by excelling all your Sex.

Every individual of it who knows you, or has heard of you, seems to think you answerable to *her* for your conduct" (I, 4). We know that if Clarissa is exemplary, she is certainly not unaware of her own goodness. Quite the contrary, she seems consciously to define herself as better than those whom she encounters, and her reactions to the overtures of others consistently betray this self-esteem.

Thus the tone of her rejection to Lovelace's initial interest, however appropriate that rejection may have been, illuminates the vanity of her virtue. "I thought it best to convince him, by the coolness and indifference with which I repulsed his forward hopes (at the same time intending to avoid the affectation of pride or vanity) that he was not considerable enough in my eyes to make me take over-ready offence at what he said, or at his haughty looks: In other words, that I had not value enough for him to treat him with peculiarity either by smiles or frowns" (I, 19-20). We learn that she has turned away a multitude of suitors, none of whom has been deemed worthy of her; and her reaction to the family's proposal of yet another suppliant is, until she learns that the man is Solmes, merely the weary intolerance of one who has lost patience with an imperfect world. "Whose addresses now, thought I, is this treatment preparative to?—Mr. Wyerley's again?—or whose? And then, as high comparisons, where *self* is concerned, sooner than low, come into young people's heads; Be it for whom it will, this is wooing as the English did for the heiress of Scotland in the time of Edward the Sixth" (I, 44-45).

Clarissa's pride in her virtue may be seen in almost all of her actions, but it is demonstrated nowhere more clearly than in the relationship with her brother and sister; for if she articulates her identity in the correspondence with Miss Howe by stating and restating her passivity, with her brother and sister a similar assertion of self takes the

form of a continuing affirmation of moral superiority. She
is someone, we feel, only so long as she perceives herself
better than someone else. And the penetrating Miss Howe
recognizes the import of Clarissa's behavior almost at once.
"It must be confessed, however, that this Brother and Sister of yours, judging as such narrow spirits will ever judge,
have some reason for treating you as they do. It must have
long been a mortification to them (set disappointed Love
on her side, and Avarice on his, out of the question) to be
so much eclipsed by a young Sister. Such a Sun in a family,
where there are none but faint twinklers, how could they
bear it!" (I, 182-183). Of course Clarissa expands with
praise and recognition, but insofar as she aggrandizes
herself at the expense of her brother and sister, the very
act of confirming her own sense of self precludes recognition of theirs. " 'How often,' " cries her sister Bella, " 'have
I and my Brother been talking upon a subject, and had
every-body's attention, till *you came in, with your bewitching meek* pride, and *humble* significance? And then
have we either been stopped by references to Miss Clary's
opinion, forsooth; or been forced to stop ourselves, or
must have talked on unattended to by everybody' "
(I, 316).

Once begun in this course, Clarissa cannot seem to find
it within her power to alter her behavior; and even when
she is most vulnerable to the spite of a vengeful sister (or
perhaps *because* she is perpetually threatened with reprisals), she continues in her attitude of quiet reproach.
For instance, practically every interview with Bella ends
with Clarissa's mild reminder that Lovelace, who has become her suitor, began by paying his addresses to the elder
sister. Bella's reaction to this bit of torment is always
violent, for she has clearly been insulted by his slight; yet
Clarissa never refrains from reopening the wound. She
never stoops to open hostility, seldom allows herself any

overt expression of anger. Still her attitude is not entirely consistent with the passive mien we have come to expect of her. As her uncle remarks, "Was this the way you used to take to make us all adore you as we did?—No, it was your gentleness of heart and manners, that made everybody, even strangers, at first sight, treat you as a Lady, and call you a Lady, tho' not born one, while your elder Sister had no such distinctions paid her. If you *were* envied, why should you sharpen envy, and file up its teeth to an edge?' " (II, 96).

Clarissa's character, then, is a peculiar mixture of passivity and aggression; and the articulation of both is essential to an expression of her own identity. In her relationships with others she always displays a "womanly" passivity. She is never moved to an overt expression of will or self-determination save in her resistance to the will of others, but this behavior belies the fact that she has a very strong sense of her own worth and her own desires. In a deeper sense, then, she is determinedly willful, despite her conscious passivity; but she effects her desires not by acting but by manipulating others.

When we meet Clarissa at the beginning of the novel, there is no intrinsic reason to suppose that she will not continue to be successful in her dealings with the world. She has, by all accounts, been exemplary in her duty, preserving a quiet and submissive attitude towards her parents and showing no obvious symptoms of rebellion. Unlike Pamela, whose reputation grew only after her marriage, Clarissa has already acquired a reputation for excellence while still single; and the worldly reward that is bestowed as the culmination of Pamela's trials has already come to Clarissa, who is a considerable heiress in her own right. We may deplore her tendency to strike a superior attitude before her brother and sister; but the traditional, religiously conservative society of latter-day

Puritanism has always encouraged the virtuous to reprove their errant brethren, and there is no doubt that Richardson intended us to see her as virtuous—"an Exemplar to her Sex" (Preface). Indeed, much of Clarissa's nature, especially as it is summarized for us by Anna Howe at the end of the novel, can be seen as the typical embodiment of Puritan virtue; and, as we have seen earlier, however disagreeable the conduct of such people may seem to us, there had certainly been considerable public approval of it.[14]

While it would indeed be mistaken to view Clarissa's nature merely as the *product* of certain social and religious forces, it would be equally mistaken not to recognize the importance of these forces in *sustaining* her character. Passivity is viable as a mode of behavior only when the figures of authority to whom one turns are benevolent in the exercise of their power. The humble practice of virtue will bring praise and recognition only in a society whose dominating values are religious or ethical; and moral superiority will prevail in the world only as long as it is not opposed to some inimical force—either monetary or physical. While society remained unambiguous in its approval and support of those qualities which defined Clarissa as "good," there would be no conflict and no unhappiness in her life. However, when society's rules and expectations begin to change (when, for instance, we find the curious conflict between differing notions of behavior that Defoe mirrored so vividly in his religious works), then the kind of conduct that had formerly found credit may suddenly be deemed inappropriate or wrong; and the personality that once acted effectively in the world may no longer be able to function. When Clarissa's quandary develops, it is occasioned by the breakdown of the values of the society to which she belongs. She has been taught passivity and a conscious sense of her own moral worth; yet she suddenly discovers that submissiveness brings only tyranny and that the assertion of her moral superiority is followed with angry reprisals. She is capable of recognizing the harsh injustice of her family's behavior, but nothing in her upbringing and very little in her character can indicate a solution; the very identity which had been nurtured by its environment is now rejected, and a viable solution to the resultant dilemma can only come from a reconstruction of the self.

Within the system of mutual duties and obligations postulated by the Puritan and conservative Anglican view of family government, there were, of course, provisions for the failure of one party to perform his part of the contract. Parents were obliged to make the child's moral welfare their primary concern, and in the case of marriage they were also expected to make their own adjudged choice coincide as much as possible with the daughter's preferences and personal inclinations. Should they, for whatever reason, neglect this duty, the daughter could oppose them, for "if any parent shall be so wicked, as to require his child . . . to do any unlawful thing, the child then offends not against his duty, though he disobey that command, nay, he must disobey. . . . Yet when 'tis thus necessary to refuse obedience, he should take care to do it in such a modest, and respectful manner, that it may appear 'tis conscience only, and not stubbornness moves him to it."[15]

Clearly, in Clarissa's case, Richardson means us to understand that the Harlowes are going beyond their rights as parents in forcing Solmes on their daughter. He is a man whose moral character would not permit her to fulfill her obligations to him conscientiously, for in marriage the daughter must transfer her duty of obedience from

the father to the husband, and if the proposed husband
be immoral or if for some other reason his nature be such
as would prevent the wife from doing her duty, then her
parents have no right to urge the union. "How much
easier," Clarissa exclaims of her family's behavior, "to
bear the *temporary* persecutions I labour under, *because*
temporary, than to resolve to be *such* a man's for *life*. . . .
A *month* will decide the one, perhaps: but what a *duration
of woe* will the other be!—Every day, it is likely, rising to
witness to some new breach of an altar-vowed duty!"
(II, 71). In such a situation Clarissa's only recourse would
be a steadfast refusal to marry him; this much she would
be permitted—nay, enjoined—to do in order to protect
herself from a moral injustice. In fact, as we learn later in
the novel, had she persisted in her rejection of Solmes,
the Harlowes were prepared to give in to her wishes at
the last moment. She would never, however, have the
right to leave home (as she rashly does) nor to contract a
marriage with anyone else against her father's wishes. On
the purely ethical or religious level of the novel, then,
Clarissa's most obvious sins are the disobedience of leaving
her parents' home and the violation of her duty to them.
Lovelace in this rather simple context represents the devil,
that agent who instigates sin; and the repeated epithets
of Lucifer, Devil, Demon, and the like which are applied
to him throughout the novel underline this role, as does
the elaborately treacherous strategy by which he tricks
Clarissa into running away.

   If there were no more to the situation than the plight of
a daughter whose rash disobedience led to her destruction,
the story would have made a nice moral tale, but it would
scarcely have grown into the brilliant study of character
that Richardson provides. The tragedy is precipitated not
simply by the parents' refusal to do their duty, but by the
particular nature of their failure—not merely by Clarissa's

inability to adhere to the pattern of conduct which had hitherto shaped her life, but by the internal forces which drove her to reject that pattern. The events in Richardson's novel, then, chronicle the breakdown of a social system, the disappearance of a way of life; and Clarissa's "sin" of deserting her parents' home is merely the first step in a search for new values with which to give her existence meaning.

The Puritan notion of family government which is implicit in the Harlowes' relationship functions most efficiently in a small, theocratic community. Not surprisingly, the dissenters and devout Anglicans of the sixteenth and seventeenth centuries had frequently segregated themselves from the larger social system of England in an attempt to create such a group. (And, of course, the Commonwealth movement in England and the colonial society of America had each in its differing way moved toward this notion of social organization.) In such a system the primary values would be religious, and the probability that one individual's control over the actions or life of another would be unselfish or benevolent might, hopefully, be maximized. In the case of parents making decisions for their children, these decisions would, under optimal conditions, be governed by the moral values of the community. Furthermore, a small group, one in which everyone was well-known by the other members, would allow parents to have sufficient personal knowledge of the young people to choose an appropriate partner for their child.

However, the eighteenth century brought changes to this way of life, as the dissenters, for monetary, political, or socially ambitious reasons, were gradually drawn into the life of England as a whole. This assimilation brought temptations to woo one from the old ways, as Dodderidge, Watts, and Defoe all point out—the lure of money and of the possibility of a way of life which had previously been available only to those who inherited wealth and title, or the inevitable temptations offered by increased contact with those of other faiths and those of no faith at all. Such threats to piety could be countered by renewed emphasis on religious education and on the importance of duty, and these were the battle cries of the eighteenth-century Puritan; however, most were vain, for the religiosity of the increasingly successful merchant could seldom prevail against the attractions of the secular world he was growing to know. The property won by hard labor and virtuous industry began to exert a force of its own. As Weber has suggested, the accumulation of money became an end in itself, and all other aims were frequently subordinated to it. One very efficient mode of gaining money or enlarging one's estate was the judicious "property marriage," and the Harlowes are of course aware of this possibility. Christopher Hill has explored the monetary aspects of *Clarissa* in a nicely penetrating study,[16] tracing the prudential reasons which made a marriage between Clarissa and Solmes so very attractive and which, at the same time, made her inheritance from the grandfather abhorrent and the possibility of her marriage with Lovelace unthinkable. As Hill says, "What the novel does is to examine the effect on individuals of property marriage and all that goes with it. How do individuals react to this monstrous perversion, which we must take as given? How does it affect their relations with other human beings?"[17] There is no doubt that this strain runs strongly throughout the novel; but it is not the whole picture, for the concern about the degrading effects of a "property marriage" and about the increasing importance of money and land is just one more aspect of the religious view of the novel, which would see it as one group within the family failing to do their duty (here the failure of the parents who have

yielded to the sin of avarice). That Richardson was concerned with this tendency is undeniable; as he says in the
conclusions to the novel. "The unhappy Parents and
Uncles, from the perusal of these Extracts, too evidently for
their peace, saw, that it was entirely owing to the avarice,
the ambition, the envy, of her implacable Brother and
Sister, and to the senseless confederacy entered into by the
whole family . . . that she ever thought of quitting her
Father's house" (VIII, 279). But quitting her parents' home
was merely the first step in Clarissa's tragedy, and her
family's rapacity is only one part of the eventual crisis.

Other much more important changes which shaped the
life of the latter-day Puritan cannot be subsumed so easily
under the traditional headings of sin and temptation. For
instance, the entrance of the relatively parochial dissenter
into a larger and more varied life made it impossible for
him to know all the members of his growing social sphere.
Close acquaintance with the residents of his country village
or with the members of his urban congregation could lead
to an intimate personal knowledge of them; however, the
process of meeting and becoming acquainted with a
larger number of people, often people who were quite
unfamiliar in their ways and beliefs, made intimate knowledge of their character increasingly difficult. A more
heterogeneous, perplexing society necessarily forced
people to judge others by relatively external signs. Thus
even parents who wanted to do their duty in choosing an
appropriate partner for their children might be quite unable to assess the essential nature of a man or his true moral
character; and perhaps, like Pamela, they would even be
reduced to judging him by his clothes.[18] Lovelace is admitted in good faith as a respectable suitor for the older
daughter on the recommendation of his money and position. However self-seeking the Harlowes may have been, it
is difficult to imagine that they would ever have con-

sidered Lovelace, no matter how great his wealth, had they known of his depravity. That they did not know is due partly to their self-deluding avarice and partly to the increased complexity of the society in which they lived.

In addition to the increasingly complicated social pattern of one's life, the increasing popularity of another custom in the eighteenth century proved a much more serious threat to the order of family government; this was the gradual undermining of the authority and importance of the role of the father. In his discussion of marriage settlement during this period,[19] H. J. Habakkuk describes a cumulative tendency, dating from the mid-seventeenth century and coming into dominance during the first part of the eighteenth century, to focus power and importance in the family on the oldest son. This change was effected by a form of inheritance arrangement called the "strict settlement." The aim of this innovation was to insure that the family estate should pass from generation to generation; and the function of the strict settlement (as opposed to the entail, which could be broken with relative ease) was to prevent a legatee from obtaining absolute ownership of an estate and then selling off some portion of it. According to this procedure, a grandfather would settle his estate on the oldest son of his own oldest son. In such an arrangement the father would be by-passed; and his claim in the estate of his own father would be reduced to that of a life tenant, receiving income from the property but unable to sell or mortgage it for any period longer than his own life. In a time of a changing economy—a period during which business investments yielded a higher income than land, despite the fact that land was still more heavily taxed—there was often pressure to pay debts by mortgaging or selling land which had become a diminishing source of profit. Yet the man who had inherited under the strict settlement was not free to do so, for the control of his estate was in the hands of his son. Nor was this an uncommon form of inheritance. Habakkuk asserts that strict settlement was the most normal procedure for willing an estate of any size and estimates that by mideighteenth century about one-half of all the land in England was held under these provisions.[20]

The result, of course, was the development of a general family pattern in which the authority and status of the father diminished as he lost the power to enforce his wishes in the event of any dispute. As Hill observes, "The eldest son came to occupy a unique position of authority,"[21] and the strong paternalism of traditional family government began to disappear. If we remember, now, the Harlowes' situation, we can easily see this change mirrored in Richardson's portrayal of their relationships. The question of a strict settlement is not raised (the grandfather's estate having gone to Clarissa), although there is every expectation that the estates of the uncles will be left to Clarissa's older brother; but the arrogance of the son James, the general effort to aggrandize his position, the extent to which his family regards him as the center of their interests, and his own complete domination over his father all demonstrate the breakdown of traditional notions of family government which was associated with this economic change.

All of these forces combine in their effect on Clarissa. She is acutely aware of the fact that she is being used as a pawn in a vicious and ambitious game, treated more like an object than a person whose rights are to be respected. "I never can be . . . I never *ought* to be, Mrs. Solmes.—I repeat, that I *ought* not: For surely, my dear, I should not give up to my Brother's ambition the happiness of my future life" (I, 136). She endeavors to evade the traps of his family's greed, observing that Solmes' "chief, or one of his chief motives in his address to me, is, as I have reason to believe, the contiguity of my Grandfather's Estate to his own. I will resign it; for ever I will resign it: And the resignation must be good, because I will never marry at all" (II, 98-99). But all such strategems fail; Clarissa continues to be considered only as an object to be bartered, despite her increasingly frantic efforts to resist such treatment. "I will claim the protection due to a child of the family, or to know why I am to be thus treated. . . . I will know . . . *why* I am to be constrained thus?—What is intended by it?—And whether I am to be considered as a *child* or a *slave*?" (I, 332). In seeking redress for injustice, Clarissa naturally applies herself to her father, only to find that he has given over his authority to be guided by an arrogant and selfish son; and at this point her position seems to have gone beyond help. She is not freed of her obligation to her father; but she cannot appeal to him for mercy or relief because he has himself chosen to obey the dictates of her imperious brother. The resultant chaos and misrule leaves her searching frenziedly and vainly for some inkling of returning order, as she sees her fate more and more thrust into her brother's hands. "Something is strangely wrong somewhere!" she exclaims to Anna Howe, "to make Parents, the most indulgent till now, seem cruel in a child's eye; and a Daughter, till within these few weeks, thought unexceptionably dutiful, appear, in their judgment, a rebel!—Oh! O my ambitious and violent Brother! What may he have to answer for to both!" (II, 133-134). Something is wrong, of course. The order Clarissa has always known is slowly crumbling away, and the final and inevitable stage of despair with her family is reached just before her flight. "You can not imagine what my emotions were behind the yew-hedge, on seeing my Father so near me. I was glad to look at him thro' the hedge, as he passed by: But I trembled in every joint, when I heard him utter *these* words: Son James, To You, and to Bella, and to You, Brother, do I wholly commit this matter. That I was meant, I cannot doubt. And yet, why was I so affected; since I may be said to have been given up to the cruelty of my Brother and Sister for many days past?" (II,252).

The combination of these changes—the temptation of money leading a family to a violation of their duties, the growth of a confusing and complex sphere of personal relationships, and the ultimate crumbling of the structure of power and authority within the family—all lead to the disintegration of a social system. The older order in which Clarissa had thrived and won acclaim is disappearing, and in its stead is a new, confusing, and much more demanding world.

In the light of this situation, it is easy to understand Clarissa's attraction to Lovelace. Perhaps the central factor in her break with her family is the failure of her father. The mother is weak, yes, but one scarcely expects any decisive action from her; Clarissa repeatedly defends her passive behavior to Miss Howe. "Would not LOVE and PITY, *excusably*, nay *laudably*, make a good Wife . . . give up her own will, her own likings, to oblige a Husband, thus afflicted, whose love for her was unquestionable?" (I, 194). A woman was not supposed to contradict her husband's will; but by the same token, the husband and father was expected to exert that will decisively. Such behavior was deemed appropriate and even attractive in a man, for as Clarissa tells us, "They were my Father's lively spirits that first made him an interest in [my mother's] gentle bosom" (I, 194). The father's abnegation, then, is the crucial factor in Clarissa's break with her background, for in a literal sense, sound family government depended on his continuing guidance and control. In addition, he was the very symbol of steadiness, strength, protection, and order. Certainly there is a sexual component in Clarissa's adoration for Lovelace; however, we must not permit our interest in the sexual attachment to obscure the fact that she is desperately seeking a man who is strong in the ways that her father had seemed strong. Only by finding such a man and subjecting herself to his authority can she revert to the passive role which she finds familiar and gratifying.

Clarissa's fears and fantasies both before and after her flight center on the contrarieties of her father's nature: it is her father's weakness in failing to act which has thrown her into despair, and her father's potential for violence which later makes her fear his curse. By contrast, she initially perceives Lovelace as appealingly and unwaveringly strong. He begins to make his addresses at just that time when Mr. Harlowe's indecisiveness is becoming apparent; and as the father's will grows weaker and weaker, as his authority has less and less real meaning, Lovelace's suit becomes increasingly pressing. Clarissa turns to Miss Howe for guidance, but her friend's advice to abandon her submissive stance is the last thing Clarissa wants to hear. Lovelace, on the other hand, is full of plans which would permit him to take care of her, relieving her from torment without demanding from her any more direct action than retreat. As the novel moves slowly towards Clarissa's flight, the antiphonal attractions of the lover and the father urge her first in one direction and then in another, and the structure of the novel mirrors her indecision beautifully. Clarissa will describe a stormy scene with her family, avowing her continued dutifulness and detailing the disappointment of her fruitless appeals to an impassive father; her following letter will reveal the substance of a proposal by Lovelace. The next letter again treats the family harshness—perhaps with an increasingly desperate sense of frustration; this is again followed by a letter transcribing Lovelace's urgent promises. At

the beginning of the novel there is no contest between the
forces, for Clarissa is determined in her duty. However, as
she gradually feels herself betrayed by her father, Lovelace increasingly displaces him in her affections as the
masculine embodiment of power and will.

There is danger, of course, in Lovelace's strength. As
Clarissa says of him early in the novel, "In short, my dear,
like a restiff [sic] horse (as I have heard described by sports-
men) he pains one's hands, and half disjoints one's arms,
to rein him in" (I, 180-181). Yet there is a fascination even
in this very potential; and if Lovelace is violent in his
strength, there is at least a magnificence in his violence.
When he is compared with the family's candidate, there
can be no doubt as to Clarissa's preference. "Constitution
was to be considered. . . . A man of spirit would act like
one, and could do nothing meanly. . . . A creeping mind
would creep in every-thing, where it had a view to obtain
a benefit by it; and insult, where it had power, and nothing
to expect" (II, 195-196). In contrast to the majestic animal
images used to describe Lovelace—he is a horse, for instance, or a hawk—the beast mostly clearly associated
with Solmes is a reptile or some other creeping, crawling,
cowering thing. He sits "asquat" a chair (I, 99), enters a
room "cringing to the ground" (II, 202), and attempts to
assure the sincerity of his protestations by an agony of
indecision and awkwardness. "The poor man's face was
all this time over-spread with confusion, twisted, as it
were, and all awry, neither mouth nor nose standing in
the middle of it. He looked as if he were ready to cry"
(II, 230).

Solmes' clumsy ineffectuality (he scarcely ever speaks
for himself, and allows the Harlowes to do his courting
for him) is inevitably contrasted with Lovelace's self-
confidence in its potential effect on Clarissa's role as wife.
"He is allowed to be brave," Clarissa muses of Lovelace.

"Who ever knew a brave man, if a man of *sense*, an universally base man? And how much the gentleness of our
Sex, and the manner of our training up and education,
make us need the protection of the Brave, and the countenance of the Generous, let the general approbation which
we are all so naturally inclined to give to men of that
character, testify" (I, 293). In such a man even the cruelty
of his strength might provide a certain gratification in
both the sexual and the non-sexual areas of marriage, and
Clarissa naively tantalizes and excites herself with the
prospect of such a relationship. Perhaps the wife "must
practice as well as *promise* obedience, to a man so little
used to controul; and must be careful to oblige. And what
Husband expects not this? . . . And how much easier
and pleasanter to obey the man of her choice, if he should
be even unreasonable sometimes, than one she would not
have had, could she have avoided it?" (I, 292).

In a very real sense, then, Clarissa's flight from home
is intended as a journey toward, rather than a journey
away from, the order which she had always known. If her
father's strength has failed her, Lovelace will not waver
in his; if her family has ceased to appreciate the value of
her gifts, Lovelace ardently offers himself in admiration.
Thus escape with her lover, and the subsequent marriage
implicit to her in that act, would re-establish the old relationships and the old patterns of behavior. Passivity
would again be demanded of her, and obedience (because
Lovelace is, according to Clarissa at least, a *brave* man and
a man of *sense*) would bring reward and praise. Finally,
even the very fact of Lovelace's faults recommends him to
her, for they are the means by which she can again assert
her own moral superiority (as she had asserted it before
with her brother and sister). "And then has the secret
pleasure intruded itself, to be able to reclaim such a man
to the paths of virtue and honour: To be a *secondary*

means, if I were to be his, of saving him, and preventing the mischiefs so enterprising a creature might otherwise be guilty of, if he be such a one" (I, 293).

Clearly Clarissa lacks insight into Lovelace's potential for depravity. Indeed, perhaps the dominant theme of the first portion of the novel is its heroine's ignorance, both of her own nature and of Lovelace's. Her attention and energy are almost exclusively focused on the family problem: she still wants to act out the old, familiar patterns— still seeks praise by methods which have long since proved ineffective, remaining unaware even of the need for self-recrimination. This self-centeredness is a moral failing, and it is at the root of her increasing distress. Immersed as she is in her own needs, she scarcely perceives Lovelace at all; he exists merely as a figure in her fantasies. Because Clarissa does not consider Lovelace as an important moral force, she mistakenly assumes that he is incapable of having an adverse effect on her. She sees him as a man who could become a positive figure of authority, one to whom the transfer of her duties of obedience might eventually be appropriate; and she learns of her mistake only after it is too late to correct it.

CHAPTER V

Clarissa and Lovelace

The premise that underlies Clarissa's initial thinking about Lovelace is that there is some basic sense of moral and social order informing all of his behavior. On the basis of such an assumption, she can interpret all acts of violence and cruelty as atypical variations from the norm. (It is important, in this context, to notice that she speaks of *re-claiming* him, taking him back to some former state of virtue.) Clarissa's problem arises when Lovelace proves not to have this moral groundwork; and unlike Mr. B., whom Pamela can woo from his sinful ways by a virtuous display of strength, Lovelace is fated to remain malevolent in the exercise of his power.

Lovelace serves a number of functions in the novel, and his character is traced much more completely than that of Mr. B. in *Pamela;* indeed, so many letters in the second half of the novel are devoted to his ruminations (much more than would be needed merely to offer another view of the action) that a modern reader might wonder why Lovelace's character figures so prominently in Clarissa's tragedy. Surely one answer is that Richardson is offering a complementary portrait to that of his heroine: if she is to represent a member of the Elect, an "early Saint,"[1] then Lovelace is a portrait of the damned. The description of his death, defended by Richardson in a letter to Edward Moore, was explicitly intended as contrast to Clarissa's glorious departure. "Have I not then given rather a dreadful than a hopeful Exit, with respect to Futurity, to the unhappy Lovelace! —I protest I have been unable to reperuse the act: of his Death *with this great Circumstance* in my Head, and to think of the triumphant one of my divine Clarissa, without pity—and I did hope that the contrast if attentively considered would be very striking."[2] The desire to characterize the cursed as well as the blessed has precedent: in the Puritan religious tradition of the seventeenth century we find the portrait of Mr. Badman, who is traced "in his life, from his childhood to his death; that thou [the reader] mayest, as in a glass, behold with thine own eyes the steps that take hold of hell; and also discern, while thou art reading of Mr. Badman's death, whether thou thyself art treading in his path thereto."[3] Moreover, such portraits were not limited to the religious tradition of the Puritans. The Anglican, Gilbert Burnet, wrote the *Life and Death of the Right Honourable John, Earl of Rochester* in order to reform "a loose and lewd Age."[4] Richardson's repeated assertions throughout the letters that he *intends* Lovelace to be unamiable and profligate, that Richardson has combined the worst qualities of some two or three known rakes in an attempt to make this evil seem life-like, that he deliberately blackened Lovelace's character when over-tender female readers clamored for a wedding—all of this merely points to the deliberateness with which Richardson set about portraying his member of the Accursed.

Lovelace shares several qualities with the traditional religious portraits of unrepentant sinners; and ironic as it may seem in the light of Clarissa's expectations of him, perhaps the central element in all such characters is misrule, the violent rejection of any form of order.[5] In Lovelace, this affinity for deceit is most readily seen in his use of language: he uses words contemptuously, for deceit rather than for discovery, delighting to make up new expressions and deliberately plaguing his correspondent *"with* out-of-the-way *words and phrases"* (III, 131). [6] In the matter of dress, too, he aims at disguise and intrigue; thus his public manner is frequently one of conscious dissimulation. As he boasts to Belford, "Ovid was not a greater master of metamorphoses than thy friend" (III, 52).[7] At the beginning of his courtship he spends a great deal of time around the Harlowe estate in disguise, and as the narrative progresses, this theme of deception becomes increasingly important. Clarissa is introduced as his sister to the keeper of the inn where they spend their first night; later in London she is to pretend to be his wife. The prostitutes of Mrs. Sinclair's establishment are presented as virtuous, and several of them engage with Lovelace in a cheap plot to convince Clarissa that she has met his relatives. Tomlinson is disguised as a friend of Clarissa's uncle, and Lovelace himself again takes to false dress when he recaptures Clarissa after her first escape.

Misrepresentation through dress and use of language is, of course, only one part of Lovelace's passion for intrigue and manipulation. Throughout the novel one frequently senses that his exhilaration in the pursuit of Clarissa derives primarily from his enjoyment of plotting and that plotting for its own sake, without regard for the possible prize to be won, is an essential part of his nature "Thou knowest nothing, Jack," he tells Belford, "of the delicacies of intrigue: Nothing of the glory of outwitting the Witty and the Watchful: Of the joys that fill the mind of the inventive or contriving genius, ruminating which to use of the different webs that offer to him for the entanglement of a haughty charmer" (III, 77-78). His outward behavior is, of course, calculatingly geared to the execution of his schemes, and his letters to Belford are filled with self-congratulatory accounts of his efforts to deceive Clarissa. "But all gentle shall be my movements: All respectful, even to reverence, my address to her—Her hand shall be the only witness to the pressure of my lip—my trembling lip . . . . As soft my sighs, as the sighs of my gentle Rose-bud. By *my* humility will I invite *her* confidence" (I, 256). Calculation, deception, and scheming are the standard characteristics of many traditional portraits of the devil, and it seems entirely likely that at least part of the inspiration for Richardson's representation of this arch-fiend came from some portrait of Lucifer such as the one in Milton's *Paradise Lost*. Thus Lovelace combines his fascination for deception and intrigue with that protean changeability conventionally associated with the devil. "What a matchless plotter thy friend! —Stand by, and let me swell! —I am already as big as an elephant; and ten times wiser! —Mightier too by far! Have I not reason to snuff the moon with my proboscis?" (III, 201).[8]

By rejecting the accepted standards by which one judges another—distorting language, consciously attempting to change his identity by changing his clothes, and altering his speech and manners to disguise meaning and deceive his listener—Lovelace defies the very notion of restricting and governing social norms; and not surprisingly, he expresses general contempt for social institutions and socially defined relationships. Richardson is sometimes driven to ludicrous lengths to demonstrate the distortions of his villain's perverted sense of duty; for instance, Lovelace boasts of his conquest of women—taking them at will and laying himself under obligation to none. Yet should an unfortunate girl die giving birth to his bastard, he will always go into mourning, "a distinction I have ever paid to those worthy creatures who died in Childbed by me" (III, 250). Such a parody of the mutual duties attendant on personal relationships is worse than total neglect of them, for Lovelace betrays the fact that he at least knows the meaning of obligation.

His remarks on marriage follow this same pattern. He never completely rejects the notion of a sustaining man-woman relationship, always referring himself by way of contrast to the socially accepted form; yet he consistently rejects that form, perverts it and distorts it. He constructs fantasies of a ten-year cohabitation in which he and Clarissa live together as man and wife, no one to know that they are not really married save themselves. He formulates a scheme of marriage by which the contract would be renewed each year with a different partner, an arrangement deemed suitable to his Protean nature. "O Jack! with what joy, with what rapture, would the *changelings* (or *changeables*, if thou like that word better) number the weeks, the days, the hours, as the annual obligation approached to its desirable period!" (V, 293-294). Yet even here he parodies genuine regulations, making "provision" for the encumbrances of such an arrangement (the children of such unions to be considered as "children of the public") and, in the manner of a Mandeville, even postulating social benefits: no jealousy, fewer murders and less duelling, fewer rapes, fewer quarrels between husband and wife. This attitude is not unlike Mr. B.'s notions of polygamy in its tendency to flaunt social customs and restrictions. Yet in the case of Mr. B. these fantasies might well be viewed merely as aberrations from a firmly fixed and socially well-defined character, whereas in the case of Lovelace there is no such stability. His character has no fundamental coherence because he has thrown off *all* limitations, distorted *all* meaningful social roles.

At first the reader may be deluded—believing, with Clarissa, that the disguises merely serve to hide the real Lovelace from our view. As the novel progresses, however, we gradually come to realize that there is no real Lovelace behind the mask, that the mask itself is Lovelace, and that the formlessness of his nature, the very absence of a coherent identity, makes it impossible for him to limit himself by engaging in any social role. He has a kind of freedom, but it is the spurious freedom of a lost soul, damned to toss forever in a hell of chaos and darkness.[9]

Once we recognize Lovelace's plight, we can see that marriage with Clarissa is impossible for him—not because he is unwilling to submit to it, but because he is incapable of entering into *any* meaningful relationship. The pathos of his plight is not unlike that of a fallen angel, condemned always to know the value of the paradise he has lost. The implicit references to an orderly society, the insistent comparisons between his own conduct and the customs of the world he has rejected, represent his own half-submerged desire to rejoin the community he has left; and much of his raving, despite its incoherence, does have this unifying theme. He dreams of seeing Clarissa with his son at her breast; he tempts himself as well as Clarissa with the shammed intention to marry, even to the point of obtaining a license and drawing up a settlement; and he admires and esteems Clarissa's virtue all the while lamenting his own incapacity to meet it. "I know not the subject on which she does not talk with admirable distinction; insomuch that could I but get over my prejudices against Matrimony, and resolve to walk in the dull beaten path of my ancestors, I should be the happiest of men—And if I cannot, perhaps I may be ten times more to be pitied than she" (IV, 345).

Richardson gives a standard religious explanation for the deformity of Lovelace's nature—he was indulged too much as a child and never made to suffer any rule of control over his passions—and it is the same excuse which was given earlier for Mr. B.'s behavior. To a certain extent the characterization of both men is an exaggerated portrait of the profligate nobility of the Restoration and early eighteenth century, for Richardson could well remember the licentious misrule of the court wits; and in addition to public scandals, there was always the rake-hell behavior of Richardson's early employer, the Duke of Wharton, to serve as a model. However, there is more to Lovelace's problem than this stereotyped picture might suggest.

If we compare Lovelace with Mr. B., for instance, the differences are striking. In *Pamela*, Mr. B.'s behavior could plausibly be seen as the passionate indulgence of the basically moral man; he is always uncomfortable about his attempts on Pamela (never delighting in his own deceptive cunning). His unwillingness to sanction the satisfaction of his desires by marrying her seems to stem only from differences between their stations, and this essential commitment to morality is attributed to the influence of a mother whose kind instructions shaped Pamela's character as well. Lovelace, by comparison, seems quite inhuman in his vice. There is, for instance, a striking absence of passion in his nature. He is capable of great resentment, but it grows in him like a virulent cancer, nurtured by his own corruption instead of bursting out naturally as anger. Indeed, his most characteristic form of behavior is to mask anger, just as he dissimulates all incipient feeling, for the purpose of manipulating others. Thus his grudge against the Harlowe family is, one feels, merely an excuse for his behavior, not a cause of it; the slight was so minor and the memory of it so assiduously kept alive. Similarly, his relationship with Clarissa has little or no *real* sexual content, and actions which might seem at first the natural manifestation of great desire are gradually shown to have some darker and more vicious origin. Belford recognizes this trait in Lovelace, remonstrating, "Thou, Lovelace, has a Soul, tho' a corrupted one; and art more intent (as thou even gloriest) upon the preparative stratagem, than upon the end of conquering" (IV, 370). Even Clarissa, despite her sexual fantasies, is faintly aware of Lovelace's lack of humanity. Very early in the novel she discusses his character with Miss Howe, musing "Sometimes we have both thought him one of the most undesigning *merely* witty men we ever knew; at other times one of the deepest creatures we ever conversed with. So that when in one visit we have imagined we fathomed him, in the next he has made us ready to give him up as impenetrable. . . . But I used to say, and I still am of opinion, that he wants a *heart*: And if he does, he wants everything. A wrong *head* may be convinced, may have a right turn given it: But who is able to give a *heart*, if a heart be wanting? . . . Should not one fly the man who is but suspected of such a one? (I, 295-296)."

The man thus warped and lacking any vestige of human feeling does have one passion, and that is the passion for power. To put it most simply, Lovelace is an embodiment of unrestrained will. He is the shrieking, completely selfish child grown older but not wiser; his vision of the world begins and ends with himself, and his fantasies all have the story-book illusion of personal omnipotence. The selfishness of the child, however, has grown suddenly diabolical and threatening; for Lovelace is an adult, and he has wealth, power, and cunning. Thus the child whose will was never checked has become a man with the force to insure that his desires are carried out.

One of the most infantile expressions of Lovelace's distorted view of the world is his inability to distinguish between his own welfare and the welfare of those who are in some way connected with him, a confusion which is manifested most clearly in his attitude towards his estate. The ostensibly prudent manner in which he manages his land holdings is seen by Clarissa as a point in his favor when she is attempting to assess his character (I, 24). However, as the novel progresses, we learn that the solicitude for his tenants is merely another way of safeguarding his own appearance and reputation. "Take this," he says, giving money to a poorly dressed couple whom he encounters at church. "I will abate you five pounds a year for seven years, provided you will lay it out upon your wife and self, that you may make a Sunday-appearance *like* MY *tenants*" (I, 83). His seeming benevolence becomes brutality when his inclinations run contrary to those of his tenants; his farmers hide their pretty daughters from him, and Lovelace himself says of his dependents, "I . . . think I have a right to break every man's head I pass by, if I like not his looks" (III, 132). In truth, there is neither benevolence nor even conscious malice in Lovelace's attitude, merely the incapacity to acknowledge that the claims of anyone else might be separated from or superior to his own desires or rights.

As one might expect, his fantasies all run to illusions of omnipotence and omniscience. The phrase "in my power" occurs obsessively in his letters to describe his relationship with others, especially with women; and the numerous seductions and rapes are seen by him simply as the means by which he brings the intended victim into his "power." There never seems to be any sensual pleasure associated with sexuality. The sexual act itself becomes almost identical to the notion of ingestion in his demented view, for it is the means by which the woman is incorporated into the extended and unstructured notion of self which is implied in his use of the notion of power. Thus he speaks of wishing to "devour" Clarissa's hand when he kisses it (III, 178) or refers to himself as "a notorious womaneater" (IV, 382). In his planning against Clarissa he seems possessed by the necessity of knowing everything that passes, or at least of knowing more than any of the others concerned, as if there were a latent force in knowledge itself. The elaborate network of spies, of course, serves this purpose, as Joseph Lemen, the girls at Mrs. Sinclair's, Tomlinson, and all the others plot in his favor; and the violent resolve to intercept Clarissa's correspondence is at least partially dictated by his compulsion to omnipotence.

In a very real sense knowledge does become power for Lovelace as he manipulates the various characters in Clarissa's tragedy to suit his diabolical fancy. For instance, he plays upon the emotions of the Harlowe family as a virtuoso upon an instrument, inflaming their jealousy and perpetuating their anger. "I knew that the whole stupid family were in a combination to do my business for me," he exults. "I told thee that they were all working for me, like so many underground moles; and still more blind than the moles are said to be, unknowing that they did so. I myself, the director of their principal motions" (III, 1-2). However, the real successes of his convoluted plotting lead imperceptibly to greater and greater *delusions* of omnipotence. "Had I been a military Hero," he exclaims, "I should have made gun powder useless; for I should have blown up all my adversaries by dint of that strategem, turning their own devices upon them" (III, 114). Speaking of a spy who goes by the pseudonym Captain Mennell, he gloats, "I have changed his name by virtue of my own single authority. Knowest thou not, that I am a great Name-father? Preferments I bestow, both military and civil. I give Estates, and take them away at my pleasure.

Quality too I create. And by a still more valuable preroga-
tive, I *degrade* by virtue of my own imperial will, without
any other act of forfeiture than for my own convenience.
What a poor thing is a monarch to me!" (IV, 44).

The climax to this phantasmagoria is his extended fantasy of the rape of Anna Howe and the following trial. In
Lovelace's fevered, ego-centered vision it becomes the
ultimate fantasy of his triumph over conventional morality and social order (and is, in this respect, an intimation
of his eventual real intentions towards Clarissa). He envisions the arraignment, "the people, the women especially, who on this occasion will be five-sixths of the
spectators, reproaching her [for having brought him to
trial]" (IV, 274). He, the prisoner, is to be the focus of a
wild adulation; "Even the Judges, and the whole crouded
Bench, will acquit us in their hearts; and every single
man wish he had been me! —The woman, all the time,
disclaiming prosecution, were the case to be their own"
(IV, 274). The procession to court is to have the trappings
of a triumphal march, enough "to make a noble heart
thump it away most gloriously, when such an one finds
himself attended to his tryal by a parade of guards and
officers, of miens and aspects warlike and unwarlike; himself their whole care, and their business!" (IV, 274-275). And
when he comes to trial, Lovelace boasts, "I know I shall
get off for one—were it but for family sake: And being a
handsome fellow, I shall have a dozen or two of young
maidens, all dressed in white, go to Court to beg my life—
And what a pretty shew they will make, with their white
hoods, white gowns, white petticoats, white scarves, white
gloves, kneeling for me, with their white handkerchiefs
at their eyes, in two pretty rows, as his Majesty walks thro'
them and nods my pardon for their sakes!" (IV, 277).[10]

Indeed, the more one learns of Lovelace, the less magnificent his splendid rebelliousness becomes; and when we

reach this abomination, he seems less a muscular stallion than a poisonous swollen toad, stuffed with the corruption of his own selfish desires. Richardson portrays a man too infantile to appear attractive, too undeveloped in his notions of the world even to acknowledge the separate order of other personalities. His vision of the society in which he lives is monstrously distorted, for he sees himself as the center and cause of all that occurs; he is intended as a portrait of one inevitably doomed to collapse into the chaos of his own soul.[11]

There is tragic irony, then, in Clarissa's flight from home: the atmosphere of disintegrating order which had bred dissension and pain drives Clarissa to seek another world and another chance for harmony; yet the very act which was to have been her salvation plunges her into an abyss more terrifyingly incoherent than the disorder of her wildest nightmares. Clarissa in her father's home has, after all, a social position and a socially delineated identity. She is mistreated, and the terms by which she defines herself and her relationship to others are no longer accepted or workable. Yet Clarissa's self-image still has the virtue of internal consistency, and she is still able to formulate a clear statement of the public role which she has apparently lost. Thus the novel begins, at least, in a society of sorts; and when Clarissa leaves that society to seek an order which actually exists only in the projections of her own desires into her image of Lovelace, she is quitting a real (if increasingly imperfect) social arrangement for chaotic illusion.

Miss Howe can see the import of the action Clarissa meditates, and her warnings take the form of pointing out the inevitable disruption of the rules which govern social behavior ('punctilio') and the attendant abandonment of

any notion of public approval. Indeed, Anna Howe knows
—as Clarissa in her self-delusions cannot—the awful threat
of allowing Lovelace to trap one "in his power." "Give
this matter your most serious consideration. Punctilio is
out of doors the moment you are out of your Father's
house. I know how justly severe you have been upon those
inexcusable creatures whose giddiness, and even want of
decency, have made them, in the *same hour* as I may say,
leap from a Parent's window to a Husband's bed—But
considering Lovelace's character, I repeat my opinion, that
your *Reputation* in the eye of the world requires that no
delay be made in *this* point when once you are in his power"
(II, 308).[12] Clarissa is justly frightened by Miss Howe's
ominous warning and she ritualistically repeats her
friend's words in suitably awed italics. "When . . . you
represent, *that all punctilio must be at an end the moment
I am out of my Father's house,* . . . who can bear those
reflections, who can resolve to incur these inconveniences,
that has the question still in her own power to decide
upon?" (II, 319). She says of her projected flight with
Lovelace, "For a few moments I doubt I must, lest he
should take some rash resolutions . . . But here your
words, *That all punctilio is at an end, the moment I am
out of my Father's house,* added to the still more cogent
considerations of Duty and Reputation, determined me
once more against taking the rash step" (II, 329).

The conflict could scarcely be more clearly drawn: the
order of a father's house, with the exercise of that order
vested in the father himself, and the regulations of a
society whose notions of punctilio and reputation can
serve as guides, balanced against the prospect of social
anarchy and the threat of being "in the power" of Lovelace. Reason manifestly dictates that Clarissa should stay;
and yet she flees.

She flees, one feels, because she can neither understand

nor accept the real meaning of her action; and though she has left social proprieties behind in her rash decision, she stubbornly continues to demand the recognition of them by Lovelace. Miss Howe, on the other hand, realizes that until Clarissa has reestablished her social position, she must be an outcast from society with no right to avail herself of its protections and sanctions; thus her initial advice (advice which is repeatedly offered throughout the novel) is that Clarissa become Lovelace's wife. "If you are *not* married by this time, be sure delay not the Ceremony. Since things are as they are, I wish it were thought that you were privately married before you went away. If these men plead AUTHORITY to our pain, when we are *theirs* —*why should we not, in such a case as this*, make some good out of the hated word, for our reputation, when we are induced to violate a more natural one?" (II, 342). Even Clarissa seems to recognize her anomalous position, re-marking (when it is too late to go back), "At *every* Age on this side of Matrimony (for then we come under an-other sort of protection, tho' that is far from abrogating the Filial duty) it will be found, that the wings of our parents are our most necessary and most effectual safe-guard from the vulturs, the hawks, the kites, and other villainous birds of prey, that hover over us with a view to seize and destroy us the first time we are caught wandering out of the eye or care of our watchful and natural guar-dians and protectors" (III, 216). And immediately after the elopement she acknowledges that in such a position as hers, "there are, my dear Miss Howe, a multitude of punctilios and decorums, which a young creature must dispense with" (III, 17).

Yet despite her knowing statements, Clarissa continues blindly to demand of Lovelace the courtesies, the reserve, the respect, the reticence, the virtue that she had demanded when under her father's roof. For instance, even on their very first morning together (when she must have been painfully aware of her delicate position), she overhears him using strong language and self-righteously accuses him of swearing like a trooper. "I am sure they deserve chastisement," she remonstrates, "for Swearing is a most *unmanly* vice, and Cursing as *poor* and *low* a one" (III, 21). Lovelace's immediate resentment of her presumptuous attitude breaks out in his letter to Belford. "She finds fault with my protestations; with my professions, with my vows: I cannot curse a servant, the only privilege a master is known by, but I am supposed to be a trooper. —I must not say, By my soul; nor, As I hope to be saved. Why, Jack, how particular this is!" (III, 78).

In the portion of the novel before the elopement, almost all the letters included are from Clarissa's correspondence, and there are only two from Lovelace to Belford; however, in the first hundred or so letters following the flight, the letters are divided almost exactly evenly between Clarissa's and Lovelace's correspondences. This shift in the balance of their differing points of view parallels the increasingly abrasive effect which their personalities have upon one another; the pattern of mutual antagonism and misunderstanding which has been set on this first morning continues with increasing intensity and acrimony. Caged together with neither rules of decorum nor sympathetic friends to mediate between them, they grow increasingly bitter in their demands and accusations; and the incompatibility of their separate images of themselves and of the world destroys whatever relationship they may previously have had. As Lovelace says to Belford, "Thou knowest the whole progress of our warfare: For a warfare it has truly been; and far, very far, from an amorous warfare too. Doubts, mistrusts, upbraidings on her part; Humiliations the most abject, on mine" (III, 31).

Clarissa's unfortunate stance is one of peevish, self-righteousness. She takes no blame for the elopement (though, as Richardson states several times in his letters, she is meant to share the responsibility for the moral infraction), choosing instead to blame Lovelace for everything. The air of confident superiority that had dominated so much of her relationship with her family becomes now petty, captious, and querulous when her position is no longer secure. "I thought myself, I said, extremely unhappy. I know now that to determine upon: My reputation now, no doubt, utterly ruined; Destitute of cloaths; unfit to be seen by any-body; My very indigence, as I might call it, proclaiming my folly to everyone who saw me" (III, 8). Here, as before in Clarissa's behavior with her brother and sister, Miss Howe points out the imprudence of such an attitude. "When the Lover is exalted, the Lady must be humbled. He is naturally proud and saucy. I doubt, you must engage his *pride*, which he calls his *honour:* And that you must throw off a little more of the veil. And I would have you restrain your wishes before him, that you had not met him, and the like. What signifies wishing, my dear? He will not bear it. You can hardly expect that he will" (III, 98). However, Clarissa again ignores the advice. The pattern of self-deluding righteousness seems to grow more fixed and more rigid with each new humiliation and each failure to find the ideal embodiment of strength that she had sought.

Unwilling to face her own mistakes, she turns an even more venomous tongue on Lovelace. *He* is wanting in honor; *he* has led her to ruin; and once her illusions have been shattered, no insult becomes too great, no resentment too bitter. "Every woman of discernment, I am confident, knowing what I know of you now, would say as I say . . . that your politeness is not regular, nor constant. It is not *habit*. It is too much seen by fits, and starts, and sallies, and those not spontaneous. You must be *reminded* into them. . . . Upon my word, Sir, you are not the accomplished man, which your talents and opportunities would have led one to expect you to be. You are indeed in your Noviciate, as to every laudable attainment" (III, 164-165). These are, of course, the very sentiments that Clarissa had expressed to Anna Howe before the elopement; these are the traits that she would have reformed. Yet her notion of reformation has become inextricably confused with her desire to assert her own moral superiority and her unfortunate tendency to lecture.

Lovelace's immorality is, of course, beyond question. Yet if any check to his vicious behavior were possible, it would not come from these angry accusations, for (as we have seen) even apparent benevolence in Lovelace must *begin*, at least, in pride and self-esteem. Clarissa's suspicions and her scorn serve only to increase his tyranny. "I fansy, by her circumspection, and her continual grief, that she *expects* some mischief from me. I don't care to disappoint any-body I have a value for" (III, 32). And the villainy that Lovelace has not completely decided upon is more and more thrust upon him by Clarissa's captious nature.[13] "Is it prudent, thinkest thou, in *her* circumstances, to tell me, *repeatedly* to tell me, 'That she is every hour more and more dissatisfied with herself and me? That I am not one, who improve upon her in my conversation and address?' (Couldst *thou*, Jack, bear this from a captive!) 'That she shall not be easy while she is with me? . . . That if I think she deserves the compliments I make her, I may pride myself in those Arts, by which I have made a fool of so extraordinary a person? . . . That she will take care of herself; and since her friends think it not worth while to pursue her, she will be left to her own care?' " (III, 79-80).

Thus the two labor at cross-purposes, struggling against one another; and each ironically defeats himself in the very act of attempting to overcome the other. Clarissa demands that Lovelace admit his faults and become the man of strength and bravery that she has imagined him to be, whereas Lovelace would have Clarissa acknowledge her moral pride and submit unquestioningly to his power. Yet his attacks on her only confirm her scornful opinion of him and fan her pride to new heights, while her own, condescending attitude evokes nothing but renewed tyranny from him.

This parallel situation would seem to imply a parity between Clarissa's and Lovelace's positions, and to a limited extent there is some similarity. Each, after all, is self-deceived, and the behavior of each is ironically suited to evoke a response directly opposite to the one which is apparently desired. However, here the similarity ends; for Clarissa, despite her evident faults, still appeals to an order which Richardson would identify with moral righteousness. She is mistaken in her proud illusions of converting Lovelace, but she would at least convert him to a morally coherent set of values; whereas Lovelace is not only deluded in his estimation of Clarissa's strength, but adds to this mistake in judgment the more serious error of moving consistently away from any notion of goodness. Beneath the superficial barrage of peevishness and the generally berating tone, there runs in all of Clarissa's objections the consistent theme of her desire to return to order and justice; and it is Lovelace's inability to conform in this respect that poses the crucial obstacle. "Had you not been an unmanageable man, I should not have been driven to the extremity I now every hour, as the hour passes, deplore—With this additional reflection upon myself, that I ought not to have *begun*, or, having begun, not *continued* a correspondence with one, who thought it not worth his while to clear his own character for *my sake*, or to submit to my Father for *his own*, in a point wherein every Father ought to have an option" (III, 151).[14]

Lovelace, not unaware of Clarissa's beliefs, uses them against her. Freed as he is from the restrictions of moral order, he deliberately plays upon her unwillingness to divorce herself from them. "How unequal," he exults, "is a modest woman to the adventure, when she throws herself into the power of a Rake! —Punctilio will, at any time, stand for reason with such an one. She cannot break thro' a well-tested modesty. None but the impudent little rogues, who can name the Person and the Church before you think of either, and undress and go to bed before you the next hour, should think of running away with a man" (III, 182). Thus when he proposes to her immediately and in a manner which makes his proposal unacceptable, Clarissa observes, "Having . . . declared to him in my Letters . . . that I would not think of marriage till he had passed thro' a state of Probation, as I may call it—How was it possible I could encourage, with *very* ready signs of approbation, such an early proposal?" (III, 74). He next adopts a manner of exaggerated awe and courtesy whenever the matter of marriage comes up, and Clarissa (now hoping to obtain a proper declaration from him) is endlessly frustrated. "Would to Heaven he might, without offending!—But I *so* over-awed him! . . . And so the over-awed, bashful man went off from the subject" (III, 145).

Yet even if Clarissa had been willing to "throw off the veil" of her notions of propriety, one wonders whether Lovelace could ever have been brought under society's regulations, given that he is incapable of submitting the chaos of his own identity to any order. Marriage itself imposes restrictions and limitations; and the swelling, distorted identity which Lovelace had displayed in all his actions is capable of no such limitation. There could be no partial concessions to the distortions of his personality in the name of love, only complete submission and total anarchy.

Richardson would have us see that love itself, indeed *any* relationship between two people, presupposes fully formed, coherent personalities and the willingness to conform them to reasonable rules of behavior. As Clarissa says, "If Love, as it is called, is allowed to be an excuse for our most unreasonable follies, and to lay level all the fences that a careful education has surrounded us by, what is meant by the doctrine of subduing our passions?" (IV, 298). Yet for Lovelace, love means misrule and serves as the excuse to violate all order; and in keeping with his egocentric, infantile personality, he envisions love as a state in which he is the *object* of adoration, controlling his environment by the exertion of his will (or his power over his partner), while passively absorbing a limitless supply of affection. Mutual obligations have no place in such a fantasy, nor does the commitment to any governing moral code. In speaking of Clarissa's attitude he complains, "What mortifies my pride, is, that this exalted creature, if I *were* to marry her, would not be governed in her behavior to me by Love, but by Generosity merely, or by blind Duty . . . I would have the woman whom I honour with my name, if ever I confer this honour upon any, forego even her *superior duties* for me. I would have her look after me when I go out, as far as she can see me . . . and meet me at my return with rapture. I would be the subject of her dreams, as well as of her waking thoughts. I would have her think every moment lost, that is not passed with me: Sing to me, read to me, play to me when I pleased; no joy so great as in obeying me" (IV, 264). However romantically appealing this vision may have seemed (and there were many of Richardson's readers who could not perceive the perversion of Lovelace's nature) it is no more than an illusion, a fantasy relationship which could never be sustained in the real world because it denies meaningful existence and personal right to anyone outside of Lovelace himself.

The unrealistic selfishness of romantic love was a subject that Richardson discussed both in his novels and in his private correspondence, and he always saw the placing of personal gratification above community or general happiness as intrinsically wrong. His intellectual friend Miss Mulso objected to his rather stringent view, saying that *true* love is unselfish because "it must desire the happiness of its object preferably to its own."[15] However, Richardson shrewdly saw that such a view merely pushed the problem of selfishness one step further. "Yet what means the person possessed [by love], but to gratify self, —or self and proposed company? Is a man who enters into a partnership to be regarded, who declares that his ardent thirst after accumulation is not for himself, for his own sake; but for his partner's, whom he loves better than himself?"[16] There is always, as Richardson well knew, an identification between lover and loved one; and even this identification or union, to the extent that it excludes the just demands of the rest of society, becomes selfish and unjustified. "Dear Madam, is not the object pretended to be preferred to self, a single object? a part of self? And is it not a selfishness to propose to make all the world but two persons, and then these two but one; and, intending to become the same flesh as well as spirit, know no public, no other private?"[17]

Lovelace, then, is the supreme embodiment of all that is selfish in love, for by his love he would deny not only society's rights but Clarissa's as well; and true affection, as defined by his distorted set of values, would make his lady's will indistinguishable from his own. "When I should be inclined to Love [she would] overwhelm me with it; when to be serious or solitary, if apprehensive of intrusion, retiring at a nod; approaching me only if I smiled encouragement: Steal into my presence with Silence; out of it, if not noticed, on tiptoe. Be a *Lady Easy* to all my pleasures, and valuing those most who most contributed to them" (IV, 264). Thus by cruel (but scarcely inexplicable) coincidence, Clarissa has chosen a man who treats her as an object, who disregards her own desires and rights, who, in short, shows all of the faults that had marred her family's dealings with her. His notion of a wife's duty becomes as perverted as her father's notions of the duty of a daughter, each seeing the 'duty' to exist on one side only. "A tyrant-husband makes a dutiful wife," declares Lovelace, "And why do the Sex love Rakes, but because they know how to direct their uncertain wills, and manage them?" (IV, 265). Not only has Clarissa failed to better her state, she has not even changed it—save, perhaps, that she has made it worse.

It is characteristic that Lovelace views love so one-sidedly; if Clarissa truly loves him, he reasons, her volition will become indistinguishable from his. (It never occurs to him that, having rejected the moral framework which had formed the basis for the notion of wifely duty and subjection of the woman's will, he should be as willing to identify himself with *her* desires as he expects her to be ready to sympathize with his. Even conventional notions of romantic love, such as the version given to Richardson by Miss Mulso, dictate that the lovers should live for *each other,* not that both of them should live for one.) In his earlier relationships with women, Lovelace had viewed them merely as objects to be governed by his own sense of power; and the sexual act had represented the definitive exertion of that power—in Lovelace's warped fantasies, the literal ingestion or incorporation of the woman into himself. When the notion of love enters his mind, he thinks of it in much the same way: satisfaction of his own love would require that he possess Clarissa entirely; proof of her love for him would come only if she relinquished her own will and her own separate identity to make them one with his. This is, for Lovelace, the ultimate expression of his own nature, for it is the most appalling and most extreme disruption of order—the violation of the integrity of another human identity.

Initially Lovelace justifies his persecution of Clarissa by deeming it the only method of determining her true character. He has, after all, a certain degree of penetration, and he is capable of discovering her weaknesses. "Is not, may not her Virtue be founded rather in *Pride* than in *Principle?*" he wonders (III, 86). "Is Virtue to be established by common Bruit only?—Has her Virtue ever been proved? . . . What must be those inducements, how strong, that were *too strong* for Duty, in a Daughter so *dutiful?* . . . Is then the divine Clarissa capable of *loving* a man whom she ought *not* to love? . . . May not then the Success of him, who could carry her *thus far*, be allowed to be an encouragement for him to try to carry her *farther?*" (III, 86-91). There is an ironic truth here, for Clarissa's trials do reveal her nature to herself—and then secondarily to Lovelace. In this as in all of his dealings with Clarissa, however, Lovelace's primary aim is only self-aggrandizement; and alliance with her, victory over her, becomes a way of assessing his own value. "Is it not the divine CLARISSA . . . whom I am thus by application threatening?—If Virtue be the True Nobility, how is she enobled, and how would an alliance with her ennoble" (III, 85). The encounter with Clarissa appeals to Lovelace, then, as another way of attempting to define his own position; and he measures his own identity by the value of the character he is attempting to devour. "But let me ask, Has it not been a constant maxim with us, that the greater the *merit* on the woman's side, the nobler the victory on the man's?" . . . And will ye not now all join to say, that it is more manly to attack a Lion than a Sheep?—Thou knowest, that I always illustrated my Eagleship, by aiming at the noblest quarries; and by disdaining to make a stoup at wrens, phyltits, and wag-tails" (IV, 23-24).

Such notions are inevitably self-defeating. If Lovelace succeeds in his attempted conquest, then Clarissa's value will be reduced by the evidence of her moral weakness, and there will be no triumph for Lovelace, no credit to his own character, in defeating her. If on the other hand, she prevails against him, she will have proven her worth, but in doing so she will have rejected him. Neither of the possible results can possibly benefit Lovelace; yet he is unable to see the flaw in his fantastic plans.

The more desirable Clarissa becomes in his eyes, the more inflamed becomes Lovelace's passion to possess her entirely. Thus the repeated contact, the inevitable intimacy that grows up despite the warfare between them, merely hardens him in his resolution; he seems incapable of pity or of sympathy, and his growing "love" only increases the urgency of his desire to conquer her will. He seems eventually to resign himself to the notion of marriage (though he frequently appears to equate it with mere co-habitation), and the lines of battle are drawn about the meaning of such a marriage; as Lovelace says, "the struggle only, Whether I am to have her *in my own way*, or in *hers*?" (V, 162). Triumph would come for Lovelace if Clarissa were to submit to his sexual advances outside the sanctions of marriage because such a violation of moral order would indicate that she had placed him above duty, above all considerations of principle. The physical act itself is of minor importance; it is Clarissa's will that Lovelace desires; and though the threat is both physical and psychological, even Clarissa herself soon realizes that the primary danger is to the integrity of her personality. "How much unhappier am I already with him than my Mother ever was with my Father after marriage! Since (and that without any reason, any pretence in the world for it) he is for breaking my spirit *before* I am his." (IV, 59).

Moreover, once he has committed himself to the struggle, Lovelace cannot withdraw before the battle is decided. He believes that ceasing his treachery would be tantamount to a victory for Clarissa. Lovelace's notions of his own character are so unclearly defined, so completely dependent upon his ability to see himself reflected in his power over others, that any failure to achieve that power represents a diminishing of himself. Thus he fears the example of Clarissa's goodness, saying she "half-*assimilates* me to her own virtue" (IV, 241; the italics are mine); and when he finds himself writing in praise of her, he has an horrific delusion that she has invaded his very being, perhaps even unmanned him. "But she was a thief, an imposter, as well as a tormenter. She had stolen my pen.—While I was sullenly meditating, doubting, as to my future measures, she stole it; and thus she wrote with it, in a hand exactly like my own; and would have faced me down, that it was really my own handwriting" (V, 240). Such distorted fantasies serve further to display the unstructured (the Satanic) nature of Lovelace's character. A will that was never checked has become the instrument of a deformed mind, and Lovelace has no clear concept either of the checks to his own power or of the limitations to the potential power of others over him. He is the embodiment of misrule, and in this sense is truly extra-social. His fleeting desires to find some order are inevitably thwarted by his proud, indomitable willfulness.

Lovelace well knows that physical force can demonstrate no more than a physical control. Yet as his stratagems and temptations continue to fail him, the urgency of his quest for total possession of Clarissa pushes him to consider increasingly extreme courses of action. "*Force* answers not my end—And yet it may, if there be truth in that part of the Libertine's Creed, *That once subdued, is*

always subdued!" (IV, 187). In the face of renewed assaults
Clarissa's resolution seems only to increase, and as she
grows stronger, Lovelace himself grows more distraught.
"Her emotion . . . was not owing to perverseness, to
nicety, to ill-humour; but to *weakness of heart.* She has
not *strength of mind* sufficient, she says, to enable her to
support her condition. Yet what a contradiction!—*Weakness of heart,* says she, with such a *strength of will!*—O
Belford! she is a lion-hearted Lady, in every case where her
Honour, her Punctilio rather, calls for spirit" (IV, 217).
Still Lovelace resists the temptation to descend to physical
violence. "Abhorred be *force,* be the *necessity* of force, if
that can be avoided! There is no triumph in *force*—No
conquest over the will—No prevailing by gentle degrees,
over the gentle passions!—*Force* is the devil!" (IV, 238).
Yet there is always the deluding hope that once she has
been subdued by force, the subjection of the will can follow;
and while Clarissa draws strength from her trials, the
frustration of Lovelace's attempts upon her character ren-
ders him more and more desperate. "Is not *this* the hour
of her trial—and in *her,* of the trial of the virtue of her
whole Sex, so long premeditated, so long threatened? . . .
Whether her virtue be principle? Whether, if *once subdued,
she will not be always subdued?* And will she not want the
very crown of her glory, the proof of her till now all-sur-
passing excellence, if I stop short of the ultimate trial? . . .
(*Abhorred be force!—Be thoughts of force! There's no
triumph over the Will in force!*) This I know I have said.
But would I not have avoided it, if I could?—Have I not
tried every other method? And have I any other recourse
left me?" (V, 305). The rape is, then, in every sense a final
measure—the ultimate physical violation and the last
resort of a demented and desperate man; and when this
attempt fails, too, the agony of Lovelace's final defeat re-
sounds like the pronouncement of his own doom. "And

for what should her heart be broken? Her will is unviolated. . . . There must be something more than a *name* in virtue!—I now see that there is!—*Once subdued, always subdued*—'Tis an egregious falsehood!—But Oh, Jack, she never *was* subdued" (V, 381, VI, 28).

The first two-thirds of the novel is a chronicle of the journey from social order to anarchy, and the disregard for rules of behavior that Clarissa first encounters in her father's house is merely the dreadful prelude to a disintegration of all coherence more terrifying than any of her anxious presentiments. Lovelace is lawlessness, and even his earliest addresses are characterized by deception and fraud. Once he has separated Clarissa from her family, this anarchy becomes the prevailing mode. Nothing is as it seems in the universe of Lovelace and Mrs. Sinclair, and the parade of prostitutes cloaked in the garb of gentility begins to assume the proportions of some hellish mummery. There are the whores who masquerade as waiting maids, the whores who pretend to be Lovelace's relations, and the whores who make up the dreadful card party—all presenting a mask of innocence and hiding behind it the face of evil. There are Lovelace's feigned attacks of sickness which so arouse Clarissa's sympathy and the very genuine fire whose existence Clarissa doubts. And providing the setting for all, there is the infernal world of the bawdy house itself.

Once Clarissa has entered this underworld, society and all of its supporting controls have been left irrevocably behind, and gone with them are the relationships which have formed her nature. Duty has no meaning in a world of total sham; duty, honor and merit all depend upon real distinctions between people. Unwilling as she evidently is to relinquish the familiar and safe patterns of behavior which had served to define her, eventually Clarissa is forced to do so, for her liaison with Lovelace has led her hopelessly beyond the boundaries of established order. Her struggle is no longer a futile attempt to perpetuate the old ways—these are acknowledged as lost to her now forever; instead it has become the more desperate effort simply to preserve the unity of her own personality. She is assaulted on two fronts. From outside there are the attacks of Lovelace, driven by an obsessive desire to subdue her will and possess her completely. The more serious threat, however, comes from within; for in being prevented from playing those roles by which she had articulated her character, she has lost the very means by which to define herself. If she is to preserve her identity, she must first discover its nature and find some coherent expression of it. She must see herself apart from all social order, stand alone, and in that intolerable isolation look into her soul to trace meaning and coherence. Only when she has had the honesty to view herself thus stripped of all social vestments, to discover the individual and unique meaning for her of the roles she has been playing, can she begin the journey back to order; for to preserve identity she must find new roles to play, and before she can determine these roles, she must understand the meaning in her own individual life of the ones she has been forced to give up.

Faced with this unavoidable burden of self-examination and threatened always by the impending disintegration of her own personality, Clarissa quite characteristically turns once again to her background and the socio-religious order from which she has come to provide the terms in which to frame her supreme effort; and she finds them in the isolating, introspective literary form of the Puritan diary. Indeed, the diary is doubly appropriate to her situation. It is, of course, the traditional mode of self-examination, a way of seeing individual character without the comforting and deceiving gloss of custom to offer a spurious explanation or justification for behavior; and the understanding gained from seeing her life chronicled in such a way might well lead Clarissa to some inner truth about her actions which goes beyond the easy excuse of doing what is conventional or expected. Furthermore, and in this case perhaps more important, such a diary inevitably becomes an objective embodiment of the self which is the subject of examination. For Clarissa (increasingly threatened by a loss of identity) the unity of the objective 'self' contained in the letters or diary could prove a stay against the continuing danger to the coherence of her personality. Thus although at the very beginning of the novel, the exchange between Clarissa and Anna Howe does seem to have very much the air of a correspondence (the letters are short compared with the ones which are to follow, and they seem designed to give information about the strange events which are taking place at the Harlowe house), its primary function quickly becomes less communication than self-examination; it soon begins to take on most of the characteristics of the diary or journal.[18]

Certainly Clarissa's obsessive need to write is closely linked with the struggle to hold her fragmenting self together; and when she admits to Anna Howe, "Indeed, my dear, I know not how to *forbear* writing . . . I must write on, altho' I were not to send it to anybody" (III, 221), she is merely giving testimony to the urgency of the task confronting her. Without coherence, without unity, there is only death and oblivion; and the theme of death that runs throughout Clarissa's struggles may aptly be seen to begin here with the struggle to maintain personal integrity.

The identification in Clarissa's mind between being prevented from writing and dying is strikingly illustrated early in the novel. The chambermaid Betty has come to impart the family's displeasure and to transmit the order that Clarissa leave off her composing. Clarissa reacts instantly and with an hysteria quite disproportionate to the objective situation. "What will they do, Betty," she cries. "They won't kill me? What *will* they do?' 'Kill you! No!—but you will not be suffered to stir from thence, till you have complied with your duty. And *no pen and ink will be allowed you*' " (II, 121). Several days later Betty makes the threat again, and again Clarissa displays her acute anxiety. "This hint [of losing my writing materials] alarms me so much, that I shall instantly begin to conceal, in different places, pens, ink, and paper; and to deposit some in the Ivy Summer-house, if I can find a safe place there; and, at the worst, I have got a pencil of black, and another of red lead, which I use in my drawings; and my patterns shall serve for paper, if I have no other" (II, 237-238). Immediately following these precautions, the family does in fact confiscate her writing materials, and the scene takes on the character of a ritual act. " 'I must do as I am bid,' " the maid declares. " 'I can't help it—Don't be angry with me, Miss. But I must carry down your pen and ink.' 'By whose order?' 'By your Papa's and Mamma's.' 'How shall I know that?' She offered to go to my closet: I stept in before her: Touch it, if you dare. Up came my cousin Dolly—'Madam!—Madam!' said the poor weeping, good-natured creature, in broken sentences—'You must—indeed you must—deliver to Betty—or to me—your pen and ink' " (II, 245-246). This elaborate parade over pen, ink, and paper would indeed be ludicrous were it not for the significance they bear. Gaining control of Clarissa's writing becomes, for the avaricious family, a way of controlling her nature; Clarissa's precautions, the secreting of her writing materials in every conceivable hiding place, are merely her way of maintaining independence.

When Clarissa finds herself in Lovelace's hands, the same pattern continues, but the import becomes more ominous; for the act of stealing letters, forging letters, and reading letters that she had already written is part of Love-

lace's larger scheme of invading her personality. His preoccupation with the letters begins soon after they have
arrived in London, and the language he uses with regard
to them has clear sexual overtones. "If I could find out
that the dear creature carried any of her Letters in her
Pockets, I can get her to a Play or to a Concert, and she
may have the misfortune to lose her Pockets. . . . As to her
Pockets, I think my mind hankers after them. . . . But
they cannot hold all the Letters that I should wish to see.
And yet a woman's Pockets are half as deep as she is high.
Tied round the sweet *Levities,* I presume, as Ballast-bags,
lest the wind, as they move with full sail, from whale-
ribbed canvas, should blow away the gypsies" (IV, 45-46).

As the novel progresses, Lovelace's attempts to invade
the correspondence between Clarissa and Miss Howe become (along with the sexual attempts on Clarissa's body)
incorporated into his general desire to possess her, and
the invasive imagery of the lock and key is used to describe both.[19] Lovelace steals his glimpses of Clarissa
through the keyhole of her room, a room which is always
locked against his advances. Unlocking this door becomes
fused with the notion of sexual violation, and both are
seen as a preparatory to a ravishing of her will. The letters,
too, are locked away, and Lovelace provides the servant
Dorcas with a "master-key which will open every lock in
this chest" (IV, 47), declaring, "I must, I must come at
them. This difficulty augments my curiosity. Strange, so
much as she writes, and at all hours, that not one sleepy
or forgetful moment has offered in our favour!" (IV, 48).[20]

In part, at least, the letters become as people in the novel;
Lovelace would rape them, and Clarissa would protect
them at any price, locking them away and even sewing
them into her clothes for protection. They are not merely
the 'passive' means by which character is revealed or events
are told, but have become active forces themselves, the

object and source of action; and this importance stems partially from the fact that they are embodiments of personality. Thus Lovelace's desire to possess Clarissa's letters is certainly an extension of his desire to possess her. However, the fury of his attitude toward the correspondence between Clarissa and Miss Howe may still have another source.

At the beginning of the novel there is postulated an extraordinarily close relationship between Clarissa and Miss Howe which suggests that Clarissa's friend is viewed more as an extension of Clarissa herself then as a separate individual. As the situation becomes more trying for Clarissa and the letters begin to be a journal or diary of that trial, Anna Howe's function becomes more clearly defined. She is an embodiment specifically of the correcting mind; for she has perspicacity and intelligence and is more capable than Clarissa herself of understanding the devious motivation behind Clarissa's behavior. Her voice, then, becomes the voice of conscience, urging self-examination, remaining satisfied with nothing less than complete honesty from Clarissa, and pressing the truth of Clarissa's motivation upon her with irresistible strength. Clarissa recognizes and repeatedly confirms this role. "As I ask for your approbation or disapprobation of my conduct, upon the facts I lay before you," she tells Miss Howe, "I should think it the sign of a very bad cause, if I endeavoured to mislead my judge" (I, 312). Appropriately, the language which Clarissa uses to describe her situation to Miss Howe echoes the traditional language of the Puritan diarist; and the struggle with Lovelace is, in part at least, the typically Puritan battle with her own inherent sinfulness and the deceptiveness of the human heart. Thus only complete honesty, brutal clarity, will conquer. "Nothing less than the knowledge of the inmost recesses of your heart, can satisfy my Love and my Friendship," the voice of conscience warns. "Surely, you are not afraid to trust *your-self* with a secret of this nature: If you are, then you may the *more* allowably doubt *me*" (I, 275). And Clarissa assents in this view. "I hope, my dear, I do not deceive myself, and, instead of setting about rectifying what is amiss in my heart, endeavour to find excuses for habits and peculiari-ties, which I am unwilling to cast off or overcome. The heart is very deceitful: Do you, my dear friend, lay mine open (*But surely it is always open before you!*) and spare me not, if you think it culpable" (IV, 103).

Such casuistical language might come from any of a number of the diaries or devotional works. The necessity for self-examination, the unavoidable snares and strate-gems of the heart—all of this is clearly in the Puritan tra-dition. The letters from Clarissa to Miss Howe are truly the communications of a human trying to see herself ob-jectively and honestly, no matter what the price; and Clarissa's repeated pleas for Miss Howe's moral judgment are poignant testimony to the pain of such an undertaking. "I am a very bad Casuist," she confesses, "and the pleasure I take in writing to you, who are the only one to whom I can disburden my mind, may make me, as I have hinted, very partial to my own wishes [to continue the corres-pondence]. . . . I would be glad methinks to be per-mitted still to write to you; and only to have such *occa-sional returns* by Mr. Hickman's pen . . . as might set me right when I am wrong, confirm me, when right; and guide me where I doubt" (III, 220). Yet even con-science cannot always inform the sinner in time, and Miss Howe seems doomed to know more than Clarissa, failing to save her from the disastrous punishment for her own sinfulness. "It was plain to me," she laments, "to whom you communicated all that *you knew* of your own heart, tho' not all of it that *I found out*, that Love had pretty early gained footing in it. And this yourself would have discovered sooner than you did, had not his alarming, his unpolite, his rough conduct, kept it under" (V, 40).

It is surely significant, then, that throughout much of the early part of the novel Lovelace is as concerned to deceive Miss Howe as he is to trap Clarissa. Later, his frenzied attempts to interpose himself between them by intercepting their letters may be seen as a literal attempt to come between Clarissa and the voice of her conscience. (And, of course, the vituperation that he continuously heaps upon Miss Howe is anger directed not at the woman herself but at the moral insight and advice associated with her.) In the final analysis, however, even the success of Lovelace's plots, his breaking into the correspondence by forging letters from both Clarissa and Anna Howe, is a mere mechanical victory much like the advantage sustained by drugging Clarissa before the rape. Possessing a diary is, after all, not the same as possessing the will of the diarist—however much the diary itself might represent an objective embodiment of its author.

However, perhaps the most important element in the correspondence between Clarissa and Miss Howe is the *way* in which it reveals personality; and the illumination which may be given to the novel as a work of art by viewing it in terms of the Puritan tradition from which Richardson came is most important precisely here in the matter of characterization. Miss Howe's insights, and Clarissa's after them, all depend on the same source—the 'self' which is projected into the letter-diary. There is no other way to judge her, especially in the specific case of her dealings with Lovelace, for neither Miss Howe nor the reader ever sees her directly.[21] If we turn our attention to this correspondence, we can see with reasonable clarity the manner in which Miss Howe's assessments are made. She does not fix upon any single incident as the decisive, signifi-

cant, or ultimately illuminating one; nor does she follow
the progression of Clarissa's actions to predict a fitting or
logical conclusion for them. Rather she examines the unself-conscious, rambling, apparently disorganized series
of confidences and confessions that comprise the correspondence. These provide the material from which she
must draw all of her conclusions; and both she and Clarissa acknowledge as much, a fact which explains the often
repeated injunctions for complete honesty. Thus Clarissa
and her friend are seeking to discover truth by discerning
the *pattern* of character. Neither ever doubts the manner
in which they will find this truth; and, significantly, even
when Clarissa would deny the validity of her friend's
conclusions, she does so without impugning the way by
which those conclusions were reached. "Let me enter into
the close examination of myself which my beloved friend
advises. I did so; and cannot own any of the *glow*, any of
the *throbs* you mention.—*Upon my word* I will repeat, I
cannot. And yet the passages in my Letter upon which you
are so humorously severe, lay me fairly open to your agreeable raillery. I own they do. And I cannot tell what turn
my mind had taken to dictate so oddily to my pen" (I, 68).

Miss Howe's function as conscience is to perceive the
pattern which is latent in Clarissa's letters, both by understanding the significance of repeated incidents and by
noting the manner in which these incidents are recorded,
while Clarissa in turn must understand Miss Howe's insights and learn the process by which she herself can begin
to detect the order which informs her spontaneous notations. Thus it is absolutely essential that no extrinsic order
should be imposed on the letter-diary, no "lesson" taught
in it, no general truth about the world consciously embodied in it; any such disruption of the natural and
unrestrained expression of self would serve only to distort

or obscure the "self" which did emerge, imputing to it attributes which it might not possess and giving an inadequate and therefore inaccurate explanation for behavior. As we have seen earlier, these were the problems that beset Pamela.[22] Richardson imposed order on her story, making it an encomium of virtue rewarded. In *Clarissa* there is no such apparent order. The novel rambles interminably, and the letters are drawn to extreme, perhaps (one might feel) even absurd lengths. Yet these seeming flaws lie at the very heart of Richardson's literary skill; for the reader (with Miss Howe and Clarissa) must *discover* the truth, the order which unifies both Clarissa's nature and the letter-diary that embodies it. The complexity of the novel is a mirror of the very complex mind speaking through it; the laborious repetitions are important precisely because they are repeated; and the reader's commitment to the novel must in the final analysis be a commitment to Clarissa herself.

Perhaps the first insight which emerges clearly from the study of Clarissa's character provided in the letter-diary is understanding the role that pride has played in her definition of self. As we have seen earlier, Clarissa at the beginning of the novel is praised, petted, and renowned for her exercise of virtue; and the assertion of her own value, even when it is articulated by a deliberate attempt to reveal herself as *better* than those around her, is merely part of Clarissa's conception of her role as dutiful daughter and conscientious Christian. She never considers her motivation because it never occurs to her that she is doing other than what is proper and expected of her; and one of the first effects of her changed environment is to make her recognize the significance of attitudes that she has always taken for granted. "Thus are those imputed qualifications, which used so lately to gain me applause, now become my crimes," she laments, "So much do disgust and anger alter the property of things" (II, 103). Once she is confronted with the fact that the standards for acceptable behavior may vary, the way has been opened for a consideration of her own actions; and very early in the novel she has the passing thought that her nature—even the conscious exercise of virtue—might be motivated by a sense of pride. "It is true, thought I, that I have formed agreeable schemes of making others as happy as myself, by the proper discharge of the Stewardship entrusted to me. . . . But let me examine myself: Is not Vanity, or secret Love of praise, a principal motive with me at the bottom?—Ought I not to suspect my own heart? If I set up for myself, puffed up with every one's good opinion, may I not be *left* to myself?" (I, 134-135).

However, this fleeting thought does not linger. It is significant, for instance, that when the notion of pride first occurs to Clarissa, she frames it in terms of the pride that would be involved in taking possession of her estate (something that she would never do anyway) rather than seeing the very real arrogance of her manner toward others. The theme of Clarissa's tendency to self-aggrandizement is not dropped, however, for Anna Howe consistently points out the detrimental effects of Clarissa's flaunting her virtue before her brother and sister. "Why, my dear, they must look upon you as a prodigy among them: And prodigies you know, tho' they obtain our Admiration, never attract our Love" (I, 183). Even the relationship between the correspondents is not untainted, and when Clarissa is obstinately set upon being over-generous in her reward to one of the Howe's servants, Anna Howe flares out, "Indeed I *am*, and I *will be*, angry with you for it. A year's wages at once well nigh! . . . *I must give you your way in these things*, you say. . . . But why should you, by the nobleness of your mind, throw reproaches upon the rest of the world? Particularly, upon your own family—and upon ours too? . . . Why blush you not, my dear friend, to be thus singular?—When you meet with another person whose mind is like your own, then display your excellencies as you please: But till then, for pity's sake, let your heart and your spirit suffer a little contraction" (II, 181-182). Anna Howe's insistent voice urging moderation and temperance upon Clarissa in her attitude toward others runs in counterpoint with the violent outbursts that mark Clarissa's encounters with her family. Taken together they delineate a pattern of behavior which emerges with ever-increasing clarity. Virtue, as it is defined by the Clarissa whom we meet at the beginning of the novel, is a comparative quality: one can be virtuous only by being better than others. Thus to express personal goodness, one must simultaneously articulate the inferiority of others. Such is the theme that runs throughout Clarissa's relationships, and it becomes more and more evident when the social roles which had supported or masked it have disappeared. Though Clarissa intermittently wonders about her tendency to pride, she never comes to any real understanding of the problem while she is living with her family; and her elopement is perhaps the grandest gesture of that sinful complacency, placing her above not only her relatives but Miss Howe as well, for all of the friend's entreaties that she be allowed to help Clarissa are summarily rejected. Anna Howe argues, "If, by a *less* inconvenience to ourselves, we could relieve our friend from a *greater*, the refusal of such a favour makes the refuser unworthy of the name of Friend" (II, 309). Yet to allow Miss Howe a share in the adventure would be to accord her a threateningly equal claim to the moral victory implicit in Clarissa's denial of her family, and so she is refused.

The intrigue with Lovelace merely reinforces Clarissa's

pride. The angry series of recriminations and accusations perpetuates the mode of behavior which had been set earlier with her brother and sister, and Anna Howe's injunctions for moderation are again ignored as Clarissa continues to repeat the patterns which have become a part of her nature. Even her assertions of freedom from Lovelace's control are dangerously dependent on proving herself his moral superior, and Lovelace himself can see the folly of such a position. "If impeccable," he muses, "how came she by her impeccability? The pride of setting an Example to her Sex has run away with her hitherto, and may have made her till *now* invincible" (III, 86). This kind of virtue must be tested to be revealed; and the person whose goodness is of such a nature must perforce court temptation if he is to prove superiority. Lovelace is no fool (the Devil is traditionally seen as a dangerously cunning adversary), and he perfectly well understands the deadly irony of Clarissa's committing the sin of pride in the very act of vowing virtue. After all, he reasons, "Am I not justified in my resolutions of trying *her* Virtue; who is resolved, as I may say, to try *mine?*" (III, 94). Such rationalization becomes a perverse parody of Clarissa's own thinking, and one cannot help recognizing that even if Miss Howe's rhapsodical estimation of Clarissa is correct, it emphasizes the unpleasant dependence of the notion of goodness upon evil. "Upon the whole," she says, "there seems, as I have often said, to have been a kind of fate in your error, if it *were* an error; and this perhaps admitted *for the sake of a better Example to be collected from your* SUFFERINGS, *than could have been given, had you never erred:* For, my dear, the time of ADVERSITY *is your* SHINING-TIME" (IV, 67). And if Clarissa shines in adversity, it would certainly be fair to say that she defines her afflictions as God's special tribute to her nature. "Indeed, my dearest Love," she admits to Miss Howe, "I am

afraid I am singled out (either for my own faults, or for
the faults of my family, or perhaps for the faults of both)
to be a very unhappy creature! —*signally* unhappy!"
(II, 263).

The belief that God in His infinite wisdom can wrest
good from apparent evil has a long and respected religious
sanction; yet there is an equally strong tradition (dating
back at least to the temptations of Christ) that to court
temptation for the purpose of demonstrating moral
strength is itself sinful. Such a view is certainly the religious basis for Richardson's portrayal of Clarissa's pride;
but this tendency in her nature has interesting psychological significance as well. Her definition of self, her
estimation of her own worth, must always be predicated
on relationship to others. Thus she cannot be "good";
she can only be "better than." And so long as she persists
in this error, she and Lovelace are bound in a kind of infernal, self-defeating, union—he delineating his greatness
in terms of the worth of those whom he incorporates into
himself or controls, she in turn basing her evaluation of
herself on the superiority demonstrated by her resistance
to his temptations.

The critical break in this vicious circle comes just after
Lovelace has succeeded in stealing a portion of Clarissa's
correspondence. The act is, in an objective and mechanical
sense, his first genuine "violation" of her integrity; and
the knowledge of her character that it gives him infuriates him. He attempts to mask his anger, but Clarissa
senses it despite his precautions; and the violence of his
reaction gives her an unprecedented insight into the
viciousness of his nature. She recoils in horror from it,
but is enabled, through this vision of *his* depravity, to
recognize the folly and the sinfulness of her position. "My
temper, I believe, is changed. No wonder if it be. I question whether ever it will be what it was. . . . I tremble

to look back upon his encroachments. And now to give me cause to apprehend *more evil from him, than indignation will permit me to express!*" (IV, 208-209). Her insight sweeps over the whole of her character as it has been revealed through the letter-journal, and events which had seemed isolated and independent of each other come now to have a dreadful significance as the pattern of her own presumption emerges with unmistakable clarity. "You, my dear," she cries to Miss Howe, "could not be a stranger to my most secret failings, altho' you would not tell me of them. What a pride did I take in the applause of every one! —What a pride even in supposing I had not that pride!- Which concealed itself from my unexamining heart under the spacious veil of *Humility,* doubling the merit to myself by the *supposed,* and indeed *imputed,* gracefulness in the manner of conferring benefits, when I had not a single merit in what I did. . . . So desirous, in short, to be considered as an *Example!* A vanity which my partial admirers put into my head!—And so secure in my own virtue" (IV, 209-210).

This, Clarissa's first great triumph over the sinfulness of self, becomes not a castigation of identity but a correction of it and—finally—a celebration of it. Despair would be an even greater sin than pride; thus Clarissa must use her increased understanding as a means of hope, relying on God's help to support her. "Let me, however, look forward," she resolves. "To despond would be to add sin to sin. And whom have I to raise up, whom to comfort me, if I desert *myself*" (IV, 210). The most immediate result of Clarissa's self-knowledge is the ability to distinguish just pride from sinful pride, to have an appropriate appreciation of her own value without placing unwarranted confidence in her own abilities and without being forced to denigrate others by comparison. Once she has achieved this ability, Clarissa can turn on Lovelace with the scorn he so manifestly deserves; her judgment of him has become independent of her definition of self, and for the first time in their relationship, she becomes genuinely free of him. Lovelace recounts her rejection. "She would have flung from me: 'I will *not* be detained, Mr. Lovelace. I *will* go out.' . . . I cast myself at her feet. —'Begone, Mr. Lovelace,' she said, with a rejecting motion, her fan in her hand; 'for your own sake leave me! —My soul is above thee, man!' with both her hands pushing me from her!—'Urge me not to tell thee, how sincerely I think my soul above thee! —Thou hast in mine, a proud, a too proud heart, to contend with! —Leave me, and leave me for ever! —Thou hast a proud heart to contend with!' Her air, her manner, her voice, were bewitchingly noble, tho' her words were so severe" (IV, 215-216).

Still, despite this alteration in the relationship, despite the fact that Clarissa no longer *needs* the reassurance of Lovelace's iniquity to prove her own value, she does not leave; indeed, she even continues to partake in the projected marriage settlements. The reason for her behavior is a simple one: she no longer needs him, but she still desires him.

The second principal element in Clarissa's nature that is revealed in her relationship with Lovelace is the sexual or passionate component. This, like pride, is a quality which was originally manifested in her dealings with her family; and like pride, it is transferred into the liaison with Lovelace. However, its sources, its nature, and even its moral significance are much more complex than the rather straightforward descriptions that we have been given of pride. For instance, as we have seen earlier, passion properly directed was desirable, even necessary in a man. "They were my father's lively spirits that first made him an interest in [my mother's] gentle bosom" (I, 167), Clarissa observes; and Solmes is condemned as a man with a "creeping mind"—hardly a man at all. The fact that women universally admire a man of spirit or passion is acknowledged throughout the novel. Yet passion to be beneficial must be controlled. The violence of Mr. Harlowe's black moods demonstrates the danger of uncontrolled passion, as does the cold rage which Lovelace directs at the Harlowe family. Clearly Clarissa fears strong emotion at least as much as she desires it, for she cautions even her friend Anna Howe, "Learn, my dear, I beseech you learn, to subdue your own passions. Be the motives what they will, Excess is Excess. Those passions in our Sex, which we take no pains to subdue, may have one and the same source with those infinitely blacker passions, which we used so often to condemn in the violent and headstrong of the other Sex" (III, 381). Education, then (and this is a doctrine taken unchanged from the Puritan creed), must involve the control of the passions; and it is this education that Lovelace lacks. "If he be really so much concerned at his past faults, as he pretends . . . must he not, of course, have corrected, in some degree, the impetuosity of his temper? The first step of reformation, as I conceive, is to subdue sudden gusts of passion, from which frequently the greattest evils arise, and to learn to bear disappointments. If the irascible passions cannot be overcome, what opinion can we have of the person's power over those to which bad habit, joined to *greater* temptation, gives stronger force?" (II, 127).

One danger of passion is, of course, the possibility that it may lead to sin. In the Puritan creed, sin is of the body, and the body is the seat of the passions; failure to exercise control over the body and its passions must inevitably lead to sin. In personal relationships, uncontrolled passion may have yet another danger, and Anna Howe, discussing Lovelace's spirited nature, points out that danger. "We are too apt to make allowances for such tempers as *early* indulgence has made uncontrollable; and therefore habitually evil. But if a boisterous temper, when under *obligation*, is to be thus allowed for, what, when the tables are turned, will it expect? . . . The suiting of the tempers of two persons who are to come together is a great matter: And yet there should be boundaries fixed between them, by consent as it were, beyond which neither should go: And each should hold the other to it; or there would probably be encroachments in both. To illustrate my assertion by a very high, and by a more manly (as some would think it) than womanly instance—If the boundaries of the Three Estates that constitute our Political Union were not known, and occasionally asserted, what would become of the Prerogatives and Privileges of each other? The two branches of the Legislature would encroach upon each other; and the Executive power would swallow up both" (II, 148-149).

Thus the control of passion is directly related to the problem of defining one's nature. Anyone who is prey to his own uncontrolled emotions is less than human, for virtue, character, identity itself all depend upon restricting the passions; furthermore, so Miss Howe points out, anyone who has no self-control will always be a threat to the integrity of other's characters as well. It is not surprising, then, that Clarissa invariably associates strong passions of any kind with death or the loss of identity. She is both attracted by passion and terrified of it; and her feeling about her father, her fantasies about the relationship between Lovelace and her brother, and her own sexual feeling for Lovelace all partake of this double nature.

As we have seen in our earlier discussions, Clarissa is often able to recognize passion in others (although she cannot always assess its extent); however, she is completely incapable of realizing the hold that passion has over her. Her sexual feelings for Lovelace are revealed to us very early, and Miss Howe sees them too and tries to inform Clarissa of their danger. "It is my opinion, and that from the easiness of his [Lovelace's] heart and behaviour, that he has seen more than *I* have seen; more than you think *could* be seen;—more than I believe you *yourself* know, or else you would let *me* know it" (I, 66). There would be no shame, of course, in an attraction to a man of character, one worthy of becoming Clarissa's husband, for this would be a passion controlled by reason. Thus Clarissa avoids Miss Howe's inquiries, deeming her affection a "conditional liking only" (conditional, one supposes, upon Lovelace's proving his worthiness). Yet as more and more of Clarissa is unself-consciously revealed through her letter-journal, we soon come to perceive that passion dominates reason in her relationship with him and that it is, moreover, a passion which has not been divorced from the sense of inevitable violence which Clarissa habitually associates with strong feelings.

The flight itself, for instance, is occasioned by an ambivalent mixture of motives; the sounds that emanate from the garden portend an angry encounter which Clarissa would avoid, while at the same time the physical presence of Lovelace seductively urges acquiescence. Neither the reader nor Clarissa herself can ever be sure whether it was fear or desire which motivated her; and the answer is that it was clearly both, for they are inextricably related in her mind, as the mixture of sexual imagery and violence in her dream (occurring immediately before the elopement) clearly indicates. "Methought my Brother, my Uncle Antony, and Mr. Solmes, had formed a plot to destroy Mr. Lovelace; who discovering it, and believing I had a hand in it, turned all his rage against me. I thought he made them all fly into foreign parts upon it; and afterwards seizing upon me, carried me into a church-yard; and there, notwithstanding all my prayers and tears, and protestations of innocence, stabbed me to the heart, and then tumbled me into a deep grave ready dug, among two or three half-dissolved carcasses; throwing in the dirt and and earth upon me with his hands, and trampling it down with his feet" (II, 283). If, as this portentous dream would seem to indicate, Clarissa was at some level of her being aware of the mortal danger inherent in her flight from home, it must have seemed only the natural accompaniment of unloosed passion. The conceit that sexual fulfillment is "death" takes on for Clarissa a terrifying literal meaning; for being possessed by passion can only mean an ultimate loss of self.

Here, as in the case of Clarissa's pride, the theme of passion is stated and reiterated throughout the correspondence, and by this repetition we come to see it as a part of Clarissa's character. From the beginning Anna Howe is insistent in her demands that Clarissa acknowledge her feelings; and these warnings of conscience are consistently matched by actions which articulate Clarissa's true emotions—her refusal to break off the correspondence with Lovelace, her obvious fascination with his physical appearance, and the elopement itself. Moreover, this pattern of desire is never dissociated from the insistent threat of violence and death. Thus Clarissa's imprudently scornful and unconsciously self-punishing attitude toward Lovelace during the early days of their mutual imprisonment inevitably brings down upon her an anger and a violence of response which she would assume to be a natural component in any relationship based on sexual attraction; and it is certainly significant that Clarissa's feelings are for the first time completely revealed to both Lovelace and the reader during a feigned attack of sickness when her fears that he might die inadvertently expose the strength of her affection for him.

As we have remarked earlier, Lovelace himself is not a

man of sensuality; he wants possession for the sake of possession and not for the satisfaction of his own physical
cravings. However, he is certainly perceived by Clarissa
as a sensualist, and we might postulate that she sees him
thus because he represents an embodiment of her own unacknowledged feelings. His assaults on her identity, then,
take on added significance: they are external threats, the
actions of a being who would wholly incorporate her into
himself; yet they are also representations of the battle that
Clarissa must wage with her own inherent sinfulness, and it
is this second form of menace which provides the most dangerous temptation. Unlike Pamela, who was so secured
against Mr. B.'s enticements that there was never any
genuine internal pressure on her to yield, Clarissa is
tempted by her own desires each time Lovelace makes an
advance; in rejecting him she must also repress the desires
in herself that he awakens; and so long as she persists in
viewing the sexual threat as entirely external to herself,
she will be deluded as to the true nature of her character.
Of course the moments of greatest peril come precisely
when Lovelace (or the sinful tendencies that he represents)
threatens to invade her character, and such moments of
crisis can lead to self-knowledge; thus Clarissa's pride is
discovered as the result of Lovelace's encroachments into
her letter-journal. In the same way, the far more destructive
series of violations that culminates in the rape finally
leads Clarissa to at least a partial understanding of her
own passionate desires.

Appropriately enough, Clarissa's dreaded journey into
the dark complexity of her passions begins with a very
real fire whose existence Clarissa denies. The full account
of the incident is given in Lovelace's letter to Belford. Dorcas raises the cry of fire, and "no sooner had she made this
dreadful outcry, but I heard her Lady's door, with hasty
violence, unbar, unbolt, unlock, and open" (IV, 389). With

the door now open, Lovelace confronts Clarissa, equally terrified by the fire and by the presence of the man whom she had locked out of her heart. *We* know that at this moment Lovelace has no thought but her safety (indeed the failure to press his advantage infuriates him once the incident has passed). Clarissa is near collapse as Lovelace "lifted her to her bed, and sat down by her upon the side of it, endeavouring with the utmost tenderness, as well of action as expression, to dissipate her terrors" (IV, 390). His manner is not violent; he avows, "in my own account, I was both decent and generous" (IV, 391)—and certainly his behavior is less threatening and less offensive than it had been on many previous occasions. Yet Clarissa cannot contain her terror. She is thrown into frenzied struggles and pleading. "She protested, that she would not survive what she called a treatment so disgraceful and villainous; and, looking all wildly round her, as if for some instrument of mischief, she espied a pair of sharp-pointed scissors on a chair by the bed-side, and endeavoured to catch them up, with design to make her words good on the spot" (IV, 391). The tumult continues and Clarissa grows more incoherent in her terrified ravings. Lovelace is her "dear Lovelace"; she implores his pity. She screams to Heaven against his "treachery." She is desperate and will not be pacified; and though she begs for assurance of mercy, she will not let him speak. The horror is now upon her; the bolted door has been thrown open from within; and Clarissa's passions have betrayed themselves in her terrified delusions. It is not Lovelace she fears, but the power of her own feeling, a power which is revealed in all of its implacable fury. Clarissa offers violence to herself in unmistakably sexual terms and immediately thereafter dementedly imputes the same violent motives to Lovelace. "*Am* I then a villain?" Lovelace demands. "O no!—And yet you are!'—And again I was her *dear*

Lovelace!—Her hands again clasped over her charming bosom:—'Kill me! Kill me!—If I am odious enough in your eyes to deserve this treatment; and I will thank you! —Too long, much too long, has my life been a burden to me!'—Or, wildly looking all round her, 'give me but the means, and I will instantly convince you, that my Honour is dearer to me than my Life!' " (IV, 394). She cried out to God, imploring that the curse of a violent and angry father not be visited upon her; and at last, Lovelace, struck by the fury of her protestations, withdraws. Once away from her he rues his failure to subdue her and returns to press his demands, but "her door was fast. . . . I thought I heard her coming to open the door, and my heart leapt in that hope; but it was only to draw another bolt, to make it still the faster; and she either could not or would not answer me, but retired to the further end of her apartment, to her closet probably; And more like a fool than before, again I sneaked away" (IV, 397). The interlude is over; the door is once more safely locked.

Of course, it would be mistaken to ignore the objective dangers. Clarissa *is* in a state of undress, and Lovelace does embrace her repeatedly. However, the villainy that Clarissa would impute to him is quite manifestly not there: the fire was real; his concern for her was genuine; and he does withdraw at her insistence without offering violence to her. Indeed, the double report of the scene—Lovelace's admiration and desire mixed with a sense of bewilderment at the vehemence of Clarissa's reactions contrasted with Clarissa's own certainty that this was at last the ultimate attempt upon her—underlines Clarissa's mistake quite explicitly; moreover, her reactions afterward merely confirm the shock she suffers at having thus revealed herself. She locks herself in her room, refusing to come out and refusing to admit Lovelace, as if she could somehow nullify the terror of that unguarded moment; and at the earliest possible opportunity, she makes her first effective attempt to escape him.

But escape has come too late. There is no refuge from the terrors of the mind once they have been roused. Clarissa has nowhere to go; the sexuality and potential violence that lay beneath her notions of duty and submission to a demanding father had been transferred to Lovelace, and his actions in turn have indicated the desires that lie hidden in the dark recesses of her own character. There is danger now not only from a father who fails in his duty or from a Lovelace who batters at the barriers of her reserve. Danger is everywhere; for she carries it within her and cannot escape. As Clarissa says to Miss Howe during her brief liberation, "my terror is not yet over: I can hardly think myself safe: Every well-dressed man I see from my windows, whether on horseback or on foot, I think to be him" (V, 56). Lovelace's rediscovery of her, then, is inevitable; and Clarissa, caught in the fatal pattern of events, becomes increasingly incoherent in her expression of fear. The vengeance of Lovelace, the anger of a father, desire, and death rise and fall as vivid images in her troubled mind. " 'Surely, surely, faulty as I have been, I have not deserved to be *thus* persecuted!!—I resume, therefore, my former language: 'You have no right to pursue me: You *know* you have not: Begone, then; and leave me to make the best of my hard lot. O my dear cruel Father!' said she, in a violent fit of grief (falling upon her knees, and clasping her uplifted hands together) 'thy heavy curse is completed upon thy devoted Daughter! I am *punished*, dreadfully punished, by the very wretch in whom I had placed my wicked confidence!" (V, 132).

The pace of the novel quickens as Clarissa is caught in the vortex of her own chaotic mind and swept down and down to the forbidden regions of unknown horror. Society is at its furthest reach now, and the brothel becomes a world of fantasy, nightmare, and delirium: Lovelace, inflamed and literally demonic, "his sentences short, and pronounced as if his breath were touched" (VI, 188), triumph in his glittering eyes; Clarissa herself, wracked with thirst, gasping, unable to control her vision or her speech, and breaking into incoherent frenzies; and the rape, the ultimate violation with the unspeakable apparitions that haunt Clarissa's memory, "visionary remembrances I have of female figures, flitting, as I may say, before my sight" (VI, 191). These are the terrors of unleashed passion; and after this there is nothing further left to fear.

Now that Clarissa's character has been stripped bare of its social identity so that her nightmarish fears might become reality; her initial response is incoherence and the confessed inability to define and control the terrifying forces that have been loosed. "I am tired of myself," she tells Miss Howe brokenly. "I sat down to say a great deal— My heart was full—I did not know what to say first—And thought, and grief, and confusion, and (O my poor head!) I cannot tell what—And thought, and grief and confusion, came crouding so thick upon me; *one* would be first, *another* would be first, *all* would be first; so I can write nothing at all. —Only that, whatever they have done to me, I cannot tell; but I am no longer what I was" (V, 327). Her hysterical appeals to her father are reiterated, and she continues disjointedly to associate him with the violence which has been visited on her. But throughout all there runs the pervading, spectral vision of destructive passion unleased and uncontrolled.

> A Lady took a great fancy to a young Lion, or a Bear. I forget which—But a Bear, or a Tyger, I believe, it was. It was made her a present of, when a whelp. She fed it with her own hand: She nursed up the wicked cub with great tenderness; and would play with it, without fear or apprehension

of danger: And it was obedient to all her commands: And
its tameness, as she used to boast, encreased with its growth;
so that, like a Lap-dog, it would follow her all over the
house. But mind what followed: At last, some-how, neglect-
ing to satisfy its hungry maw, or having otherwise dis-
obliged it on some occasion, it resumed its nature; and on
a sudden fell upon her, and tore her in pieces.—And who
was most to blame, I pray? The Brute, or the Lady? The
Lady, surely!—For what *she* did was *out* of nature, *out* of
character, at least: What *it* did, was *in* its own nature. (V, 329).

Here the animal imagery that has been used throughout
the novel to describe Lovelace becomes fully meaningful
in this beast fable. Clarissa had feared that she could not
rein him in, but she discovers that it was the beast within
her own breast whose viciousness she had always feared,
her own passion whose nature she has so tragically mis-
judged. Here, then, is where Clarissa's desperate fantasies have led her. Lovelace has become an agent of darkness much more powerful than she had originally feared
—evoking her own deep passions and turning her righteous nature vengefully inward. Yet Clarissa's greatest
struggle must exclude Lovelace. Having been tempted,
having recognized the secret yearning to respond to temptation, Clarissa must now prove her right to move beyond
this stage of despair.

CHAPTER VI

Clarissa Triumphant

After the rape death advances upon Clarissa—death as
defeat, death as the violent rape of self and the loss of
identity, death as the dread devourer of all that she had
valued. " 'Twill be a mercy,' " she cries, "the highest act
of mercy you can do, to kill me outright upon this spot.'
. . . Then, baring, with a still more frantic violence, part
of her enchanting neck—'Here, here, said the soul-har-
rowing Beauty, let thy pointed mercy enter!' " (V, 375).
"Would but they kill me, let them come, and welcome. I
will bless the hand that will strike the blow!" (VI, 25).
Again and again she offers injury to herself in sexual
terms, as if the physical defilement she has suffered were
indistinguishable from oblivion itself. "She held forth
a penknife in her hand, the point to her own bosom,

grasping resolutely the whole handle, so that there was no offering to take it from her. . . . She withdrew to the door, and set her back against it, holding the pointed knife to her heaving bosom; while the women held me, beseeching me not to provoke the violent Lady—For their *house* sake" (VI, 67-68).

Clarissa's identification of death with sexuality has been consistent throughout the novel, but here death takes on added meaning. It becomes not just the final physical violation but the loss of that very self which the letter-diary and the struggles recorded in it had been designed to preserve; and Clarissa's longing for death is born of despair and selfcondemnation. We can find such sentiments in Puritan diaries—sentiments that range from a vague sense of anxiety and alarm, unspecific and pervading all consciousness to an articulated desire for death and even to attempted suicide itself. We might identify a partial cause for such behavior as a revulsion from the sinful "self" which has been discovered through introspection and the accompanying desire to escape from it. Yet there is another factor here, again a characteristic element in the Puritan dilemma and a theme of the diaries we have examined, which would prove an even more dangerous reinforcement of the suicidal tendencies inspired by Clarissa's unleashed sexual drives, and this is the form of self-destruction which Emile Durkheim has termed "egoistic suicide."

According to Durkheim, suicide is less probable when an individual is well-integrated into a society, when its goals and its values may be identified with his and when his definition of himself may be expressed in terms of his meaningful relationship to the society of which he is a part. Conversely, "the more weakened the groups to which he belongs, the less he depends on them, the more he consequently depends only on himself and recognizes no other rules of conduct than what are founded on his private interests. If we agree to call this state egoism, in which the individual ego asserts itself to excess in the face of the social ego and at its expense, we may call egoistic the special type of suicide springing from excessive individualism."[1] When an individual becomes separated from those groups which have been meaningful to him without at the same time attaching himself to new groups to replace the ones he has lost, he suffers a sense of isolation which, if it becomes complete enough, may drive him to self-destruction. Durkheim explains this phenomenon in the following way:

> If . . . as has often been said, man is double, that is because social man superimposes himself upon physical man. Social man necessarily presupposes a society which he expresses and serves. If this dissolves, if we no longer feel it in existence and action about and above us, whatever is social in us is deprived of all objective foundation. All that remains is an artificial combination of illusory images, a phantasmagoria vanishing at the least reflection; that is, nothing which can be a goal for our action. Yet this social man is the essence of civilized man; he is the masterpiece of existence. Thus we are bereft of reasons for existence; for the only life to which we could cling no longer corresponds to anything actual; the only existence still based upon reality no longer meets our needs. Because we have been initiated into a higher existence, the one which satisfies an animal or a child can satisfy us no more, and the other itself fades and leaves us helpless. So there is nothing more for our efforts to lay hold of, and we feel them lose themselves in emptiness. In this sense it is true to say that our activity needs an object transcending it. . . . It is implicit in our moral constitution and cannot be even partially lost without this losing its raison d'etre in the same degree. No proof is needed that in such a state of confusion the least

cause of discouragement may easily give birth to desperate resolutions.[2]

Thus the individual in crisis, the individual who has been severed from the values which he holds as meaningful will always be threatened by the desire for death.

The suspended state of the Puritan, never sure whether he might safely define himself in terms of the community of God's Saints, is an example of just such an isolated and terrifying condition. We can see it in the diaries and autobiographies, and Isaac Watts in his treatise *Against the Temptation to Self-Murther* portrays the resultant uncertainty and sense of worthlessness with dramatic intensity. "Some poor melancholy creature may say . . . 'I am surrounded and overwhelm'd night and day with such a crowd and tumult of distracting fears and dismal imaginations that I can hardly get a moment's rest. . . . I am importuned with the endless buzz and clamor of diabolical suggestions to put an end to my life; almost everything I see is proposed to me as an instrument of self-destruction, and I fear I shall not be able always to resist; sometimes I am tempted to believe if I would but once comply, I should sleep in silence, and there would be an end of these disquietudes.' "[3] Durkheim confirms Watts' intuitions, establishing that Protestants commit suicide more frequently than Catholics and others who belong to more cohesive, highly organized religions and that among Protestants, those whose religion demands isolated intensive introspection are the most vulnerable. "The proclivity of Protestantism for suicide," Durkheim says, "must relate to the spirit of free inquiry that animates this religion. . . . Reflection develops only if its development becomes imperative, that is, if certain ideas and instinctive sentiments which have hitherto adequately guided conduct are found to have lost their efficacy."[4] In the case of the Puritans, of course, the notion of isolation became itself almost a dogma; and the one most characteristic element of the Puritan mind was its unrelieved separateness. In the life of the individual Puritan, his own relentless conscience was specifically intended to take the place of an established church authority; however, "if individual consciences keep reaffirming their autonomy, it is because a new opinion has not been formed to replace the one no longer existing."[5] The Puritan psychology was an inherently unstable one, for it postulated *process* as a continuing state with no recognizable or attainable goal to reach during life on this earth, no stable set of instinctive ideas or sentiments to reassure an individual in his own life. Puritanism, then, would be that form of Protestantism in which the individual was least well integrated into a meaningful group, and the absence of such a relationship was in and of itself dangerous. As Durkheim says, "We thus reach the conclusion that the superiority of Protestantism with respect to suicide results from its being a less strongly integrated church than the Catholic church."[6]

Thus the very process which is recorded in the diary form Clarissa uses is a threatening and potentially destructive one. Indeed, anything that isolates the individual, forcing him to redefine his values and his personality, is accompanied by an inherent risk. Social change, too, is menacing. As Durkheim says, "Society cannot disintegrate without the individual simultaneously detaching himself from social life, without his own goals becoming preponderant over those of the community, in a word without his personality tending to surmount the collective personality,"[7] and the social changes which necessitated Clarissa's self-evaluation also reinforce her suicidal tendencies. Thus Clarissa's despair and temptation to self-destruction have three separate but related causes: she has been isolated from her traditional background by social changes which made the definition of her identity no longer viable; she has turned for help to a religious tradition which demanded relentless and unending introspection, and by engaging in this process she has isolated herself still further; and finally, in the process of her self-examination she discovers that there are already loathsome, self-destructive tendencies inherent in her nature. Thus in the infernal world of Mrs. Sinclair's brothel, exiled from all that has been meaningful and confronted on all sides with the terrifying power of her own passions, Clarissa is more than half in love with death.

Richardson's increased skill as a novelist is nowhere more clearly shown than in his handling of Clarissa's despairing desires for death. After all, in *Pamela* we find much of the same fearfully anxious sentiments; and Pamela, like Clarissa, seems frequently to see the world as pervaded by a kind of inimical power. Mrs. Jewkes, for instance, "has a hoarse, man-like Voice . . . with a Heart more ugly than her Face" (*Pamela*, I, 151); and when Pamela might escape from Mr. B., she fears to do so because she is frightened by the presence of a grazing bull in a pasture she must cross, declaring, "I shall be as much frightened at the first strange Man that I meet with" (*Pamela*, I, 206). Indeed, Pamela's apparent fears even drive her to contemplate suicide. "God forgive me! but a sad Thought came just then into my Head!—I tremble to think of it! Indeed my Apprehensions of the Usage I should meet with, had like to have made me miserable for ever! O my dear, dear Parents, forgive your poor Child; but being then quite desperate, I crept along, till I could raise myself on my staggering Feet; and away limp'd I!—What to do, but to throw myself into the Pond, and so put a Period to all my Griefs in this World!" (*Pamela*, I, 233).

Yet in *Pamela* all of this terror and despair is diffuse and ineffective; we never believe in her fears, for her virtue is too securely assured. She is not really separated from society (she always has, we must remember, the implicit identity of a natural lady, despite the many changes of clothes); her letter-journal does not really engage in isolating and relentless introspection; and she discovers no self-destructive tendencies within her own nature. (Significantly, her suicidal tendencies are not expressed in sexual terms.) Thus in this first novel, when Richardson's heroine expresses fear or the desire to die, she does so because she is speaking within the conventions of the Puritan diary and autobiography which Richardson has adopted; such conventional expressions of terror are unconvincing precisely because they are *only* conventional, and it is indicative of Richardson's inexperience and clumsiness that he includes these sentiments without exhibiting their origins in Pamela's character or situations. However, when he comes to portray Clarissa, the very same kind of statement takes on real significance. Richardson now portrays the psychological state which underlies a generalized sense of anxiety and the desire for death; and what were in *Pamela* mere ritual utterances become in *Clarissa* genuine expressions of the dangerous isolation of the personality in transition, terrified responses to a relentless conscience, and the formulation of Clarissa's own most feared destructive passions.

Violent suicide is for Clarissa a real possibility as it never was for Pamela; but death under these circumstances would be defeat, and the battle she has waged would have been fought in vain should she yield to it. Success is still possible—even success in death—but if it is to come, Clarissa herself must find a way to transform death from a loss of identity and a violent usurpation of self to an assertion of self.

The strength for this final exertion originates in Clarissa's recognition of the power and integrity of her own will and in that appropriate admiration for herself which began when she learned to separate a just pride in her virtue from the sinful pride which had governed so much of her early behavior. As she learns increasingly to judge herself independently of her estimation of Lovelace, the vitality of her character increases; and (just before the rape, which is Lovelace's last, desperate effort) she can reject marriage to him with finality, desiring justification from no other source save her correspondent and God Himself. " 'For myself,' " she tells Lovelace, " 'if I shall be enabled, on due reflection, to look back upon my own conduct, without the great reproach of having wilfully, and against the light of my own judgment, erred, I shall be more happy, than if I had all that the world accounts desireable' " (V, 251).

This just admiration or love of self continues—despite the violation and the nightmarish horrors which follow— in Clarissa's sustaining confidence that her will itself has never been defiled. Lovelace, too, recognizes after the rape that "her will is unviolated" (V, 381), and even in the frenzied, incoherent ramblings which immediately follow his attack, she can rescue this one element of self from the terrifying spectacle of passion and disorder which confronts her. "Yet, God knows my heart, I had no culpable inclinations!—I honoured Virtue!—I hated Vice!—But I knew not, that you were Vice itself!" (V, 332). This, then, is a core of self which has not been touched; and this is a self, an identity, which may prevail, command respect still, even be loved. Thus Clarissa clings to the notion of her own inviolate will in the harrowing days that follow the outrage, even during her fits of near-madness and even when the temptation to suicide threatens her most strongly. " 'Compulsion shall do nothing with me,' " she assures Lovelace. " 'Tho' a slave, a prisoner, in circumstance, I am no slave in my will!—Nothing will I promise thee!— With-held, compelled—Nothing will I promise thee' " (VI, 27); and when she has escaped from her imprisonment for once and all, this confidence in herself grows. She can reject her sins, reject the passionate impulses that have been revealed in her nature, without rejecting the self entire, for a continuing identity which is independent of these faults can be defined by this notion of her prevailing will; and she can love her character and wish to preserve it thus defined while still endeavoring to eradicate the malignant elements of it. "The injury I have received from him is indeed of the highest nature," she writes, "And it was attended with circumstances of unmanly baseness, and premeditation; yet, I bless God, it has not tainted my mind; it has not hurt my morals. No thanks indeed to the wicked man that it has not. No vile courses have followed it. My will is unviolated. The evil (respecting *myself*, and not my *friends*) is merely personal. No credulity, no weakness, no want of vigilance, have I to reproach myself with. I have, thro' Grace, triumphed over the deepest machinations. I have escaped from him. I have renounced him" (VII, 232).

The psychological importance of being able to separate the essential self (which Clarissa desires to preserve) from the sinfulness of the passions that beset it is manifestly clear; however, such a process has a vital religious function too. According to Puritan doctrines (or, indeed, to any theological system which postulates Original Sin as the source of man's iniquity), no one can be completely exempt from evil, and all men will inevitably fall victim to the curse of flesh. For the Christian who believed in predestination, the problem of determining whether or not one was saved became especially vexing. All men would sin, for sin was an unavoidable part of man's nature. How, then, might the regenerate sinner, the Saint of God, distinguish himself from others who sin? The usual answer given to such questions was based on a man's ability to separate his will from the sinful actions he might commit.

Thus one could count himself saved, even when he had
sinned, if in his heart he genuinely loathed and rejected
his own sinfulness. As Dent says, in *The Plaine Man's
Pathway to Heaven,* "When once we feel the work of
grace within us (that is, that we are washed by the new
birth, and renewed by the Holy Ghost, finding in ourselves an unfained hatred of sin and love of righteousness),
then are we sure and out of all doubt that we are pre-
destinated to life."[8] And Baxter deals with the problem in
much the same way. "When you strongly hate sin and live
in universal, constant obedience, you will easily discern
your repentance and obedience."[9] Once the Christian has
so perceived himself, he may set about attempting to perfect his life and hoping to bring his body and its sinfulness
to complete submission, for "the rigor which made it so
impossible to our nature before, is now to the new-born
so mollified by the spirit, that it seems facile and easy. The
apostles indeed pressed on the unconverted Jews and Gen-
tiles, the impossibility of keeping the law by the ability of
nature corrupted; but when they have to do with regenerate Christians, they require to the law, which is the rule
of righteousness, true obedience in word and deed: the
mortifying of their members; the crucifying of the flesh,
with the affections and lusts thereof; resurrection to new-
ness of life."[10]

The preservation of the will becomes for Clarissa not
only a desperate measure by which she has maintained the
self intact, but a positive step in the formulation of a new
statement of her identity. In religous terms, as well as in
psychological terms, Lovelace's attempted invasion represents the ultimate, the final threat; and withstanding this
temptation has an undeniably purifying effect. Even during the continued seige that follows, there are perceptible
differences in her manner. She begins, for instance, to
dress in the white clothes that she continues to wear until

her death, and she is increasingly seen by those who write of her as an angel in her purity. Later, in her reflections about the incidents which comprised her trial, Clarissa manifestly senses that the grace of God has been working through her. Thus she says to Anna Howe, "I have reason to think my punishment is but the due consequence of my fault, and I will not run away from it; but beg of Heaven to sanctify it to me" (VI, 412). The letter-diary fulfills in the strictest religious terms, the function for which it was intended. It records the trials to which Clarissa was subjected; it provides an objective embodiment of the self which may be studied; and it offers the means for introspective questioning which leads to a revelation of individual sinfulness. Having passed through this preliminary period and having finally perceived the workings of grace within her, Clarissa has at last found a new self; for she may now at last redefine her nature in terms of the community of God's Saints. Certainly this was the transition that Richardson intended, for he himself says of her trials, "I laid indeed an heavy hand on the good Clarissa. But I had begun with her, with a view to the future saint in her character: and could she, but by suffering, shine as she does?"[11]

The changes in her manner after the rape clearly mirror this ever more explicitly defined sanctification, and her character becomes increasingly like the standard Puritan notion of the Elected Saint. There is, for instance, an increasing desire on her part to have done with the things of the body. When the Puritan considered the sins of the body, he often confused the various bodily functions; now we find this same confusion here. Clarissa's sin was specifically the sin of lustful passion. She deals with that fault by suppressing passion, but in the act of so doing, she mortifies with other bodily functions too; she eats less and less, despite the pleas of her physician and Miss Howe, and

she seems to require little or no sleep.[12] Indeed, like so
many of God's Elect, she would apparently rid herself entirely of the body and its demands. "How this *body* clings!"
she writes to Miss Howe. "How it encumbers!" (VII, 254).
Death itself becomes not a loss of self but the only way to
realize identity completely—not a defeat but a triumphant
affirmation of her newly discovered self. Thus she longs
for death now as a gift of God, distinguishing it from that
sinful impulse to self-murder which had threatened her
earlier. "As I am of opinion, that it would have manifested
more of Revenge and Despair, than of Principle, had I
committed a violence upon myself, when the villainy was
separated: so I should think it equally criminal, were I
now *wilfully* to neglect myself; were I *purposely* to run
into the arms of death (*as that man supposes I shall do*),
when I might avoid it. . . . I often say: —Lord, it is thy
will; and it shall be mine. Thou art just in all thy dealings
with the children of men; and I know thou wilt not afflict
me beyond what I can bear. . . . But I am sure, if I may
say it with as little presumption as grief, That God will
soon *dissolve my substance; and bring me to death, and to
the house appointed for all living*" (VI, 411-412).

This shift from the view of Clarissa as sinner to the
delineation of her as Saint is mirrored in the literary
methods by which her character is defined as well as in
the specific judgments of her self she makes. Thus during
her period of introspection and trial, we see her through
her own eyes or reflected in the observations of her confidante and conscience, Anna Howe. After the discovery of
her sinful pride, the number of her own letters begins to
decline; and after the rape, we see her almost entirely
through the admiring eyes of others. Lovelace's letters become a testament to her beatific goodness. Belford figures
more and more prominently in the novel, providing a
point of view which has no direct personal involvement

with the outrage: and the clear function of his letters is to give independent and impartial affirmation of her growing goodness. This shift in point of view, of course, originates in the traditional literary forms of Puritan private devotion. During the period of trial, the sinner sees himself in order to judge and to analyze; however, once earthly trials have ceased and the sinner has been accepted into the community of the Saints, his character is delineated by an admiring outsider (in the case of the Puritan literature, by the funeral minister or the biographer). Even during her most trying moments, Clarissa's potential glorification could be predicted from the grudging admiration of her virtue in Lovelace's letters, and certainly one function which is served by the alternating series of letters that constitute the novel is precisely this balancing between the view of Clarissa as a relentless introspective transgressor and the picture of her as redeemed. The supreme trials, the moments of most intense isolation, are fittingly enough narrated by Clarissa, who probes deep within herself to find meaning; but as she moves back into a community and is once more able to define her nature meaningfully in terms of her relationship to a system outside of herself (now, the *other*-worldly society of the Saints), she is seen by an external observer.

When death comes for Clarissa, she greets it eagerly with arms outstretched like a happy bride. Death becomes for her the triumph over life—life which inheres in sinful flesh—and through it her soul eludes forever the unending death of sin. Fittingly, then, the inscription on her funeral urn reads, " 'Thou hast delivered my soul from death; mine eyes from tears; and my feet from falling' " (VII, 338); and in death Clarissa finally finds the identity which she has been denied at the beginning of the novel. For her, then, the cycle is complete. She has triumphed over those who would rob her of self, by fashioning a new self whose lifetime is forever.

Richardson's fidelity to the character he has created is the supreme achievement of his novel, and his refusal (in the face of passionate appeals from his readers) to transform his heroine by some feat of specious dexterity into a well-adjusted female Grandison, who lived to tell the tale of her trials to a host of happy grandchildren reveals a comprehension of her nature which one might expect of the artist who could create her. There clearly is no place in this world for Clarissa; to claim one for her would be a violation of her nature more deadly than any with which she has been threatened in the novel. Yet in remaining true to his heroine, Richardson has failed at least partially to solve the problems with which he begins the novel. Thus as a novel of character, an example of psychological realism, the work is superb; as a novel which attempts the further task of placing character into a coherent moral or social framework, the narrative leaves us not completely satisfied.

For instance, let us consider the problem of pride. This is the first major fault which Clarissa discovers in her nature, and she deals with it by distinguishing between sinful pride and just pride. Sinful pride, according to her judgment, is a rejoicing in one's superiority over others as if that superiority were inherent in one's own power; just pride comes in perceiving that virtue is one of God's blessings and in rejoicing in personal goodness without denigrating others. Thus sinful pride depends on the comparison between self and others, while just pride focuses on the relationship between self and God. These are, according to Richardson (and according to traditional Christian thought), valid distinctions; in making them Clarissa has proceeded with complete honesty, and it would be inaccurate to say that she has failed to reveal her true self in this respect. The problem of religious pride, however, is a vexing one; and while Richardson may have defined Clarissa's actions correctly, he leaves unsettled a series of questions about the general notion of pride which have been raised indirectly by his treatment of her.

Even if goodness comes to her through the grace of God, it still makes her different from (certainly better than) others who have not been thus blessed. An awareness of her singularity still infuses her actions and is manifested both in her consistent desire to be reliant *only* on God and in the related attempts to distinguish herself from others who are apparently less favored by God: she sells her clothes rather than accept money from Miss Howe; she writes letters to the members of her family which serve to justify her actions posthumously; and she longs to go to "her Father's house," even making all of the preparations for that important journey herself so that she will not have to rely on others. *"God will have no rivals in the hearts of those he sanctifies,"* she declares. "By various methods He deadens all other sensations, or rather absorbs them all in the Love of Him" (VII, 404). Indeed, God is a jealous master. "All I wished was pardon and blessing from my dear Parents," Clarissa says. "Easy as my departure seems to promise to be, it would have been still easier, had I had that pleasure. BUT GOD ALMIGHTY would NOT LET ME DEPEND FOR COMFORT UPON ANY BUT HIMSELF" (VII, 459).

How genuinely different is this sense of superiority from the sinful pride which a sinner must reject? The answer to such a question is neither simple nor readily discernible; and the attempt to find some answer has proved the nucleus of many modern treatments of such saints as Becket or Joan of Arc. Perhaps a solution can be found only after we have decided whether virtue is primarily a worldly or an other-worldly quality. If its effects serve only to unite an individual with his God, then one must follow his own sense of distinguished goodness without regard for the effect of his actions upon the world or its members. However, if virtue may be identified by the good that it effects in the lives of others, then to the extent that religious righteousness separates a man from his fellow men, even his "virtue" may be a source of sin.

The same kind of ambiguity remains in Richardson's treatment of the problem of passion. Passion is a condition of the body; according to Puritan doctrine it must be repressed in all of its forms, and complete goodness would presuppose absolute restraint of the passions. Clarissa's experience, however, demonstrates that the actual realization of this ideal would in practice not be consistent with life in the world. It is clear, for instance, that Clarissa has not eradicated the demands of the body. Even after her escape from Lovelace following the rape, she still reveals the existence of passion by her obsessive fear of all men; she has repressed the expression of lust in herself, but in doing so she has merely projected it into her perception of others. Similarly, she has not overcome the need for food and sleep; and when she dies, no medical cause is given for her expiration save that she has gradually stopped eating and sleeping. If Clarissa were to continue to live in the world, she would have to find some acceptable outlet for her human desires and needs; the "virtue" revealed by denying them completely is consistent only with an otherworldly existence.

Both of these questions are part of the larger problem of adapting a religious, spiritually oriented notion of morality to the needs of a secular society. It is a difficulty which seems consistently to have interested Richardson; and even his earliest works, the *Apprentice's Vade Mecum* and *Familiar Letters,* were embryonic attempts to assert a relationship between social utility and moral good. In the novels Richardson narrows the question somewhat, choosing to deal primarily with the problems which arise when an essentially good or moral person must define his identity in terms of a secular society.[13] *Pamela* adopts one standard Puritan solution to the problem of worldly morality: it equates earthly reward with Divine reward, and Pamela is paid for her chastity. Clarissa offers a second alternative, and this too comes from the Puritan tradition: earthly values are transcended, and the individual defines himself purely in terms of a community of Saints. However, this too proves an unsatisfactory solution to the problem of giving virtue a social definition.

Richardson has started with what is an essentially sociological quandary—economic and societal changes have taken place which make a certain kind of personality and certain expressions of virtue no longer possible—and given it a purely religious answer. Thus while Clarissa may well have found the key to her own individual personality through her trials, she has hardly offered a solution to the problem of defining identity which would help anyone who wanted to remain in the world. Moreover, even the definition of a new identity which is finally postulated for her is incomplete insofar as it does not in any genuine sense replace the earthly identity she has been denied.[14] Certainly Richardson's portrait of Clarissa is brilliantly realistic; we feel that we have come to know her thoroughly and accurately. However, we may be left in some doubt about the judgment we ought to make of her actions. Does the heavenly role she assumes transcend her previous earthly ones to offer her the highest possible moral state; or might it have proven an even greater moral good if she had found some new definition of her personality which would have replaced the one she lost and allowed her to express her goodness while remaining in the world?

If the novel has any flaw, then, it is not in Richardson's accuracy in the realization of Clarissa's nature, but in the ambiguity of his attempt to expand the personal significance of her experience to answer the more general question, "How does the essentially moral individual express himself and his own goodness in this world?" Richardson's desire to answer this question may be seen both in the manner in which he has initially posed Clarissa's problems and in his consistent attempts to give her new-found nature social meaning, even after she has left the world. It is certainly significant that the novel does not end with her death. Presumably, then, we are intended to be concerned with the meaning which her trials may have for others. Yet though we may perhaps infer a partial solution to this problem, Richardson does not provide us with a clear answer. His uncertainty stems from a conflict between the two definitions of virtue that we have mentioned earlier—the notion of virtue as a quality which is revealed primarily in one's relationship to God and the notion of virtue as a quality which is revealed in one's dealings with the world. This conflict runs throughout the Puritan literature that Richardson adopted; the diarist always looked to his inner self and his dealings with God for reassurance of salvation—praying well, feeling enlarged, and sensing God's grace in his own soul—while the biographer saw the Puritan Saint as virtuous because of his works within the world. Even the same man's virtue might be defined differently, depending on where one found it described. The diarist would see himself as virtuous because of his feeling of sanctification, while his biographer might point to his good deeds as evidence of salvation.

When *Clarissa* makes the transition from letter-diary to biography, a corresponding shift is made in the tacit definition of virtue that Richardson offers; and as the novel approaches its end and Clarissa assumes the role of Saint, Richardson tends increasingly to define virtue in terms of its social utility. From Clarissa's point of view death is not just an appropriate climax to her struggle, it is also the only means of assuming the most glorious identity which God could bestow upon her. The world and all that is in it has become meaningless, and her virtue can be completely realized only when she has finally returned to "her Father's house." However, for Miss Howe, Belford, and all those who remain behind, Clarissa's life, like the life of the Puritan Saint, was important precisely because it had an earthly significance, her virtue noteworthy because they could find in it a lesson for their own lives. If the reader sees the events through Clarrisa's eyes, her death will seem an unqualified triumph. If he has identified with Miss Howe or Belford, he might well sympathize with their pleas that Clarissa remain in the world for a while longer. Whatever our feelings, it is certainly the case that Richardson makes a very great effort in the latter portions of the novel to give Clarissa's goodness a social significance. The most rudimentary expression of this conception of virtue originates in the notion that a Saint's life could serve as an ideal for others, and the exemplary value of Clarissa's trials is affirmed repeatedly at the end of the novel; indeed, the "life" of Clarissa appended by Miss Howe is the very model of a typical Puritan Saint's orderly and controlled existence.

Perhaps the most explicit lesson of social virtue taught by the example of Clarissa's suffering is the value of the capacity for pity; and the development of this capacity is directly related to Clarissa's success in overcoming the sin of pride. Once she has ceased to look upon others as competitors in virtue and her sense of her own goodness has been secured, she can genuinely wish good for others and feel pity rather than triumph when they fail. The increase in this sympathy for others is evident in all of her relationships, but most evident in her feelings about Lovelace. Against all of Miss Howe's insistence, for instance, Clarissa refuses to prosecute Lovelace for his villainy, for she has no need to revenge herself upon him.

She no longer feels lust for him; and she makes this fact quite explicitly clear. Yet she feels compassion for him as another human being. "Let me then repeat, that I truly despise this man! If I know my own heart, indeed I do! — I pity him! —*Beneath* my very pity as he is, I nevertheless pity him! —But this I could not do, if I still loved him" (VI, 410). Later, she defines her feelings even more precisely. "Poor wretch! I pity him, to see him fluttering about; abusing talents that were given him for excellent purposes; taking inconsideration for courage; and dancing, fearless of danger, on the edge of a precipice!" (VI, 459). This same pity is extended to her family as well, as she both asks forgiveness from them and offers hers to them for the treatment she has suffered.

Closely related to the ability to feel pity is the increasing selflessness with which Clarissa relates to the world about her. If Lovelace's villainy was an expression of selfishness in its most extreme and pernicious form (his "love" for Clarissa merely an expression of his own self-interest) then this picture of vice is balanced by Clarissa's virtuous attempts after her escape from Lovelace to consider other's needs before her own. " 'Tis a choice comfort, Mr. Belford, at the winding-up of our short story,' " she declares, " 'to be able to say, I have rather *suffered* injuries *myself*, than *offered* them to *others*' " (VII, 438). Indeed, her entire conception of identity changes with her growing selflessness. At the beginning of her trials identity is something which might be taken from her, something which might be possessed and destroyed by another; her whole attention is directed toward preservation of self. The crisis in her own life, however, teaches her that no one can really possess another; and she learns subsequently to think in terms not of taking, destroying, or preserving self, but of giving self. This notion of selflessness seems even to replace the virtue of duty that had governed

Clarissa's earlier life. All men are inextricably bound together, sharing with each other the mutual state of trial
which is life; and in this world, none can be independent
of others. Thus the rather limited notion of the relationships among members of a family is replaced by this more
extended notion of the relationship of all to all. Selflessness, or the ability to pattern one's inescapable interactions
with others on the ability to understand and supply their
just needs and desires, can become a positive moral act in
much the same way that obedience was earlier. Even the
final beatification reinforces this notion of selflessness,
for the setting of an example within one's individual life
becomes a way of giving that life to others. "SELF is an
odious devil" the reformed Belford attests (VI, 430); and it
is Clarissa's ability to overcome self in her generosity and
benevolence towards others that reclaims his soul to God.
Ironically, the more one can give to others, the more of
self (in the proper sense) one gains; and Clarissa becomes
most triumphant in her affirmation of identity when she
denies all selfish worldly claims. Conversely, the more
childishly self-centered one becomes, the less meaning one's
character has. Thus Lovelace, who is the very embodiment
of egoism, sinks, finally, into a raving, chaotic incoherence.
   The ethic which may be inferred from such a picture
(although it is never stated explicitly within the novel
itself) is the virtue of disinterested benevolence; and Clarissa's behavior in this regard is expanded to others as well
when they come to know her goodness. We can be assured
that a person is virtuous, then, when we can see that he has
a genuine interest in the welfare of others. Belford's conversion, for instance, is initially indicated by his concern
for Clarissa; and his growth in virtue is paralleled by his
ever-increasing solicitude for her safety. The heroic measure of Clarissa's personal trial is the general social good
that it works: Miss Howe is counselled; the Harlowe fam-

ily is chastened; and even the harlots repent. One might conclude that personal good will necessarily tend to social good; and although Richardson does not formulate this maxim in *Clarissa,* it is certainly implicit in the latter portions of the novel. Thus even within the novel there is a movement away from the splendid isolation of Clarissa's heroic confrontation with self toward the reintroduction of social values and a social context. This movement culminates in Richardson's final novel and in his adoption of social realism rather than psychological realism as the means for defining character. Moreover, the notion of goodness as behavior which springs from a genuine selflessness provides the basis for the moral framework of *Grandison,* Richardson's most fully developed statement of the relationship between morality and social utility.

CHAPTER VII

Sir Charles Grandison

Richardson never relinquished the desire first expressed in *Pamela* of defining private virtue in public terms. Clarissa's triumph is in her personal honesty and prevailing integrity; Richardson's success as a novelist derives from his fidelity to this honesty, even though it means the death of his heroine. When he came to write *Grandison*, however, Richardson hoped finally to formulate a coherent social expression of moral worth; and the principal indication of this intention can be found in the characterization of the hero. Grandison's nature would not be articulated in the isolation of the Self-Examiner, but in his meaningful relationships with others. Grandison was to be the perfect social creature, a man whose virtues tended to increase the general good, a man "of Liveliness and Spirit; accomplished and agreeable; happy in himself, and a Blessing to others" (I, Preface), a secular version of the Puritan Saint.

The differences between the notion of heroism and virtue here and the same qualities as they were depicted in *Clarissa* is striking. Personal honesty, strength of will, faith in God, and ardor in His service—these were the virtues of a Clarissa, and they are qualities which pertain only to her own soul and its relationship with God. How unlike such a view of goodness is the notion that there is eternal merit in the purely social virtues of being accomplished, lively, or agreeable.

Richardson was conscious of the dangers in attempting to create a social paragon. Expressing fear that he might draw "a faultless monster,"[1] he tried to temper the virtue. "I would draw him as a mortal. He should have all the human passions to struggle with."[2] Yet despite these forebodings, Richardson did not succeed in making Grandison's character consistent with reality. The man is too good, too judicious, too much the model of propriety and tact to be either likeable or believable. Grandison's only real dilemma is in choosing between the love of two desirable women, and he makes his choice seem like some protracted legal adjudication. "As a man should be a reasonable creature," Richardson protests, "Sir Charles shall, I think, be made to love like a reasonable man."[3] Yet how credible is such a display of reason; and how compelling is the hero who embodies it? Richardson tells Miss Mulso, with bitter irony, "Why yes, many girls would be glad of a Sir Charles Grandison, and prefer him even to a Lovelace, were he capable of being terribly in love";[4] but he did not seem to recognize the tragic truth of his remark.

The other elements in Sir Charles' character merely serve to confirm our image of him as something more (or less) than human. "Do we feel a certain disappointment when we meet the man whom all ladies love, and in whom every gentleman confesses a superior nature?" asks Leslie Stephen, Richardson's nineteenth-century editor.[5] Almost certainly,

> He is one of those solemn beings who can't shave themselves without implicitly asserting a great moral principle. He finds sermons in his horses' tails; he could give an excellent reason for the quantity of lace on his coat, which was due, it seems, to a sentiment of filial reverence; and he could not fix his hour for dinner without an eye to the reformation of society. In short, he was a prig of the first water: self-conscious to the last degree; and so crammed with little moral aphorisms that they drop out of his mouth whenever he opens his lips. And then, his religion is in admirable keeping. It is intimately connected with the excellence of his deportment; and is, in fact, merely the application of the laws of good society to the loftiest sphere of human duty. . . . As he carries his solemnity into the pettiest trifles of life, so he considers religious duties to be simply the most important part of social etiquette. He would shrink from blasphemy even more than from keeping on his hat in the presence of ladies; but the respect which he owes in one case is of the same order with that due in the other: it is only a degree more important.[6]

Such complete identification of personal virtue with social propriety is possible only in a society whose laws of deportment and judgment exactly coincide with the laws of morality. Thus Richardson has made the same kind of mistake that had marred Pamela, but he has made it here on a much grander scale. The novel becomes a monstrous caricature of the real world rather than a representation of it. It was to have been Richardson's triumphant exit from the literary world, and it proved only to be his greatest failure. During his own lifetime *Grandison* never achieved the popularity of the earlier novels (despite the force of the author's very sizable reputation), and today it is generally deemed the novel least worthy of critical attention. Certainly *Sir Charles Grandison* deserves much of its bad reputation. However, it is all too easy merely to criticize or ridicule and then to dismiss it altogether. After all, we know from reading Jane Austen's letters to her sister that *Grandison* was one of her favorite novels; and unless we are willing to believe that she suspended her critical judgment as soon as she laid aside her own writing, the fact alone should be sufficient to induce us to look beyond the facile condemnations of the novel. It is the first English novel of manners, and many of the literary problems which it treats with less than complete success might never have been solved by later novelists had not Richardson laid the groundwork here. Furthermore, it does answer many of the questions that had been raised in Richardson's earlier works, offering an explanation of the relationship between morals and manners, redefining the role of woman to meet the changing conditions in which she found herself, and outlining a system of benevolent sensibility which was to be the dominant influence in English fiction for the following half-century.

To a great extent, the social system that Richardson offers in *Grandison* grows out of the problems discussed in *Clarissa*. The world of the Harlowes had been a small world, a world in which duty and individual personality were both defined in terms of a limited number of fixed roles—parent, child, husband, wife, servant of God. Clarissa's trials started, really, when divisive forces began to disrupt the stability of this system. Money became increasingly important, and the acquisition of money and land occasionally took precedence over other values in determining behavior; the absolute authority of the father (and to a lesser extent the husband) deteriorated because of socio-economic changes; society itself grew larger and more complex, while personal decisions which depended upon an intimate and accurate knowledge of others grew less easy to make. In the face of these changes, the definitions of duty, woman's role, and even virtue itself became obscured and confused. *Clarissa* postulates no coherent alternative to the unsatisfactory state in which we find the heroine at the beginning of the novel, no release for the virtuous save the ambiguous release of death.

As we remarked in Chapter II, one curious quality of the Puritan view of character was the fact that sin tended to be delineated in intimate, personal terms whereas virtue was most easily designated by the articulation of certain social relationships. In *Clarissa* Richardson is strongest when he is dealing with the deficiencies of Clarissa's nature, that is, throughout the period of her temptations and trials. When the novel falters at the very end, it does so precisely because Richardson is less deft in articulating the nature of Clarissa's triumph. In the Puritan literature that provides Richardson's basis for characterization, there is an inherent clumsiness in the transition from Pilgrim to Saint (it is mirrored, for instance, in the incongruity of the two portraits of Newcome cited earlier—that of the diary and that of the funeral oration). Some of this clumsiness remains at the conclusion of *Clarissa*. Thus when Richardson turns to *Grandison*, he begins by rejecting the narrow world of the Harlowes and placing his characters into a larger, freer, and more varied environment; he also rejects the primacy of the role of Self-Examiner (with its intimate, limited focus on the interior world) and substitutes for it the more robust, social image of the moral man, that of the Saint.

Richardson intimates that the point of view of the Puritan eulogizer was right, after all, that duty and individual personality are correctly defined in terms of one's relationship to the community at large. The relationships to father, mother, and God are still important, but they are no longer the only meaningful relationships. All men owe a duty to all other men. The very notion of duty begins to lose its rigid character, and it becomes not so much a set of rules to which obedience is exacted, as a series of choices among voluntary acts of charity. Sin is not, then, just the failure to do what certain specific relationships demand; it is not even merely the failure to monitor the potentially sinful impulses of the body. Now a man may be deemed deficient for failing to take the opportunity to better the lot of others, for failing to act the part of the Good Samaritan; and the truly moral individual (according to such a system) is one who gives freely of himself to help others. Accordingly, his alternatives are much more varied than the limited set of mutual obligations that governed child and parent or husband and wife. He may perform his duty in an infinite variety of ways.[7] His primary virtue would not be obedience but benevolence, the desire to do good toward all mankind; and the personal attribute most desired in a moral individual would be the quality of sympathy, that active principle which would prompt benevolent actions by enabling one to feel the needs and desires of others. The moral shift from *Clarissa* to *Grandison* might well be expressed in the terminology of ethics as a shift from a system of perfect duties to a system of imperfect duties. Accompanying this alteration, Richardson's conception of the moral man changes too; the ideally virtuous man would be active, seeking instances in which he could appropriately exercise his freedom to do good for others, rather than passive, submitting himself to the rule of a rigid set of moral injunctions that governed his behavior.

Much of this new ethic bears unmistakable resemblances to Latitudinarian sentiments; some of it may seem pure

"Sentimental Benvolence." This infusion of sentiment is not surprising: Grandison is Richardson's ultimate attempt to adapt Puritan ways of life to a secular environment, and the acceptance of many popular notions of morality would be necessary in such an adaptation. What is more, Richardson admired the Latitudinarian Divines; he refers to them with great respect in his letters. Still, there are certain crucial idiosyncrasies in Richardson's system—qualities which clearly set him apart from others in the sentimental school and which relate directly to his Puritan background. For one thing Grandison's moral behavior is always seen as an exercise of *duty*; there is no sense that it flows from a spontaneous, innate impulse toward good. Hence Richardson consciously portrays him as a man of reason, deliberately controlling his passions (see Richardson's letter to Miss Mulso, quoted above). Virtuous behavior was certainly satisfying; one might even see it as a source of pleasure. However, the principal reason Sir Charles is virtuous is that it is his duty—not for any aesthetic or emotional satisfaction. And as is inevitably the case with duties, it is something he has *learned*. Richardson retains his conviction that the passions must be confined (Sir Charles refuses to duel) and that emotionalism is dangerous (as in the case of Clementina). Certainly we can say that the altered moral structure found in *Grandison* does not completely discard the notions that had shaped the social framework of *Clarissa*; instead, it builds upon these notions. The obligation of familial duty and obedience which is based upon blood relationship continues to be important: Sir Charles obeys his father, even though the father is reprehensible; Emily Jervois is required to honor her mother, even though the mother has flaunted her own weaknesses. However, such responsibilities now form only a part of one's general moral life.

Perhaps the most striking symptom of change is the

way in which the characters in the novel "adopt" a family by translating their social ties into terms that would previously have applied only to bonds of kinship. Harriet, when she is importuned by Sir Rowland to marry his son, turns his proposal aside by offering an alternative relationship. " 'To shew my regard for you, Sir: Let me be happy in your friendship, and good opinion: Let me look upon you as my Father: Let me look upon Mr. Fowler as my Brother: I am not so happy, as to have either father or brother. And let Mr. Fowler own me as his Sister; and every visit you make me, you will both, in these characters, be dearer to me than before' " (I, 133-134). Nor is this merely a gesture; for the parties concerned, once they have agreed to adopt the roles proposed to them, govern their behavior according to the decorum of their new ties. Thus many of the moral obligations that had formerly been imposed by a blood relationship are now extended to these newly acquired kin as well. All of Sir Rowland's subsequent allusions to marriage are blunted by the fact that he has been adopted as Harriet's father; moreover, when Harriet finally marries Grandison, Sir Rowland's attitude is that of a fond parent giving his daughter away. He presents her with a dowry of fine jewels, gifts that she would return to him but for his protests. " 'What, Sir Charles, not . . . a present from her father to his daughter, on her nuptials, and as a small token of his joy on the occasion.' . . . When Sir Charles saw the jewels, he was a little uneasy, because of the value of them. . . . '[Sir Rowland] knew,' he said, 'that I could not want any of these things: But he could not think of any other way to show his love to his daughter.' It was nothing to what he had intended to do in his Will; had I not intimated to him that what he left me should be given among his relations. 'I am rich, madam, I can tell you: And what, on your nuptials, could I do less for my daughter?' " (VI, 63-64).

Harriet, orphaned at an early age, has acquired sisters in the Grandison girls and also thoughtfully provides herself with a mother in the person of Lady D., who is pleading her son's cause with Miss Byron. " 'You delight me!' " Harriet exclaims to the older woman. " 'Talk of a bad world!—*I* ought, I am sure, to think it a good one!—In every matronly lady I have met with a *mother*; in many young ladies, as those before us, *sisters*; in their brother a *protector*' " (I, 352). Indeed, before her marriage she jestingly warns Sir Charles of her adopted kin, saying " 'You are entered, Sir . . . into a numerous family' " (VI, 5).

One might be inclined to view such behavior as the idiosyncratic manner of a lonely girl seeking the comfort of a new family were it not for the fact that all of the major characters engage in this same vigorous process of acquiring an extended family. Sir Charles is treated as a son and a brother by the members of the della Porretta family and himself adopts a familial frankness in his letters of advice to Clemintina, speaking as " 'your tutor, as you are pleased to call him; your Friend, your 'BROTHER' " (IV, 373). He controls the impetuosity of Olivia by assuming the fraternal role with her as well. Indeed, the Grandisons, Harriet, the della Porrettas, and all their friends go about establishing quasi-familial ties with such delighted enthusiasm that the reader becomes quite sincerely convinced that they are all in some fundamental sense genuinely related.

This was, of course, Richardson's intention; for the novel contends that blood relationships are ties which effectively mirror an individual's concern with society as a whole. Both Harriet and Sir Charles confirm this interdependency. " 'My grandfather used to say,' " Harriet declares at the outset of the novel, " 'that families are little communities; that there are but few solid friendships out of them; and that they help to make up worthily, and to secure, the great community, of which they are so many miniatures' " (I, 30). Sir Charles is moved to similar sentiments when he reflects upon the arbitrary behavior of his uncle after he has been freed from the power of a dictatorial mistress. " 'I then, for the first time, pitied the woman; and should have pitied her still more . . . had she not gone away so amply rewarded: For, in this little family I looked forward to the family of the State; the Sovereign and his ministers. How often has a minister, who had made a tyrannical use of power (and even some who have not) experienced, on his dismission, the like treatment, from those who, had they had his power, would perhaps have made as bad an use of it' " (II, 362). Richardson confirms the unity of public and private morality throughout the novel by adopting the ancient notion that there are public virtues and public vices which correspond to private ones. When he causes Sir Charles to declare, " 'I own no Laws but the Laws of GOD and my Country' " (I, 371), he is merely taking the opportunity to show that every truly moral man must always consider *both* the personal and the social effects of his actions. Given such a view, no man can be completely good unless he turns his virtue to the benefit of others, for an individual's obligation to all other men is a necessary part of his indissoluble relationship to them.

Such an expression of the value of disinterested, selfless concern for the plight of others is implied at the end of Clarissa's trials; given the assumptions of the earlier novel, however, one might safely assume that the private heroism and fortitude of Clarissa would weigh more heavily in the scale of divine value than the temporal effects of her suffering and that the virtue expressed through acts of charity within the world display an order of goodness which is both different from the spirituality of Clarissa's dedication to God and inferior to it. Who could count the kindness of a Belford—however generous he might have been—in any way comparable to the saintliness of a Clarissa? In *Grandison*, however, there is a clear reversal of this position. Man must still attend to his relationship with God, but he must not do so to the exclusion of his fellow men; and if he must withdraw from the world in order to make his personal peace, he has failed to realize the full potential of his goodness. Society's claims, the world's claims, must always be an object of any virtuous effort.

Judged by such a standard, Clarissa herself would have been found wanting; for her decision to renounce the world would be deemed a less complete expression of goodness than a successful effort to resume her place in the world and turn the knowledge she has gained from her trials to the benefit of society. Certainly Grandison's attitude toward the suffering of Clementina implies such a judgment. The situation in which Clementina finds herself is not unlike Clarissa's: she has fallen in love with a man who would not make an appropriate husband; she allows her passionate involvement with him to dominate her reason and even contemplates marriage with him; when the union becomes clearly impossible, she gives him up, but in doing so she temporarily loses her sanity; eventually she manages to reconcile herself to the situation, renounces him, and expresses the wish to leave the world forever (by retiring to a convent). There are, of course, very great differences between Clementina's and Clarissa's trials, for in *Grandison* the obstacles to the marriage stem from a difference in upbringing merely and not from a fundamental incompatibility of nature. Nevertheless, the coercive efforts of a family that is motivated by concern for money and power, combine with the striking similarity in situation to remind us inevitably of the earlier novel. Thus when Clementina cries, " 'O permit me, my dearest friends, still to be God's child, the spouse of my Redeemer only! Let me, let me yet take the veil! . . . What is the portion of this world, which my grandfathers have bequeathed to me, weighed against this motive, and my soul's everlasting welfare?' " (IV, 295), who among us cannot hope that she, like Clarissa, may be allowed to enjoy whatever other-worldly peace is offered to her?

Such an end is not to be permitted, however, for it is now judged incomplete. Grandison remonstrates, " 'There is often cowardice, there is selfishness, and perhaps, in the world's eye, a too strong confession of disappointment, in such seclusions. . . . You, my beloved correspondent, who hold marriage as a Sacrament, surely cannot doubt but you may serve God in it with much greater efficacy, than were you to sequester yourself from a world that wants such an example as you are able to give it. . . God requires not that you should be dead to your friends, in order to live to Him' " (IV, 380, 379, 380). Society has made its rightful claim, and we are left at the end of the novel to conclude that she will complete the expression of her goodness by marrying a virtuous man and moving once more into the world. Clementina's pleas make the strongest possible case for the primacy of other-worldliness, yet even Grandison rejects them.

As we have seen, the portrait of the Puritan Saint depends upon the conviction that a man's virtue is most adequately defined in terms of his contributions to the community of which he is a member. Yet despite the central part that this belief played in Puritan thought, there is little systematic exploration of what might be termed "good citizenship." For one thing, the notion was originally conceived in terms of a small, theocratic community; in such a setting, there would be little distinction between religious duties and secular ones. Even more important, the literary portrait of the Saint has limited aims: it was descriptive rather than prescriptive; and although it aimed at presenting an image of virtue, it presented this image as a *fait accompli*. It was a posthumous portrait, and it offered a finished vision of goodness; it did not depict the process by which one became a Saint, did not attempt to offer any explanations to show *how* the Puritan had become a member of the Elect, and thus it gave no maxims according to which the living audience might solve problems in their own lives. (When such advice is found, it is almost always offered in connection with the role of Self-Examiner, not Saint.) Thus when Richardson determines to use this image of virtue as a way of delineating Grandison's nature, he is forced to work out many of the problems which Puritan Divines had neglected.

For example, Richardson's much more extended notion of duty was inevitably linked to social status; and unlike the world of the Harlowe family or of Pamela, Grandison's world made varying moral claims upon those of differing rank. No humble cottager could be capable of the same public service as his wealthy landlord. The two might be equally pious in their worship of God, equally honest in their discovery of their own transgressions; yet the *public* benefits which they have the power to effect differ markedly. Sir Charles observes, " 'No question but a man's duties will rise with his opportunities. A man, therefore, may be as good with a less estate, as with a larger: And is not goodness the essential part of happiness? Be our station what it will, have we any concern but humbly to acquiesce in it, and fulfil our duties?' " (II, 397).

Given such a system of morality, all the rules of a society grow to have special importance, for no man can be completely moral unless he has a clear notion both of his own position in society and of the duties attendant on his rank. Thus manners and the niceties of polite behavior have a certain weight as indicators of a man's ability to make such distinctions; and while rudeness is not synonymous with immorality, it is related to it, because both stem from the same failure to understand and obey society's dictates. It is not immoral to fail to remove one's hat before a lady, but the same failure to mark the difference between the man's and the woman's role in society may well be immoral in other circumstances. Similarly, it is not sinful of Austen's Emma Woodhouse to misjudge her own position in assuming that Harriet Smith would make a fit confidante, but the same failure to estimate her rank correctly does, in the case of her relationship with Miss Bates, lead to cruelty and unkindness. Grandison's punctilious courtesy is not moral in and of itself; however, it does indicate a disposition which is inclined to obey the dictates of society in all forms. When he says, " 'I paid my duty to the Cardinal Legate, and the Gonfaloniere, and to three of his counsellors, by whom, you know, I had been likewise greatly honoured. My mind was not free enough to *enjoy* their conversation: Such a weight upon my heart, how could it? But the debt of gratitude and civility was not to be left unpaid' " (III, 210), the duty to which he refers is one of etiquette and not moral obligation. Yet the willingness to observe these laws of propriety—even at a time of severe distress—indicates a selfless desire to do what is right, despite personal inconvenience; and the same attitude leads to charity and benevolence in other situations.

The importance of manners is one corollary to this system of social morality; the importance of money is another. Personal goodness depends upon fulfilling the duties of one's social rank. A man of humble circumstances might be quite as good an individual as a nobleman, for both could do their duties with equal diligence; the nobleman, however, will be capable of greater benefit to the world because his higher social position gives him both more power for good and the greater obligation to do good. Money and power grow to have a moral potential; and the pursuit of money becomes thus legitimatized.

In the earlier novels, the process of consciously bettering one's worldly station by actively seeking money was viewed with a degree of ambiguity. James Harlowe's ambitions were seen as wicked both because they were pursued in a manner which disrupted the moral order of the family and because money and power were seen as less noble ends than other, more narrowly virtuous ambitions. Clarissa did not hold Solmes' large estate to be a factor in his favor because she counted him a man incapable of putting money to its proper use; however, in addition to this objection, there was also the clear implication in all her attitudes that monetary considerations were simply not of the same order of importance as personal integrity. Even Pamela, whose goodness was rewarded with an advantageous marriage, would have been roundly condemned had she deliberately calculated the benefits which might be effected with money and then set out to improve her lot. Yet underlying this assumption that an otherworldly commitment to goodness is superior to mundane concerns, there is, even in the first two works, a grudging acknowledgement of money's importance: Pamela was, after all, rewarded with money; and both Clarissa and Pamela rejoiced when circumstances conspired to allow them sufficient money to pursue their private charities with generosity. When we reach *Grandison*, the ambiguity has been resolved; money is a tool for promoting the general good, and as such it deserves to be weighed thoughtfully against other conflicting claims when we are making any important decision. Thus when Clementina's family urges her to marry for no other reason than to prevent her grandfather's estate from descending to another branch of the family, Clementina would assert the priority of her own spiritual desires over such considerations; yet Grandison argues in behalf of the family's position. One wonders what his decision would have been in the case of Clarissa's dilemma.

Indeed, once money has attained this good repute, it begins to play an important part in a wide variety of personal relationships. It can serve as a sign of affection or love, as in the case of Sir Rowland's wedding gift to Harriet; the generous sharing of it can become the outward sign of an equable, happy marriage, as in the resolution of the dispute between Charlotte and her new husband over the £1000 note; it can even bring a sense of freedom from personal constraint, as it does to Emily Jervois' mother when she receives a lifetime settlement from her daughter.

One can imagine how amenable such a view must have seemed to the newly prosperous merchant whose Puritan ancestors had so vigorously renounced the world and all its claims. Virtuous diligence had frequently brought capital remuneration, and in a moral system which postulated salvation by predestined faith alone, the worldly temptation that accompanied these riches could serve as a sinful distraction from man's consuming, introspective search for the signs of God's favor in his own soul. However, the creeping Arminian influence of the gospel of good works served gradually to externalize the struggle for salvation. Whereas before, man had been forced to turn ever inward to discover knowledge of his spiritual state, now he could find reassurance in tangible, external acts of charity; and the power which was often seen to make these acts possible was, quite naturally, that money which had been the fruit of his labor. The virtue which in an earlier age could be discovered only by signs of being "in spirit" was now confirmed by endowing a college or giving prudently to the needy. Once this process of externalizing the inner life had begun, it was difficult to stop with the signs of virtue and salvation; and money, which was so important as a means to charity, could, as easily, become the symbol of love, marital concord, and individual freedom as well. In *Grandison*, this use of money to express all elements of the inner life is barely begun; however, the value of the temporal world and all of its material contents is assuredly claimed more earnestly here than in any of the previous novels.

At the center of this system, the very keystone on which rests the order of the novel, is Charles Grandison himself, Richardson's vision of a secular Saint. In a general sense he is the embodiment of complete personal virtue, the image of a nearly perfect human being; in addition he also serves the more limited function of demonstrating the behavior of a man who engages in all of his specifically masculine social roles without fault. To a certain extent, the characterization of Grandison is an answer to some of the unresolved problems of the earlier works; and if Richardson consciously addressed the portrait of his hero to Fielding as a rebuke for the rowdiness and vulgarity of Tom Jones, Sir Charles' perfectly prudent conduct provides an equally appropriate response to the weakness of farmer Andrews, the failures of Clarissa's father, the milksop Mr. B., and the corrosive evil of Lovelace. Not one of these had been a complete and satisfactory man; the virtuous among them had been weak or absent, while the villains had been all too personably effective in their wickedness. Now at last in Grandison man would assume his rightful role within both the family and society at large. His rule would be just because it would be directed to the benefit of all who relied on him; and his authority over the dependent members of society, the women and children, would be warranted by his power to protect them and to effect good for them.

Richardson had begun his career as a novelist by adopting the letter-novel as the vehicle for his study of the individual in transition, and many of his most important epistolary predecessors had dealt primarily with the theme of the woman alone, bereft of parents, friends, or lover. As we can see in both *Clarissa* and *Pamela,* Richardson picks up this concern and extends his consideration of it to the solitude of the woman deprived of the guidance which would be given by those figures who embody community judgment and authority—the parents, particularly the father, and the husband. While Richardson's heroines are alone in a literal sense (they are all separated from their families), their moral isolation is perhaps even more trying than the hardships of captivity or orphanhood. Pamela's implacable resolution to have marriage or nothing, Clarissa's horror at the thought of her father's displeasure coupled with her irresistible attraction to Lovelace, and even Harriet Byron's careful acquisition of a collection of adopted relations are all external signs of the same deep-seated desire to restore the pattern of moral order that is normally associated with family government. All of these women seek a new definition of self, but all acknowledge that this new identity is dependent upon a male-dominated society which is stable and continuing. (Clarissa even sees Heaven in such terms, and when her efforts to find a place on earth have failed, she appropriately enough views death as a return to her *Father's* house.) Richardson's women cannot define their social roles until men have asserted their willingness and ability to preserve social order; and thus in *Grandison* Richardson begins his solution to the woman's problem by depicting in Sir Charles the kind of man who would establish and maintain a community which permitted her to assume her rightful place.

Only when we understand the vital importance of Sir

Charles' taking an active part in reestablishing order can we understand why Richardson causes him to behave in a manner which may seem arbitrary and officious. Grandison bustles into his uncle's home to relieve him of a plaguey mistress and present him with a dutiful wife. Such actions scarcely befit the relationship: nephews do not arrange marriages for their uncles, and men in their twenties seldom presume to dictate to men twice their age. Those are the offices which might more suitably be performed by a father for his son, and they seem appropriate to Sir Charles only when we recognize his role as an agent for establishing social coherence. It is in this role—perhaps the central role he is called upon to play—that Grandison most fully exhibits the busy-ness, the incessant (and often unrequested) activity that becomes faintly offensive to a modern reader.

Richardson is drawing on the notion of the Saint here; and several traits essential to that Puritan ideal contribute to this picture of the moral man as one who is active in the world around him. If the Self-Examiner is an image of a man whose energies are directed relentlessly inward in search of sin, the Saint, by contrast, is almost always seen as one who can successfully turn all of his energies outward to public use. Merely the density of the accomplishments listed within the *Saint's Life* contribute to this impression; and the tendency to minimize any real uncertainties a man may have had before death supports his appearance of confident productivity. What is more, the belief that it is blessed to labor in one's calling lent a religious justification to ceaseless activity of a secular sort. As Haller reports "When God called his elect to repent and believe, he also called upon them to act. The gifts and opportunities, no matter how humble and narrow, with which the saint was invested were also part of his commission from God. Whatsoever we undertake in the exercise of our talents and in the spirit of faith is good. It is what God has called us to do. Woe unto us if we do not do it, and happy the man who responds to the vocation of his own abilities."[8] Sir Charles' meddlesome nature has several sources or justifications: he must reestablish the order of family government by offering firm, moral, masculine leadership; and he lives in a society which views socially useful works as a sign of virtue and in which activity itself is deemed commendable.

It is no accident that Grandison plays father to his uncle, for this is the attitude which he adopts in most of his relationships with others. In the case of the Danbys he becomes the administrator of their estate, dispensing their inheritance with generous equity, approving of their marriages, and even giving the sister away in marriage. With Mrs. Oldham and her children he seems to finish honorably the task that had been undertaken so discreditably by his own father.

With others his position as father is affirmed even more directly. He returns home to find the dissension and disorder that has resulted from the negligent behavior of his father; and his generosity and kindness restore the confidence of sisters who term him a " 'father and a brother in one!' " (I, 208). Emily Jervois becomes his legal daughter by virtue of his accepting her as ward, and his relationship to her is a delicate combination of attitudes which are based upon a foundation of paternal authority; "The Brother, the affectionate Friend, and Father, I may say, appeared in his unreserved tenderness to her" (VI, 167). The fact of Sir Charles' youth makes some of these relationships a bit awkward; his care for his uncle and his attitude toward Emily Jervois are both made more difficult by his own relative immaturity. However, it is essential that Grandison should be of the new generation, for the wrongs he would redress are almost always the legacies of an older age; and the fact that his own father left only chaos and confusion at his death (a disrupted family situation which the younger man is forced to reorder) is the final sign that the standards and practices of a former generation had failed to deal with the problems of a changing world.

Thus in *Grandison* we are brought full circle. If Pamela and Clarissa had lost the guidance and protection which is normally given by effective parents, the orphan Harriet discovers a new sort of harmony under the sway of a father-like protector in Sir Charles Grandison. Indeed, the very first words uttered by Harriet and Sir Charles to each other delimit the most essential feature of their relationship. " 'Will you, madam, put yourself into my protection?' 'Oh, yes, yes, yes, with my whole heart—Dear good Sir, protect me!' " (I, 211). The incident would serve as a fitting climax to either of the earlier novels—Pamela terrorized by Mr. B. or Clarissa stalked by Lovelace—had the heroine only been fortunate enough to discover a protector. It is significant that Harriet finds a protector in Sir Charles, significant that they should meet for the first time even as Grandison is in the very act of rescuing her from the base designs of an unprincipled villain.

One might almost feel, reading both *Clarissa* and *Grandison*, that to a certain extent Richardson was continuing the plot of the earlier work in his last novel, for Harriet's initial adventure begins in much the same manner as Clarissa's personal crisis; she is abducted by a would-be seducer, a man of the same distinct mold as Lovelace, an egocentric, willful, selfish man who would possess her entirely. Clearly the world is still a potentially dangerous place for the virtuous innocent. Yet there is a difference here, for this is a world in which the violence can be controlled by the forces of peace and goodness which are focused into the masculine image of Grandison. Thus while Sir Charles' reticence to draw his own sword may seem ludicrous as an example of believable conduct, it has significance as an indication of the role he is intended to play. He does not conquer might with might; he invalidates physical force as an instrument of power. In his first encounter with Sir Hargrave, he does not wound the man; instead, as he says, " 'I wrenched his sword from him, and snapped it, and flung the two pieces over my head' " (I, 212). So much for Sir Hargrave Pollexfen, so much for Lovelace and the renegade libertine of the Restoration, so much for the threat of sexual violence and the doctrine of misrule. When at the end of the novel Sir Hargrave dies lamenting his sinfulness, we may quite rightly see his death as the demise of all such villainy, conquered by Charles Grandison's righteous example. Sir Hargrave's will is given to Grandison, who is its sole executor; and a large part of the estate has been left to Sir Charles and Harriet. The victory of social order is complete.

All of the traits that had marked Lovelace's sinful duplicity are inverted in the characterization of Grandison's virtue; and where Lovelace would conceal, distort, and disguise, Sir Charles wants nothing more than precise distinctions by which to define the reality of the world. Lovelace was fond of assuming disguises in order to give his protean nature the opportunity for endless change and deception. In *Grandison,* disguise is still associated with evil; the forces of destruction assail Harriet at a masquerade, and she is saved only by the intervention of Sir Charles, who comments primly, " 'Masquerades . . . are not creditable places for young Ladies [have been known] to be *insulted* at them. They are diversions that fall not in with the genius of the English commonalty' " (I, 216). He himself takes exceptional care always to dress in a manner befitting his station (the lace on his coat is just one example of this punctiliousness)—primarily, it would seem, so that his rank might be *known.* We can understand the importance of this attitude when we reflect on the notion of duty implicit in Grandison's code: if a man's duty and the propriety of his public behavior are both dependent upon his station, the outsider can make moral judgments of him only when his station is clearly discernible. Thus the stiff, awkward, and ineffective device in *Pamela* of equating changes in moral worth with changes of clothes is refined in *Grandison*, and integrated into a comprehensive and coherent moral system. What is more, this is a system which would correct the problem suffered by the Harlowes and by all those forced by an expanding society to make judgments about individuals who were not intimately known by them.

Lovelace was also fond of coining words, using language to deceive and confuse, playing with his own diction as if he were molding a piece of formless clay; words as he used them were to have no significance save the private meaning assigned by him, just as the wills of others were to have no volition save his own. Sir Charles is just the opposite. "He never perverts the meaning of words. He never, for instance, suffers his servants to deny him, when he is at home. If he is busy, he just finds the time to say he is, to unexpected visitors" (IV, 18). And he is relentless in his pursuit of meaning in important exchanges with others, never allowing an ambiguity of language to cover an evasion of truth.

> *Sir Ch.*   . . . Can you, do you think, love Lord G?
> *Miss Gr.* Love him! love Lord G.? What a question is that!—
>   Why no! I verily believe, that I can't say that.
> *Sir Ch.*   Can you esteem him?
> *Miss Gr.* Esteem!—Why that's a quaint word, tho' a *female*
>   one. I believe, if I were to marry the honest man,
>   I could be civil to him, if he would be very complaisant, very observant, and all that. . . .
> *Sir Ch.*   . . . But if *you* cannot be *more* than civil; and if *he* is

> to be very observant; you'll make it your agreement
> with him, before you meet him at the altar, that he
> shall subscribe to the woman's part of the vow, and
> that you shall answer to the man's.
>
> (II, 432)

Such attempts to be precise in the use of language are desirable in all members of any society which wishes to
preserve external distinctions because they are meaningful
ways of placing an individual. Thus Sir Charles' desire to
maintain these distinctions is the idealized reflection of a
quality which ought to be possessed by all good individuals.

Sir Charles does not probe Charlotte's use of the word
love because he wishes to know *why* she behaves as she
does; neither Grandison nor the reader of the novel ever
gains very explicit insight into the motivation behind her
actions. Instead, he wishes to discover exactly *what* she is
doing wrong—how her behavior deviates from the norm
expected of her—and then to convince her to correct her
actions. Here Charlotte's evasive use of words corresponds
to her distorted definition of the relationship between husband and wife (as Sir Charles points out); and one can safely assume that when her attitude toward marriage has
been corrected, her language, too, will be reformed.

At the root of this conscious emphasis on precision in
speech and propriety in dress are certain assumptions about
the relative importance of different elements in the human
personality. In *Clarissa*, Richardson clearly implies that
the most "real" and meaningful aspect of any individual
is that core of self which is hidden behind the various social
masks he might wear; thus the novel becomes a kind of
systematic disrobing of personality, a stripping away of
the sustaining relationships with the outside world until
this essential self stands nakedly revealed. The conflict
between Clarissa's behavior and her family's expectations
merely provides the starting point for the journey of self-

discovery; we are infinitely less concerned to know exactly how she has erred than to understand *why* she has behaved as she did. The ultimate truth about Clarissa's motivation is both the heroine's and the reader's aim. In *Grandison*, however, the external manifestations of self—what a person does, what he wears, what he says, the social roles he plays—are now taken to be the most precise way of delineating individual personality. We are no longer so much concerned with motivation as with behavior; we no longer want to know why a person does something so much as what precisely it is that he has done, no longer seek the understanding of self in isolation so much as a comprehension of the individual placed into a social setting. The results of such a shift may be seen in Richardson's characterization of the hero.

Over and over again the author expands his portrayal of Sir Charles merely by telling us one additional fact about the protagonist's influence upon those around him: Grandison delivers Everard Grandison from debt; he settles the dispute between the Mansfields and the Keelings; he urges his sister into an appropriate marriage. Moreover, when those who are mostly nearly acquainted with him seek expressions in which to describe Grandison's nature, they usually fall into a rhapsodic list of the different relationships that he has assumed. "It is my wish," Harriet confesses to her confidante, "that you were present, and saw him, The domestic Man, The chearful Friend, The kind Master, The enlivening Companion, The polite Neighbour, The tender Husband!" (VI, 38). Again, when reflecting upon her happiness in being married to Sir Charles, Harriet calls him "[Emily's] guardian, *my* guardian, my friend, my Lover, my HUSBAND, every sweet word in one" (VI, 75); and at the end of the novel, Harriet prays, "Oh, my God! do thou make me thankful for such a Friend, Protector, Director, Husband!" (VI, 316). Even at the very beginning of the novel Mrs. Shirley affirms Sir Charles' appropriateness as a suitor to Harriet merely by listing the various social roles that he plays. " 'At last . . . the man appeared to you, who was worthy of your Love; who had so powerfully protected you from the lawless attempt of a fierce and cruel pretender; a man who proved to be the best of brothers, friends, landlords, masters, and the bravest and best of men.' " (II, 18). One need never know Grandison's reasons for behaving as he does; it is enough to know what he does, for the social roles which comprise his public identity are deemed a complete and accurate index to the man.[9]

Such a procedure would never have succeeded in placing the people of Clarissa Harlowe's world. After all, Lovelace is characterized as an exemplary and diligent student,[10] and " 'a generous landlord [who] spared nothing for solid and lasting improvements upon his estate.' "[11] He is a good friend to Belford and the crew of rakes, a man whose careful dress reveals a conscious awareness of the size of his estate, a gallant whose air in company could be delicate and deferential; and if his reputation with women is dubious, he is (as everyone at the beginning of the novel assures us) at least a man of sense who might reasonably be expected to reform. Yet he is a villain. And the extent of his wickedness, when it is finally revealed, surpasses all but the most pessimistic predictions. Clearly, in this instance at least, the outward manifestations of self have been deceptive; and a true understanding of the individual can come only after we have penetrated to the inner self as it has been unconsciously revealed through the letters. To a lesser extent the same thing is true even of Clarissa, whose virtuous reputation at the beginning of the novel masks a proud and passionate nature.

The difference between these images of personality in *Clarissa* and in *Grandison* stems from a change in the degree of accuracy with which an individual can define the various social roles that he plays. In the Harlowe world there is confusion about the duties attendant on fundamental relationships. The problem that precipitates Clarissa's trial and tragedy is not so much that she is unwilling to conform to the norm of behavior expected from a dutiful daughter as that she is uncertain just what a daughter *ought* to do, not that she refuses to play the appropriate roles (as Charlotte Grandison does, for instance) but that she cannot formulate a precise definition of those roles. Similarly, Lovelace might have been called a gentleman by some even after his villainy; certainly both Miss Howe and his family still urge a marriage between him and Clarissa. Yet neither Clarissa nor the discerning reader can acknowledge him as such unless the role of gentleman has ceased to have any real meaning at all; and the very fact that people can disagree so markedly indicates just how little consensus there is about these important relationships. We can see this breakdown of coherence most pathetically in Clarissa's attempts to maintain punctilio even when all genuine meaning has left the gestures, the customs, and the ritual observances that go to make up punctilious behavior.

By contrast, Grandison's is a highly differentiated system in which the social expression of self is so explicitly and extensively defined that a knowledge of a man's public mien will in fact provide an accurate index to the inner man as well; and any truly virtuous individual will seek to preserve this correlation. Sir Charles' concern with words and dress is but one manifestation of his desire to maintain the significance of external distinctions. As Harriet declares of him, " 'He is not ashamed to avow in public, what he thinks fit to own in private. . . . Sir Charles edified everybody by his chearful piety. Are you not of opinion, my dear Lady G. that wickedness may be always put out of countenance by a person who has an established character for goodness, and who is not ashamed of doing his duty in the public eye?' " (V, 155-156). The duty of making one's actions public applies especially to members of those orders of society by whose behavior the norms of conduct are set. Sir Charles says, " 'People of fashion . . . should consider themselves as examples of the lower orders of men. They should shew a conformity to the laws of their country, both ecclesiastical and civil, where they can do it with a good conscience' " (VI, 14).[12]

When such a system is completely effective, there can be no misunderstanding, no deception unless the individual who misperceives the world does so because of personal inadequacies (as Charlotte does in the affair with Captain Anderson). All social roles will have a prescriptive as well as a descriptive definition, and for any given social roles there will be a complete set of modes of behavior, social attitudes, and moral duties which accompany it. Decorum or punctilio will be observed not as a meaningless set of rules but as a significant guide to virtuous behavior. Thus Sir Charles, who is usually so carefully attentive to society's rules, casts off the notion of etiquette for its own sake merely and explains his early proposal to Harriet by saying that he is not desirous " 'for *dull* and *cold* form's sake . . . of postponing the declaration of my affection to Miss Byron' " (V, 112). He urges her not to reject him for reasons which " 'will be found to be punctilious only' " (V, 112), for he would reinfuse the entire notion of etiquette with a new and more genuine significance. Through his example the whole formal code of behavior which was "out the window" with Clarissa's elopement will be replaced by a notion of decorum which is related to real standards of honor and mutual consideration.

Sir Charles is Richardson's portrait of the exemplary man of honor, fulfilling perfectly the duties attendant upon his various public roles, and it is from this picture that we are meant to infer a definition of the ideal social being. Grandison might well be seen as a latter-day Puritan who has escaped the rigors of self-doubt by devoting himself completely to that interest in worldly affairs and commitment to calling which Weber has so accurately described. The confidence and satisfaction which Sir Charles exudes in all of his relationships with the rest of the world derive from the evident success of his numerous projects; his identity is confirmed in each different, meaningful social role he assumes; and the anguish of the lonely Pilgrim seems far behind; Richardson, however, did not wish to discard the terms of the internal struggle entirely, for he raises at numerous intervals the faded spector of that old Puritan nemesis, the passions. Harriet speaks with awed and innocent fascination of Sir Charles' heroic ability to control his irrational inclinations while under such severe stress during his Italian voyage. " 'But you will see, that Honour and the Laws of hospitality, were Mr. Grandison's guard: And I believe a young flame may be easily kept under. . . . Sir Charles Grandison is used to doing only what he *ought*. Dr. Bartlett once said, that the life of a good man was a continual warfare with his passions' " (III, 74). No less a person than Sir Charles himself speaks of the threat of " '*passion*, which I hold to be my most dangerous enemy' " (I, 392); and he occasionally laments his inability to vanquish the adversary completely. " 'I am very much dissatisfied with myself, my dear Mr. Bartlett. What pains have I taken, to conquer those sudden gusts of passion, to which, from my early youth, I have been subject, as you have often heard me confess! yet to find, at times, that I am unequal—to myself, shall I say?' " (II, 373-374).

The incongruity of all this talk about the danger of passion coming from the mouth of a man who seems to have suffered scarcely an irrational impulse in his life reflects

Richardson's tendency to cling to the attitudes and literary traditions of the Puritan *Saint's Life* in the portrayal of his worldly hero. The Saint's most constant source of temptation lay in the irrational, passionate inclinations of his own body; and most *Saint's Lives* contained a Section describing a (successful) struggle with the sins of the flesh. Complete moral victory came when these impulses were entirely subdued; in the Puritan tradition, such a victory could come only with death and escape from the sinful body (such was, of course, Clarissa's solution). When Richardson transfers these otherworldly attitudes of ideal goodness into his characterization of Sir Charles, he inevitably produces an internally inconsistent identity. Sir Charles is nearly perfect (and, according to the traditional *Saint's Life,* this meant that his mastery over his passions was to be virtually complete). Thus, not only does he control himself, but he subdues passion in others as well, defeating the irrational Sir Hargrave Pollexfen and cautioning the fiery Latin, Olivia, with standard Puritan homilies. With all this power over his own and others' irrationality, he is still depicted as living in the world and clearly intending to remain there, at least throughout the course of the novel. Yet according to the traditional Puritan view of man, life on earth must always be a continual war with sinful forces of the body. Hence we get the confusing image of Grandison, a man who is Saint militant and Saint triumphant at one and the same time.

The image of the good man which emerges in *Grandison,* then, is a curious hybrid. It has as its clear point of reference the strict and rigidly Puritanical code of *Clarissa* and the picture of the Saint that is typically presented in the Life, but the definition of human nature it presents has been softened by the beliefs of such liberal eighteenth-century religious leaders as the Latitudinarian Tillotson (whose views about the value of presenting an embodi-

ment of ideal goodness are quoted in the novel's concluding remarks). There is, for instance, a clear rejection of the
Calvinistic notion of innate depravity and the inescapable
wickedness of the body; and for all of Grandison's talk
about the importance of controlling the passions, we
simply do not find that life and death struggle to preserve
the self against the encroachments of the devil and inherent
evil. Accompanying this move is the growing belief that
all men may be worthwhile and that both man and the
society in which he lives are potentially perfectible. It is
remarkable, for instance, that Richardson should have
chosen to make his tragic heroine a Roman Catholic. Clearly he intends this element of the novel to be one additional
confirmation of the notion that every individual has the
potential for good: as Clementina says to Grandison,
" 'You have almost persuaded me to think charitably of
people of different persuasions, by your noble charity for
all mankind: Which I think, heretic as you are, forgive me,
Sir, carries an appearance of true Christian goodness in it' "
(III, 69).

Grandison's Puritan ancestry is still evident in his sense
of self-discipline, in the commitment to a diligent pursuit
of his calling, and in his concern to control passion. However, the struggle against passion and all other irrational
impulses is no longer the major moral battle he must
wage; this rejection of the notion of innate or inborn evil
has enabled him to direct his attention outside of himself
because if he wishes to discover the nature of his own identity, he need no longer relentlessly probe the recesses of his
own heart. Accompanying this shift is a second change in
man's way of defining himself—a change which supports
the shift away from introspection—and this is the increasing ease with which he can find significant and well-
defined social roles to play. In the changing and uncertain
world of the Harlowes, even if Clarissa had wished to find

fulfillment within a secular community, she would not have been able to do so without formulating new, more precise definitions of her social roles to replace the fragmented relationships which made up her life. Thus her own introspective journey is occasioned both by the breakdown of the social system in which she lives and by the moral inheritance of the Puritan tradition which taught self-examination as the only way of defining identity; and when in *Grandison* we make a return journey back into the world, we do so because both of the forces which had compelled man to turn into himself have now been dissipated.

There is confidence now in man's ability to effect good, both in his own life and in the lives of others; and his battle with the weaknesses of the body has become sufficiently unimportant in the general moral framework of his life so that he may turn the major portion of his energy to projects outside himself. The nature of his influence on other people and on the world in which he lives grows increasingly important as a way of determining his own moral worth. Society has once more become stable, and social roles with their attendant duties are again clearly and precisely articulated. The man who wishes to express his notions of morality and his definition of himself in terms of his relationships with others may now do so without conflict. In such a world not only is it possible to turn one's attention to the complex network of ties that bind men to each other, but such action becomes both virtous and psychologically reassuring. There is a buoyant self-confidence (as Sir Charles so clearly illustrates) to be gained from an articulation of self in a series of successful interactions with others, while social welfare becomes, if not the highest moral aim, at least a primary one. Our notion of the reality of human identity has experienced a corresponding shift, and we no longer seek to discover self in complex revelations of the inner mind, pursuing instead the social man as he reveals himself in the variety of his intereactions with others.

It is easy to understand how a doctrine of benevolence and sympathy could develop in a society that postulates a complex set of relationships among men with a corresponding set of duties, and a view of individual personality which asserts that man realizes himself most effectively in his interactions with other human beings. If the welfare of others is to be our principal moral concern, then wishing well for others and engaging to do good for them would be the most evident marks of the virtuous man. These ideas did not originate with Richardson; they were bywords of the literate culture of his time, and he must have encountered them daily. For instance, the extension of the notion of family relationships into the broader expression of a social relationship among all men is expounded at great length by Shaftesbury, who also gives voice to the doctrine that man must relinquish his self-centered desires in order to feel that sympathy with others which would enable him to promote the general good; the Latitudinarian branch of the Anglican church had long preached the inherent ability of all men to be saved. One might speculate endlessly about the exact source of those notions which pervade *Grandison,* and never find any very satisfactory solution. Richardson's eyesight had failed badly during his later years; and although he continued to write, his personal letters after the publication of *Pamela* are filled with excuses and apologies for his failure to keep up with his reading. That Richardson was acquainted with the notions of the school of moral sentiment is undeniable; however, his knowledge must have been most unsystematic—bits and snatches of ideas from the *Spectator Papers* or overheard at afternoon tea. Certainly he made no claims as a philosopher himself, nor did he attempt to formulate a coherent philosophy in his own works; they were, after all, intended for amusement as well as instruction. Thus while we can perceive an unmistakable shift away from the Puritanical assumptions of the very early works (like the *Vade Mecum*) and the first novels towards the more liberal view of man which inheres in the Latitudinarian and moral sentiment traditions, we cannot trace the move with any degree of philosophical accuracy.

For whatever reasons, then, when Richardson comes to portray an ideal human being in his last novel, the principal virtue of that individual and the quality that makes him most worthy of emulation is an actively benevolent disposition; and righteousness itself is, as Grandison so often notes, that behavior which conduces to the general good. " 'Don't you think, my Lord, that it is suitable to the divine benignity, as well as justice, to lend its sanctions and punishments in aid of those duties which bind man to man?' " (II, 220). The bad man is one who, like Sir Hargrave, never becomes a "useful member of society," while the good man must reflect in some measure the untiring efforts of a Sir Charles Grandison in the cause of social welfare. Every adulatory description of him stresses this quality: as Dr. Bartlett remarks, " 'You know not, Ladies, you know not, my Lord, what a general *Philanthropist* your brother is: His whole delight is in doing good. It has always been so: And to mend the hearts, as well as the fortunes, of men, is his glory' " (II, 369). And even Grandison describes himself as one " 'who aims at an universal benevolence' " (V, 268).

The effect of such a man upon those who meet him must be (as Richardson envisioned it) inevitably to inspire in them a desire to emulate him, and many of the discussions about Grandison's nature turn on a search to discover those personal qualities which have made him as he is. Thus Lady G. remarks, " 'Is there no man, I have been asked, that is like your brother?—He, I have answered, is most likely to resemble him, who has an unbounded charity, and universal benevolence, to men of all professions; and who, imitating the Divinity, regards the heart, rather than the head, and much more than either rank or fortune, tho' it were princely' " (V, 404). Charlotte's remarks lack a certain degree of lucidity, for it is not altogether clear what she means to indicate by a preference of the heart to the head.[13]

Sometimes this connection is expressed in terms of the benefactor's own emotional response to his virtuous action; more often the example of Sir Charles Grandison seems to make other people more aware of the joy that can come from action. " 'Till I knew my brother,' " Charlotte Grandison asserts, " 'I was an inconsiderate, unreflecting girl. Good and evil, which immediately affected not myself, were almost alike indifferent to me. But he has awakened in me a capacity to enjoy the true pleasure that arises from a benevolent action' " (I, 217). In this view benevolence might be encouraged by seeking to discover in oneself the sentiments and pleasurable inclinations which accompany selfless actions; and sentiment of the proper kind, the ability to feel this spontaneous joy in goodness easily and strongly, is an attribute to be cultivated by every man who aspired to virtue. By extension, strong emotions in and of themselves might be seen as desirable characteristics; and the portrait of the man of sentiment that pervaded so much of the popular literature in the latter part of the eighteenth century derives directly from this notion of cultivating in oneself a fine aesthetic sense of the exquisite pleasure of doing good.

Although there are some intimations throughout the novel that man derives a spontaneous delight in his own proper behavior, Richardson is still too much obsessed with the rigors of Puritan theology to place much emphasis on such a belief; and unrestrained expressions of emotion or an excessive cultivation of the ability to feel strongly, are consistently portrayed as harmful or destructive. Clementina's madness is clearly intended as a warning against the possibility of being overcome by irrational desires; and the melancholy picture of Mr. Orme, languishing in the arms of some unnamed but fatal disease, is meant to contrast sharply with the robust vigor of Sir Charles' benevolence. In a lighter vein, Harriet's criticism of a poem lamenting the death of a favorite bird strikes out against the same mistake of exalting emotion merely for its own sake. Ironically, much of the literature that followed Richardson's lead in the portrayal of sentiment had exactly the lugubrious air of emotionalism that Harriet here condemns. To be sure, Richardson did, especially in this last novel, concentrate intensively on the human capacity for emotion; however, (contrary to what one might think who had read such imitations of him as *The Man of Feeling*), he imposes very explicit limitations on the role that emotion was meant to play in one's life.

Richardson never portrays emotion as valuable or desirable in and of itself. The capacity for emotion is, however, like the capacity to reason, a faculty which all men share. Harriet observes, for instance, " 'Is not human nature the same in every country, allowing only for different customs?—Do not love, hatred, anger, malice, *all* the passions in short, good or bad, shew themselves by like effects in the faces, hearts, and actions, of the people of every country? . . . And why is the Grecian Homer, to this day, so much admired, as he is in all these nations, and in every other nation where he has been read, and will be, to the world's end, but because he writes to nature? And is not the language of nature one language throughout the world, tho' there are different modes of speech to express it by?' " (I, 282). Thus a man's ability to feel emotion affirms his fellowship with all men, and the ability to feel others' concerns as he feels his own further strengthens that tie. Charlotte asserts, "We never, I believe, *properly* feel for others, what does not touch ourselves,' " and Harriet adds the moderating note of caution, " 'A compassionate heart . . . is a blessing, though a painful one: And yet there would be no supporting life, if we felt quite as poignantly for others as we do for ourselves' " (II, 68). If supreme virtue lies in overcoming the limitations of self in order to prefer the welfare and happiness of others, then anything which strengthens our bond with others may move us to an exercise of benevolence; and sympathy is important because it may serve as just such a spur to goodness.

Such is clearly the case with Sir Charles. " 'Sir Charles is setting out for town,' " Harriet observes. " 'He cannot be happy, himself; He is therefore giving himself the pleasure of endeavoring to make his friend happy. He can *enjoy* the happiness of his *friends!* O the blessing of a benevolent heart!' " (III, 39). His sensitivity to the emotions of others and his ability to feel these emotions strongly are suggested as sources for his limitless benevolence. " 'Why have I such a feeling heart?' " he laments (II, 345). " 'You know, Dr. Bartlett, that I have a heart too susceptible for my own peace, tho' I endeavor to *conceal* from *others* those painful sensibilities, which they cannot relieve' " (IV, 132); and Dr. Bartlett replies, " 'O my Grandison! how I pity that tender, that generous heart of yours!' " (IV, 140).

Although mere sensibility and the capacity to feel emotion have no value when they are divorced from any benevolent inclination, the same feelings when they awaken our feeling of communal responsibility can incline us toward virtuous action. Strong feeling alone is no indication of moral worth (Sir Hargrave and Olivia, after all, are the very embodiments of visible emotion; and Clementina in her tearful fits of madness is scarcely a figure to be emulated); but the ability to feel *with* others may very well be the mark of an inherently benevolent individual. We saw the beginning of such a belief even in *Clarissa*, for the goodness of those who were acquainted with the heroine's tragedy was almost always measured by their ability to sympathize with her suffering. The wickedness of her family, for instance, was clearly indicated by their callous dismissal of her pain (her mother, aunt, and cousin excepted, for these were at least initially affected by her plight). Lovelace's depravity is reiterated in his unvarying attempts to *resist* any pity he might feel for Clarissa, his shame at incipient tears and his anger when he detects the slightest stirring of compassion. By contrast, Belford, Miss Howe, and all who themselves feel the pain of Clarissa's trial reveal their potential for good in this sympathy.

In *Grandison* Richardson's interest in sympathy and sensibility is more fully developed, playing an important role throughout the novel; it is significant, however, that the function of emotion is always to draw people together and prompt benevolent action. *Grandison* is filled with tearful scenes, but the characters virtually never weep when they are alone. Their tears are tears of companionship and serve to reaffirm the extended familial ties that bind them in mutual duty. Thus Harriet says of Emily, "I was moved at the dear girl's melancholy tale. I clasped my arms about her, and wept on her gentle bosom. Her calamity, which was the greatest that could happen to a good child, I told her, had endeared her to me: I would love her as my sister" (II, 312). Similarly, Harriet and the Grandison sisters are bound together by a bond of mutual sympathy in the loss of a mother. "It was impossible,"

Harriet says when the Grandisons describe the death of their mother, "not to think of my own mamma; and I could not help, on the remembrance, joining my tears with theirs" (II, 29). Lady L. remarks on the appropriateness of Harriet's reaction, saying, " 'But, my Charlotte, give Miss Byron some brief account of the parting scene between my father and mother. She is affected as a sister should be —Tears, when time has matured a pungent grief into a sweet melancholy are not hurtful: They are as the dew of the morning to the green herbage' " (II, 38). Again, when Harriet's virtuous affection for Sir Charles seems doomed to disappointment, his family and friends give visible signs of their tenderness and concern for her.

The pattern is played out with endless variations and repetitions throughout the novel, and one is sometimes tempted to feel that the characters seek each other's company only so that they may share mutually in personal crises. The life of the emotions has ceased to be a private affair, and one is no longer expected to keep his sorrows and joys discreetly hidden within the recesses of the heart. To do so would be to deny others the opportunity of helping to relieve suffering and thus to deny them the chance of exercising their own benevolent inclinations. Even courtesy depends upon understanding the emotional problems of others, and Sir Charles' elaborate consideration in all of his dealings can be genuinely effective only when he is privy to the troubles and cares of those whom he would treat with kindness.

Trial and temptation concerning the sensibilities can come in two ways. For Sir Charles, whose affections are uniformly selfless and whose inclination to virtue is unwavering, the only problems are those of a mechanical nature—the difficulties that might arise in attempting to adjust the varying just claims of others upon him equitably. Such is the awkwardness he encounters in the Italian affair, where he is forced to balance his duties to an honorable family, the welfare of Clementina, the claims of his own country and religion, and the undeniable impression he has made upon the affections of Harriet Byron. Here it is neither his capacity for sympathy nor his desire to act with generosity which is being tried, but his ability to resolve the situation justly and gracefully.

However, Harriet (along with such others as Emily and Charlotte) encounters a more serious obstacle to the achievement of a genuine sympathy, and this is the difficulty in overcoming her own selfish, individual desires in order to effect an adequate identification with others. The problem is treated briefly in several phases of the novel, but it is discussed chiefly with regard to Harriet's love for Sir Charles in the face of his apparent commitment to Clementina. The question of selfish love had come up even in *Clarissa*, where Lovelace's desire to obtain complete possession of Clarissa was seen as the very embodiment of selfcentered sinfulness. Now, in order to balance that distorted picture of affection, Richardson presents a picture of true love in *Grandison*, love based on a real desire that the loved one find happiness, love which postulates as its fundamental aim the greater good of all society. Such was to be the affection of Harriet for Sir Charles.

The temptation as Richardson portrays it is fairly straightforward. Harriet has conceived an attachment to Grandison, a liking which is based on a realistic perception of his own inherent goodness and one which is approved by both families. The difficulty arises when Harriet discovers that Grandison has a prior commitment to another lady, a woman entirely worthy of his affection, and one who by her suffering and the magnanimity of her nature lays valid claim to Harriet's admiration. According to the dictates of sympathy and benevolence, Harriet ought to feel respect and compassion for the Italian lady and wish her success in solving the complex problems that stand in the way of her marriage. On the other hand, a selfish love might well incline Harriet to desire the failure of this treaty. Thus the question which Richardson would raise is whether the power of sympathy is capable of surmounting even the demands of romantic affection.

Primarily, of course, the problem is Harriet's; but it is mirrored over and over again throughout the novel. Harriet must learn to resign herself to Sir Charles' possible marriage with Clementina. Emily Jervois, who has herself developed a romantic attachment to her guardian, must face the same problem with regard to the possibility of Harriet's marriage with Grandison. The entire Grandison family is inclined to sympathize with Harriet and to exclude Clementina's claims upon him; and even the reader, who sees all of the action in the novel from Harriet's point of view,[14] must resist his tendency to identify too completely with her, lest it obscure the rightful admiration that he ought to feel for Clementina. The test is, as the characters in the novel repeatedly affirm, a measure of Harriet's magnanimity and a trial of the quality of her love. Will she, like Olivia, allow her passions to dominate and be reduced to vicious, selfish expressions of jealousy? Or can she rise above self to make her love for Grandison a true reflection of inherent benevolence?

The key element of Harriet's character in determining her behavior in this regard is her capacity for sympathy; and the account of Clementina's suffering as it is presented in the novel is deliberately intended as an example to arouse both Harriet's and the reader's feelings. Thus there is no attempt to understand the motivation behind Clementina's behavior: we see her always from the outside and in terms of her effect on others. The several Italian episodes are each followed by an account of the reactions of those in

England who are interested in the affair, and the alternation between the narrative of the Italian scenes and the description of the response to them keeps the important question of Harriet's capacity for sympathy forever before us.

Harriet's initial reaction is, quite naturally, an expression of her own disappointment; yet even here Richardson would have us believe that her sorrow is mingled with a sense of compassion for the unhappiness of Clementina and Grandison. " 'Ah my Charlotte! No flattering hope is now left me—No sister! It must not, it cannot be! The Lady is—but lead me, lead me out of this room!—I don't love it' spreading one hand before my eyes, my tears trickling between my fingers—Tears that flowed not only for myself, but for Sir Charles Grandison and the unhappy Clementina' " (III, 35-36). As the accounts from Italy continue to come back to England, Harriet's admiration is stirred by the example of Clementina's own benevolence, and as she says, "[Clementina's] motive, thro' her whole delirium, is so apparently owing to her concern for the Soul of the man she loved (entirely regardless of any interest of her own) that we all forgot what had been so long our wishes, and joined in giving a preference to her" (III, 139).

As the Italian intrigue progresses, Harriet begins even to hope for Clementina's marriage with Sir Charles. " 'I yield to an event to which I ought to submit,' " she says. " 'And to a woman, not *less*, but *more* worthy than myself. . . . Could I, do you think, Lady G., if I were to have this honour, cordially congratulate her as Lady Grandison? Heaven only knows! But it would be my glory, if I could; for then I should not scruple to put myself in a rank with Clementina; and to demand her hand, as that of my sister' " (IV, 183). Still the protracted negotiations continue, and as Harriet increasingly identifies with the worthy Italian, she grows more and more to see Clemen-

tina's problems as similar to her own. Harriet must face
the possibility of losing Grandison! Indeed so must Clementina. Clementina's grandeur derives from her complete
benevolence; so Harriet's claim to be worthy of Grandison's
affections must come from a genuine desire that the con-
templated marriage take place. " 'A woman! an angel!' "
she says of Clementina. " 'So much more worthy of Sir
Charles Grandison, than the poor Harriet Byron *can*
be!—O how great is Clementina, how little am I, in my own
eyes! The Lady will still be his. She must. She shall' " (IV,
359).

By this time, of course, Richardson has worked himself
into an indefensible position; Grandison's admiration for
Harriet is largely based on the generosity, the magnanimity
of her feelings for Clementina (feelings which prove both
her capacity for sympathy and her ultimate virtue) and
even when the Italian liaison proves impossible, Clementina's presence must continuously be evoked by Grandison and Harriet in order to sustain the proof of Harriet's
worthiness. The relationship between them takes on a
peculiar, artificial quality because they seem to relate to
each other principally by means of their mutual regard for
Clementina. For instance, Sir Charles comes to propose
marriage to Harriet and to urge an early date for their wedding, but Harriet can only reply, " 'The dear, the excellent
Clementina! What a perverseness is in *her* fate! She, and
she *only*, could have deserved you!' " (V, 221). Grandison's response only serves to affirm the contingency of the
relationship upon a shared admiration for Clementina. "He
bent his knee to the greatly-honoured Harriet—'I acknowledge with transport,' he said, 'the joy you give me by your
magnanimity; such a *more* than sisterly magnanimity to
that of Clementina. How nobly do you authorise my regard for *her*! In *you*, madam, shall I have all *her* excellencies, without the abatements which must have been
allowed, had she been mine, from considerations of Reli-

gion and Country' " (V, 221). The unnatural relationship
continues and grows. Grandison and Harriet must wait to
marry until they can assure themselves that Clementina
approves of their union; and when Clementina finally
comes to visit England, the sympathetic bond between
herself and Harriet quite clearly seems more vital and
strong than even the tie between Harriet and her husband.

Sympathy can well be postulated as the basis for benevolent action; however, the very notion of sympathy presupposes a coherent definition of self and a genuine regard
for the demands and desires of self, for clearly if we never
want anything ourselves we can never *sympathize* with
another's want. We may perceive it, understand it, respect
it, even feel rationally compelled to relieve it; but we cannot sympathize with it unless it bears some direct relationship to our own personal experience. Thus any moral
system which contends that we are moved to generous
and apparently selfless action by virtue of our ability to
feel *with* another, to identify his cares with our own, must
necessarily include in it a nice appreciation of individual,
personal desire.

The trouble with much of Richardson's last novel is
precisely that he has failed to appreciate the assumptions
that are implicit in a system of moral sentiment. He has
attempted to incorporate the best of two worlds into his
novel, and in doing so he has failed to present a convincing
picture of either. Thus, for example, Harriet declares at
the beginning of the novel, "I really think I never shall be
in love with any-body, till duty directs inclination" (I, 97).
Very well; this is a picture of reason controlling the passions, and it forms the basis for one notion of virtue—virtue as the result of man's reasonable control over his
emotions and the resultant ability to choose disinterestedly
among various courses of action in order to follow the

best of them. The characterization that Richardson supplies of Harriet confirms just such a picture. She is not swept away by her emotions; passion is always dominated by reason in her life. When she behaves virtuously with regard to Grandison's attachment to Clementina, it would be only consistent to view it as merely one more instance in which a rational exercise of goodness can overcome temptation. Yet Richardson will not let us have it that way. Instead, he insists that Harriet's altruism should stem from her sympathy—indeed her identification—with the unfortunate Clementina. Now suddenly the girl whose emotions have thus far been so perfectly controlled is deemed to make the greatest sacrifice of her life because of the overwhelming force of these same emotions. The entire situation becomes grotesquely distorted; and Harriet seems less a generous, feeling woman than a somewhat bizarre human oddity. The portrait of Grandison fails in much the same way; for Richardson has so relentlessly insisted on Grandison's rational control over his emotions that the reader is more inclined to suspect that his untiring, energetic benevolence stems from unfortunately officious tendencies rather than from a generous heart.

Richardson was clearly capable of untangling the intricate skein of human feeling; but did not seem able to make an acknowledgement of strong emotion consistent with a portrayal of the lives of good people. When emotion is loosed with all its force, as it is in *Clarissa*, Richardson denies its strength by imposing on it a rational control so rigid that it can lead only to death. In *Grandison* Richardson would have us believe that he has incorporated human feeling into a coherent moral system and that he has even made emotion the most necessary component of that system. However, despite the external displays of feeling, despite the tears and the sympathy, Richardson still manifests a Puritanical distrust of the irrational components in human nature; and while he is perfectly able to dissect man's irrational self in order to discover means of controlling it (as he does in *Clarissa*), the kind of extended, sensitive exploration and portrayal of emotion that might give support to a system of moral sentiment is manifestly impossible for him. Thus despite the explicit appeal throughout *Grandison* to emotional forces, real complexity and strength of feeling is simply never shown; and even Clementina, whose characterization comes closest to Clarissa's, is little more than a weeping stereotype.

Strangely enough, the very prevalence of tears and expressions of sympathy serves to negate the force of emotion; for these scenes seem to arise so easily, and they reflect so little in the way of genuine feeling, that they dissipate rather than intensify the reader's already uncertain perception of the characters' passions. The sheer number of external indications of strong feeling are quite out of proportion to the incidents that seem to have precipitated them. After all, the intensity of even Clarissa's hysteria might seem disproportionate when viewed only in terms of the actual events which took place; and the novel escapes the curse of sentimentality because it probes beneath the outward manifestations of Clarissa's feeling to reveal a psychological conflict sufficiently disrupting to explain her behavior. In *Grandison* we never do go beneath the surface, and the outward signs of emotion have been equated with feeling itself. While an individual who exhibits all the signs of distress may in fact be deeply disturbed, we will never credit his unhappiness unless we can discover some evidence that manifestations of emotion do represent real feelings. When a novelist presents us with *only* the public evidence of emotion, the reader may very well not believe in the alleged feeling, dismissing the visible signs of it as merely an excess of sentiment.

We might even be led to wonder how successfully a

moral code which is based on the force of sympathy can be presented in a novel which portrays its characters in terms of social realism. A system of moral sentiment depends, after all, on the assumption that a man's feelings are an important—perhaps the most important—element in his nature; and emotion usually cannot be presented convincingly when an author portrays only the external evidence of it. Some revelation of the "inner man" is almost always necessary to support a claim of strong feelings. Yet when an author chooses to see man principally in a social setting, he automatically eliminates the possibility of portraying emotion directly; and under these conditions, effusions of tears and hysterical outbursts must always carry a somewhat spurious air. Surely it is no accident that so many of the best novels of manners are based on a moral system which depends upon an individual's *rationally* placing himself within the social framework and then adequately fulfilling the obligations attendant upon his position. Such is Charlotte Grandison's problem; and her moral choices are certainly more convincingly drawn igtue is defined
by the strength of their capacity for sympathy.

Much of *Grandison* seems deliberately intended as a conclusion to the problems of the earlier works: the individual has been returned to a social setting with a new set of values which should enable him to accommodate his emotions; the narrow relationships that had defined his familial ties and duties have been expanded to embrace all mankind; and order has once more been restored by the confident assertion of male authority. With these questions settled, Richardson can now turn to the dilemma that had been the dominant theme of the two earlier novels, the difficulty of defining the woman's role.

Because Richardson continues to see woman's place in society as essentially dependent, the solution to her quandary can be found only when the other ills which have beset the world have been remedied. Just as the ideal "new" man is embodied in the person of Sir Charles Grandison, so the ideal woman may be inferred from Richardson's portrayal of Harriet Byron; however, there is more than this simple parity between them, for without a Charles Grandison, there could be no Harriet Byron. Without the assurance of a stable and essentially benevolent social order, the woman, whose welfare is contingent upon the actions of others, would always be in jeopardy.

Richardson begins the presentation of his solution by casting off some of the rigid limitations of family ties, thereby giving the woman a much greater measure of freedom in her choice of a way of life. As Harriet reflects, "What a victim must that woman look upon herself to be, who is compelled, or even *over-persuaded,* to give her hand to a man who has no share in her heart?" (III, 371). Happily, Harriet herself suffers from no such restrictions. Thus when her hand is solicited by an appropriate suitor, Mrs. Selby declares, " 'In truth . . . we are all neutrals on this occasion. We have the highest opinion of her discretion. She has read, she has conversed; and yet there is not in the country a better housewife, or one who would make a more prudent manager in a family. . . . Were she *not* our child, we should love her for her good qualities, and sweetness of manners, and a frankness that has few examples among young women' " (I, 330). The result of this change in attitude toward marriage is that a woman of intelligence, prudence, and discretion may be given a relatively free choice in the selection of her husband, though she will be expected to confer with her elders and to defer to them when their wisdom and experience demand it.

Woman's most natural role, of course, is still seen to be

that of wife and mother. Harriet declares at the beginning of the novel, "I have a very high notion of the marriage-state. I remember what my uncle once averred; That a woman out of wedlock is half useless to the end of her being. How indeed do the duties of a good Wife, of a good Mother, and a worthy Matron, well performed, dignify a woman!" (I, 30); and the suitability of the married state is argued here with more fervor than in any of the earlier novels. Even Clementina, whose spiritual inclinations would seem to make her qualified to remain single, is urged by Grandison to marry. "You, my beloved corres-pondent, who hold marriage as a Sacrament, surely cannot doubt but you may serve God in it with much greater efficacy, than were you to sequester yourself from a world that wants such an example as you are able to give it" (IV, 379).

This tendency to wish that every woman assume the role of wife and mother is part of a general recognition of the values and demands of the world: it is repeatedly argued that a woman's contribution to society is greater when she can adopt these roles successfully. Yet there are other rea-sons for urging them upon her, not the least of which is her own safety and happiness. " 'Were it not,' " Grandison says, " 'for male protectors, to what insults, to what out-rages, would not your Sex be subject? . . . All the femi-nine graces are [Harriet's] She is, in my notion, what all women should be—But wants she not a protector?' " (V, 414). The woman alone is all too liable to insult, an easy prey for unscrupulous men; and when her age is sufficient to free her from unwelcome attention, solitude and loneli-ness may make her even more miserable.

Finally, a proper understanding of the nature of mar-riage will help to resolve the antagonism which was latent in so many of the man/woman relationships that Richard-son had presented in the earlier novels and enable a woman to realize her own personal identity more fully. While men and women are *moral* equals, they are meant to assume different roles while on earth. Sir Charles says, " 'All human souls are in themselves, equal; yet the very design of the different machines in which they are inclosed, is to superinduce a temporary difference on their original equality; a difference adapted to the different purposes for which they are designed by Providence in the present transitory state. When those purposes are at an end, this difference will be at an end too. When Sex ceases, inequality of Souls will cease; and women will certainly be on a par with men, as to intellectuals, in heaven' " (V, 418). Any woman in order to maintain her distinct identity must successfully adopt the woman's role, for the sexes are distinguished, not only by their physical difference, but also by the roles they play. " 'Were it not so, their offices would be confounded, and the women would not perhaps so readily submit to those domestic ones in which it is their province to shine; and the men would be allotted the distaff, or the needle; and you yourselves, Ladies, would be the first to despise such' " (V, 415).

While marriage is, for most women, the appropriate state, Richardson would seek to dignify the position of the spinster as well. The repeated criticism of Charlotte's thoughtless pettiness on the subject of old maids is one part of Richardson's defense of the single state; and Sir Charles' elaborate plans for the institution of Protestant nunneries is another. Thus when Mrs. Reeves declares, " 'I believe in England many a poor girl goes up the hill with a companion she would little care for . . . the state of a single woman [is] here so peculiarly unprovided and helpless: For girls of slender fortunes, if they have been genteely brought up, how can they, when family-connexions are dissolved, support themselves?' " (III, 382), Grandison replies, " 'We want to see established in every county,

Protestant Nunneries; in which single women of small or no fortunes might live with all manner of freedom, under such regulations as it would be a disgrace for a modest or good woman not to comply with'" (III, 383).

If we compare this variety of alternatives to the limited notion of women's role as it was presented in *Clarissa*, we can see that a revolution of sorts has taken place. Insofar as wealth and prudence will allow, a woman is meant to be the mistress of her own fate; and she must necessarily be trained to meet with the various decisions she will be forced to make. If the woman herself is to be entrusted with the decision of choosing a way of life, then her education must prepare her for that choice. What is more, if a woman of genius is to find an appropriate husband—one whose mind will not prove substantially inferior to her own—intellect must be trained to recognize a like intelligence. Learning in and of itself is little use to her; but learning directed toward the end of making her better able to fulfill her usual obligations is not only justified but necessary.

This particular problem in the life of the gifted eighteenth-century woman is one which apparently interested Richardson greatly, and lengthy discussions of it may be found throughout the correspondence. "Learning in women," he says to Lady Bradshaigh, "may be either rightly or wrongly placed, according to the uses made of it by them. And if the sex is to be brought up with a view to make the individuals of it inferior in knowledge to the husbands they might happen to have, not knowing who those husbands are . . . it would be best to keep them from writing and reading, and even from the knowledge of the common idioms of speech. . . . If a woman has genius, let it take its course, as well as in men; provided she neglect not anything that is more peculiarly her province. If she has good sense, she will not make the man she chuses, who wants her knowledge, uneasy, nor despise him for that want."[15] The same sentiments may be found in the definition of the feminine role which is presented in *Grandison*.

A woman's primary moral choice thus lies in the selection of a way of life. Her new freedom endows her with the right of self-determination: she may marry or not, as she wills; and if she does marry, she may select a man whose nature appears most compatible with her own particular gifts and temperament. In these areas she is to employ her discretion; in this respect she is to be free from coercion. However, a woman was obliged to have her duty to God and society always before her when making the decision by which she determined her way of life; and once she had chosen a vocation, her behavior was to be governed by the restrictions attendant upon her station. A woman might be free to choose a husband for herself. Once having chosen him, she would not be free to leave him or bully him or disobey him. Education was to function as a way of training a woman's judgment and making her more adept in setting a suitable pattern for her life. Ideally, it would serve to enhance her womanly roles by permitting her to undertake them more rationally and to fulfill them with greater success.

The tone and style of the last novel reveal a sense of satisfaction. There are no tortured journeys inward, no attempts to probe the soul in order to discover order and truth. Instead, man's identity is defined in terms of his confident and successful interactions with others. Thus whereas we learned about Clarissa by way of lengthy, unselfconscious monologues whose function was not so much to convey information as to explore the endlessly complex variations of her own reactions to the world, in *Grandison* we discover character through dialogue and gesture.[16] Many of the scenes are brilliant rapier plays in which individual identity is neatly described by words and sentences which rasp against each other in stylized combat. Frequently the form of the novel falls into a dialogue pattern, with Richardson giving only the names of the characters and the speeches that they utter;[17] and much of the novel must clearly have been envisioned by him as a play: the protagonists are seen by the reader exactly as they see each other—with no intervening intelligence to direct our attention. Thus, for instance, in this angry interchange between Lady G. and her husband, the mood, the beliefs of the characters, and even their feelings about each other are conveyed through dialogue only—in the choice of words and in the irregular, quite natural pattern of speech.

> *Lord G.* You see, you see, the air, Miss Byron!—How ludicrously does she now, even now—
> *Lady G.* See Miss Byron!—How captious!—Lord G. ought to have a termagant wife: One who could return rage for rage. Meekness is *my* crime.—I cannot be put out of temper.—Meekness was never before attributed to woman as a fault.
> *Lord G.* Good God!—Meekness!—Good God!
> *Lady G.* But, Harriet, do you judge on which side the grievance lies. Lord G. presents me with a face for his, that I never saw him wear before marriage: He has cheated me, therefore, I shew him the same face that I ever wore, and treat him pretty much in the same manner (or am I mistaken) that I ever did: And what reason can he give, that will not demonstrate him to be the most ungrateful of men, for the airs he gives himself? Airs that he would not have presumed to put on eight days ago. Who then, Harriet, has reason to complain of grievance; my Lord, or I?
> *Lord G.* You see, Miss Byron—Can there be any arguing with a woman who knows herself to be in jest, in all she says?

> (IV, 34-35)

There is no need for further explanation: the taunting, superior wife, who assumes specious airs of humility and righteousness; the tormented, exasperated husband, who has employed both kindness and anger to no avail. They are revealed for what they are, and revealed entirely by their public manner.

Other elements in the novel reinforce Richardson's implicit assertion that society is now an adequate medium for the definition and expression of individual personality. Gesture becomes important: Mr. Fowler's pulling out his handkerchief is an occasion for Harriet's pity, while Charlotte's nervous fidgeting with a fan displays her impatient selfishness. We have spoken of the significance of clothes and of the precise use of language; these too are public methods of ascertaining character. Finally, the frequency with which Richardson implants set essays into the novel (usually by putting them into the mouth of Grandison or Dr. Bartlett) conveys with the greatest air of complacency his belief that merely to learn the clear and unequivocal truth about the world from the lips of an earnest and moral man is all one needs to be both good and happy.

Inevitably, perhaps, the novel begins to assume a somewhat fatuous air; no one could ever be completely sure of himself and unvaryingly correct about others. This fault results, partly, merely from Richardson's lapses as a novelist; for while his rendering of dialogue is frequently brilliant, his conception of the ideal man and the society in which he lives is insufferably priggish and self-satisfied.

Not all of the faults, however, can be laid at Richardson's door, for some of them inhere in the literary technique of social realism itself. Whenever we characterize an individual primarily in terms of his relationships with others—that is, in terms of his social roles—we are making the implicit assumption that there are meaningful, clearly defined social roles which he may adopt. Thus, when Mrs. Shirley deems Sir Charles worthy of Harriet because he has proven himself " 'to be the best of brothers, friends, landlords, masters, and the bravest and best of men' " (I, 364),

CHAPTER VIII

Conclusion

Richardson's use of Puritan modes of characterization had a number of advantages: most obviously, they were ways of thinking about character, ways of presenting a character in literature, which would have been familiar to most of his audience, both dissenter and Anglican. They would have carried an air of authenticity and credibility; in short, they would have considerably reinforced his realistic intention. Moreover, they were ideally suited to his purpose. Any serious uncertainty about one's "social" role (whether the society be a religious or a non-religious one) produces a morbid self-consciousness which can be relieved only by gaining a secure definition of one's relationship to others. Stated in this formulaic way, the problems faced by Richardson's characters and those confronting the Puritan a century earlier were analogous; and the same literary methods could properly be used to depict both.

Richardson was, however, clearly forced to go beyond his literary sources; and because his characters faced worldly rather than religious quandaries, he almost always moved in the direction of secularizing. His aim, expressed in different ways throughout the novels, was always to discover an ethic which could prove useful and practical to a secular reading public.

He is most notorious in *Pamela*, for his sensational treatment of the sin of lust and for his unfortunate equations of goodness with virginity and of blessedness with money. *Clarissa* is, in its rendering of character, most similar to the religous sources; and though Clarissa's dilemma results from social change, it is a genuinely moral one which is resolved in the traditional Christian manner. Even here, however, there are additions: the rather extensive role played by Lovelace (though it has precedent in such stock figures as Mr. Badman) converts the isolated monologue of diarist into a kind of dialogue or counterpoint. What is more, the conflict between Clarissa and Lovelace has many of the elements of the drama, and Richardson's deliberate use of this public mode of characterizing his heroine creates significant departures from the Puritan model. There is, for example, an enormously skillful manipulation of dialogue (certainly more conversation is recorded in *Clarissa* than would ever appear in a diary); and although Clarissa frequently discovers her own real motives only after she has recorded the conversations and reflected upon them, there is a union here of introspection and public behavior which serves to define crisis at least partially in terms of social dilemmas. As we have seen earlier, Richardson seems to have been unwilling to conclude his novel with Clarissa's death and the religious eulogy which he so clearly felt she deserved. He would, instead, have her public significance more universally recognized.

This need to render personal problems in socially significant ways is fully realized in *Grandison*, where Sir Charles' virtue is expressed in terms of public service, his nature in terms of social roles. *Clarissa* was an analytical novel: the heroine had to define both the nature of her problem and a solution to it by an examination of motivation. *Grandison*, on the other hand, is normative. We are less concerned to know *why* a person behaves improperly than we are simply to discover the fact that he has erred; and once the violation of propriety has been identified, we are led to assume that a "good" character is one who is capable of reforming his behavior and willing to do so.[1] In other words, *Grandison*, like other novels of manners, accepts the validity of social norms and uses them as adequate indices of moral behavior.

Clearly this is an enormous step away from the specifically religious intention of the *Saint's Life*, and in making this final secularizing move, Richardson is forced to work out many social problems which the "worldly" image of the Saint had left unresolved. Thus as we have seen, he examines the moral significance of money and of social status; he dissects the social, intellectual, and moral ambiguity of women's roles and accords women a remarkable new freedom; he makes a genuine effort to understand the specifically "masculine" and "feminine" quality of many social roles, almost completely rejecting the sado-masochistic stereotypes that had dominated the first two novels. The private, moral dilemmas in both *Pamela* and *Clarissa* had originated in social change; Grandison not only explores the implications of that social change, but develops a literary mode for rendering the successful conclusion of it.

Some of the faults of *Grandison* result from Richardson's increasing desire to provide socially viable answers to moral questions. They are faults endemic to the novel of manners (even Austen is faulted by many for her acceptance of the narrow confines of English provincial society). There is always the danger that such a work may become excessively conservative and complacent in its acceptance of social values.[2] It is perhaps for this reason that many of the best novelists of manners are led eventually to question the very assumptions that have formed the basis for their work—as Jane Austen does in *Persuasion* or Howells does in *A Modern Instance.*

Richardson's work exercised an enormous influence on the popular novel in England during the latter half of the eighteenth century; however none of his immediate successors even attempted the kind of psychological exploration that had distinguished *Clarissa*. The greatness of *Clarissa*, and, to a lesser extent, the compelling quality of *Pamela* depend upon their understanding of the problems of an age in transition. In the midst of this change the most unlikely person imaginable, a portly, middle-aged printer transferred onto paper what he saw, what he heard, and perhaps what he himself felt. The quality of Richardson's work stems from his own quick eye and faithful pen and from his unwavering allegiance to the realism of personal crisis. And when the momentous social struggle was resolved, when the rigor and strength of the Puritan movement collapsed at last, shuddering into itself and leaving only a legacy of repression, diligence in calling, and self-righteous hypocrisy to mark its passing, the struggle that had fed Richardson's imagination is once and forever gone. Significantly, then, of all those who attempted to follow in the great author's footsteps, not one (at least in England) set out to emulate the psychological exploration of *Clarissa*.

The two greatest disciples of the Richardsonian tradition in England are Sterne and Austen, and both of these were primarily influenced by *Grandison*. In Sterne's work we find the implications of the sentimental dogma expounded at length; the full force of emotion is portrayed here (as it was not in *Grandison*), and the futile, self-defeating circularity of such a moral code is revealed in all its pathos and comic tragedy. To do good, Sterne would say, we must *feel deeply*; but when we feel deeply, the very profundity of our emotion paralyzes us and prevents us from any action. Such is man's inevitable and impossible position in life. Jane Austen draws on Richardson's skill as a novelist of manners; and many of the techniques which we saw tentatively and experimentally used by Richardson in portraying his characters are adopted by Austen, developed and expanded in her work.

Other, lesser imitators of Richardson merely picked over the most obvious and external elements of his novels. Novels of abduction and rape abounded, as did novels about penitent runaway daughters. Mackenzie's *Julia de Roubigne* and *Man of the World* are perhaps the best known of these lesser novels, although for every one which is known to the eighteenth-century scholar, there are literally dozens and dozens which have been mercifully lost.[3] The image of the good man as portrayed by Sir Charles Grandison is perpetuated in such dull fiction as Jenner's *Placid Man*, and the cult of weeping which had begun in earnest with Harriet Byron and the Grandison girls is kept alive by hundreds of sensitive heroes and heroines for whom the merest falling of a flower is sufficient to start a gentle tear or two. Few, very few of these novels go beyond the most superficial rendering of character and society. The tradition of psychological realism which had its origin with *Clarissa* was condemned to lie dormant, waiting, perhaps for the social revolutions of the nineteenth and twentieth centuries which once again drove men to seek to discover within themselves a new identity with which to give their lives meaning.

NOTES

NOTES TO CHAPTER I

1. William Sale has described Richardson's debt to Puritanism in more symbolic terms, citing elements in the novels which represent class struggle. "We know that Richardson's characters and incidents were effective symbols for his contemporaries," Sale says. "This fact is attested by the avidity with which they were seized upon. He was providing new insights. He was realizing for his generation the emotions engendered by the conditions of life that defined his generation's hopes and that set limitations upon the fulfillment of those hopes . . . The Harlowes, if you will, are essentially London middle-class tradesmen with the tradesman's narrowness of soul and smallness of mind . . . Lovelace moves in a world of larger freedoms, of wider spaces." William Sale, "From Pamela to Clarissa," in *The Age of Johnson* (New Haven, 1949), 129, 134, 135.

2. R. H. Tawney, *Religion and the Rise of Capitalism* (New York, 1948), 165.

3. E. N. Williams, "Our Merchants are Princes: The English Middle-Classes in the Eighteenth Century," in *History Today*, XII (1962), 549.

4. *Ibid.*, 553-554.

5. For examples see Philip Dodderidge's *Sermons to Young Persons* or Isaac Watts' *Catechism Composed for Children and Youth and Prayers Composed for the Use and Imitation of Children.*

6. Some of the following books can expand the very simple outlines given here. Charles H. Cooley, *Social Organization* (Glencoe, Illinois, 1956). Erik Erikson, *Childhood and Society* (New York, 1963), *Identity, Youth, and Crisis* (New York, 1968), *Young Man Luther* (New York, 1958). Erving Goffman, *The Presentation of Self in Everyday Life* (New York, 1959). George Herbert Mead, *Mind, Self, and Society* (Chicago, 1937). The works by Erikson are especially helpful.

7. Erikson, *Identity, Youth and Crisis*, 23.

8. *Ibid.*, 16.

9. *Ibid.*, 165.

10. *Ibid.*, 23.

11. It has often been noted that the writing of a diary is com.non among adolescents, who are experiencing a normal period of identity crisis.

12. Almost certainly, Richardson published these manuals—see William Sale, *Samuel Richardson: Master Printer* (Ithaca, N.Y., 1950), 162-63.

13. Daniel Defoe, *The Family Instructor* (London, 1809), 5-6.

14. *Ibid.*, 16.

15. *Ibid.*

16. *Ibid.*, 29.

17. *Ibid.*, 59.

18. Daniel Defoe, *Religious Courtship* (London, 1742), 143.

NOTES TO CHAPTER II

1. Erickson, *Identity, Youth, and Crisis*, 210-211.

2. A number of critics have seen Richardson's link to the Puritan tradition. See Alan Dugald McKillop, *Samuel Richardson: Printer and Novelist* (Chapel Hill, 1936), 127, 134-135; Ian Watt, *The Rise of the Novel* (Berkeley, 1959), 167; and William Sale, "From Pamela to Clarissa" in *The Age of Johnson* (New Haven, 1949), 127-139. However, none have attempted to trace the effect of this indebtedness on his creation of character.

3. These may be traced more completely in: Cynthia Griffin Wolff, "Literary Reflections of the Puritan Character," *JHI*, XXIX, No. 1 (January-March, 1968).

4. Q. D. Leavis, *Fiction and the Reading Public* (London, 1939), 110.

5. Robert Bolton, *Some General Directions for a Comfortable Walking with God* (London, 1625), 25-26. Because of the irregularities in spelling and punctuation, both have been modernized in quotation from all seventeenth-century manuals and all manuscript material.

6. F. G., *The Groans of the Spirit* (Oxford, 1639), 197.

7. R. S. Sibbes, *The Bruised Reed and Smoking Flax* (London, 1635), 40.

8. Lewis Bayly, *The Practice of Piety* (London, 1792), 97-98.

9. Certainly we must at least allow the possibility that when Samuel Johnson cites "Knowledge of the human heart" as Richardson's greatest achievement, he was employing a phrase which had more to do with this Puritan concept of self-examination than with the kind of emotionalism that one might find in the heroic epistle or the French Romance.

10. Arthur Dent, *The Plaine Man's Pathway to Heaven* (London, 1610), 10.

11. Bolton, *General Directions*, 35.

12. All quotations from Richardson's novels are taken from the Shakespeare Head Edition (Oxford, 1930). They are cited in the text by volume and page number, and the title of the novel is cited only in cases which might be ambiguous. Single quotes have been added to indicate dialogue within the passages quoted here.

13. Most of Richardson's audience would have been familiar with these practices and with at least some of the manuals that urged self-examination, even if they were not dissenters. After all, Richardson's casual reference to Bayly's *Practice of Piety* in *Clarissa* indicates it as a book that any reader should know.

14. William Perkins, *A Golden Chain* (London, 1592), 84.

15. William Haller, *The Rise of Puritanism* (New York, 1936), 41-42.

16. Richard Rogers, *Diary* in *Two Elizabethan Diaries*, ed. M. M. Knappen (Chicago, 1933), 67.

17. Owen Stockton, *Diary*, Ms., Dr. William's Library, London, 3-4.

18. Elias Pledger, *Diary*, Ms., Dr. William's Library, London, 29.

19. *Ibid.*, 26.

20. Bayly, *The Practice of Piety*, 61.

21. Richard Bernard, *Ruth Recompense* (London, 1865), 33-34, 78-79.

22. Thomas Gouge, *Christian Directions* (London, 1742), 96.

23. Katherine Hornbeak, "Richardson's *Familiar Letters* and the Domestic Conduct Books," *Smith College Studies in Modern Languages*, XIX, no. 2 (January, 1938), 1.

24. *Ibid.*, 5. A number of recent scholars have perceived the importance of the moral or religious intention in Richardson's work. John A. Dussinger has written several essays on the subject—most notably "Conscience and the Pattern of Christian Perfection in Clarissa," *PMLA*, LXXXI (1966), 236-45 and "Richardson's 'Christian Vocation,' " *Papers in Language and Literature*, III (1967), 3-19. Dussinger confirms Hornbeak's earlier observations to the effect that Richardson infuses an essentially moral intention into what appears to be a secular form of literature. However, he stresses the doctrinal *intention*, without tracing (as we shall do) the implications of this doctrine in the creation of character. Nevertheless, his conclusions are in no way inconsistent with the ones we shall draw. Indeed, he concludes one of the essays cited by remarking, "His psychological realism, praised by critics as an achievement often surpassing his conscious intentions, may perhaps be understood in the context of his introspective Anglican religion, which traditionally stressed the authority of conscience and the burdens of following Christ's example" ("Conscience and the Pattern of Christian Perfection in Clarissa," 245).

25. Samuel Richardson, *Selected Letters of Samuel Richardson*, ed. John Carroll (Oxford, 1964), 116-17.

26. Philip Dodderidge, *Diary* in *Works*, ed. John Dodderidge Humphreys, Vol. V (London, 1831), 270, 278, 298, 310, 330-331.

27. Rogers, *Diary*, 59.

28. Henry Newcome, *Diary*, ed. Thomas Heywood (Manchester, 1849), 45.

29. Anon. (Oliver Cromwell's Cousin), *Diary* in *Atheriae Cantabrigienses with Miscellanies*, Copy made by Rev. Wm. Cole. fols. 215-221, 412.

30. Philip Henry, *Diaries and Letters*, ed. Matthew Henry Lee (London, 1882), 32.

31. *Ibid.*, 173.

32. Isaac Watts, *Prayers Composed for the Use and Instruction of Children* (London, 1728), 66.

33. Newcome, *Diary*, 9.

34. Anon. (Oliver Cromwell's Cousin), *Diary*, fols. 215-221, 412.

35. Henry, *Diary*, 169.

36. Oliver Heywood, *His Autobiography, Diary, and Letters*, ed. J. Horsfall Turner (London, 1882), I, 233.

37. *Ibid.*

38. We might wonder why, if Richardson really intended to exploit the missives *as letters*, he did not contrive to have them exchanged between the lovers—Pamela and Mr. B., Clarissa and Lovelace. There was ample precedent for this in the epistolary tradition; Hughes' "translation" of the Heloise/Abelard correspondence was probably the most famous eighteenth-century piece of letter-fiction.

39. Anthony Kearney has observed an interesting literary parallel. He sees Clarissa's need to write as one element in her struggle against the isolating captivity into which Lovelace has thrust her. Gradually, the letter-writing becomes a means for preserving sanity. "While her situation grows steadily worse, she preserves her essential self by persisting in a regard for standards that weaker persons would throw aside under similar circumstances. In epistolary terms, each of her letters, though dramatically speaking an appeal, bears the stylistic stamp of something basically moral and enduring, "*Clarissa* and the Epistolary Form," *Essays in Criticism*, XVI (1966), 53. Kearney is not, of course, making the same psychological point that we are making; however, the observation certainly supports the claim that Clarissa's letter-journal is an enduring embodiment of self which eventually serves to prevent disruption of identity.

40. G. A. Starr in *Defoe and Spiritual Autobiography* (Princeton, 1965) has demonstrated the extent of this earlier novelist's debt to the tradition of which we are speaking.

41. The only extensive collection of autobiographies of this sort is *Spiritual Experiences of Sundry Believers*, edited by Henry Walker (London, 1652).

42. Interestingly, Roger Sharrock sees a clear link between *Pamela* and the "realistic" literary methods which can be found in the gospels. "The Gospels, surely the most influential books in the whole Western cultural tradition, deal with the common life, the lives of soldiers, harlots and tax collectors, and the sufferings of the sick: all these provide a backcloth for the Incarnation. And the method of presentation is a fine example of formal realism, especially in a less literary gospel, St. Mark rather than St. Luke." See "Richardson's *Pamela*: The Gospel and the Novel," *Durham University Journal*, new ser., XXVII (1966), 70. However, Sharrock sees this debt in terms of what one might call the mythic

or parable elements in the novel. "There is a line of development running from Bunyan's *Life and Death of Mr. Badman* through Defoe to Richardson. The Puritan didactic concern with right conduct in a trading society grows increasingly more secularized once the heroic age of separatism and persecution has passed away. The larger view is worth taking because it introduces us to some of the deeper excitements in Richardson which transcend his bourgeois background. It enables us to see how the effort towards a gospel of realism affects the whole aesthetic of the novel, the manner in which it accepts historical time, the whole gamut of suffering life, not specially selected, stoically wonderful snippets, as in drama and epic, the transcendence of mean detail and humble character. . . . When he forgets his exemplary moral attitude, then all is well: he is possessed by the myth he has created" (72). Of course, much eighteenth-century *commentary* on the gospels took precisely the form of drawing elaborate moral lessons from them—making their characters exemplary. Thus the mixture of "realism" and exemplary intentions in *Pamela*, which Sharrock so rightly deplores, was a combination that would have seemed familiar to Richardson and his audience (Farmer Andrews' comments about Pamela and the *Book of Ruth* suggest the naturalness of such a coupling).

43. John Bunyan, *Pilgrim's Progress*, ed. J. B. Wharey (Oxford, 1928), 172.

44. John Milton, *The Ready and Easy Way to Establish a Free Commonwealth*, in *Prose Writings*, ed. K. M. Burton (New York, 1958), 225.

45. John Winthrop, *A Model of Christian Charity*, in *The American Puritans*, ed. Perry Miller (New York, 1956), 83.

46. It is an interesting idiosyncrasy of the Puritans that when they discussed evil they tended to speak of the *inner* life (the diary, which is designed to search out evil is essentially introspective), and yet when they talk about goodness they tend to perceive it as a *social* characteristic.

47. Samuel Clarke, *The Lives of Thirty-two English Divines* (London, 1677), 420.

48. John Chorlton, *The Glorious Reward of Faithful Ministers* (London, 1696), 26.

49. *Ibid.*

50. *Ibid.*, 26-27. The Italics are Chorlton's.

51. *Ibid.*, 27.

52. Newcome, *Diary*, 9.

53. Clarke, *Lives*, 420.

54. In *The Rise of the Novel* (Berkeley, 1959), Ian Watt has observed the connection we are about to assert. "The later part of *Clarissa*, in fact, belongs to a long tradition of funeral literature" (p. 167). However, he has drawn no inferences from this fact.

55. See *Clarissa* (V, 478). If Clarissa was accustomed to this activity and ceased it during her ordeal (as she evidently did), then the diaristic use to which she puts her letters is psychologically understandable.

56. Samuel Richardson, *Selected Letters*, ed. John Carroll (Oxford, 1964),

57. See Starr, *Defoe and Spiritual Autobiography*.

58. See Frank Gees Black, "The Continuations of *Pamela*," *RAA*, XIII (1936), 499-507 and Bernard Kreissman, *Pamela-Shamela* in *University of Nebraska Studies*, No. 22 (May, 1960). The imitation to which I refer is *Pamela in High Life or Virtue Rewarded* (1741), printed for Mary Kingman.

NOTES TO CHAPTER III

1. *Pamela* is very much like *Jane Eyre* in this respect.

2. Perhaps this was the reason so many eighteenth-century readers steadfastly refused to acknowledge that the work was a novel.

3. See Simon O. Lesser, "A Note on *Pamela*," College English, XIV (1952), 13-17.

4. This is not to claim that Richardson was employing (either consciously or unconsciously) the highly complex structure of the Puritan autobiography as Defoe does in *Moll Flanders* (see G. A. Starr's *Defoe and Spiritual Autobiography*). Rather one might say that Richardson's conception of character in Pamela draws heavily on that notion of exemplum which may be found in the Puritan autobiography.

5. Samuel Richardson, *Selected Letters*, ed. John Carroll (Oxford, 1964), p. 47.

NOTES TO CHAPTER IV

1. See M. Kinkead-Weekes, "*Clarissa* Restored?" *RES*, new series, X (1959), 156-71.

2. M. G. Jones, *The Charity School Movement* (London, 1964), 98-99.

3. *The Whole Duty of Man* (London, 1676), 300.

4. Thomas Gouge, *Christian Directions* (London, 1742), 108-109.

5. *The Whole Duty of Man*, 280.

6. Gouge, *Christian Directions*, 120.

7. Samuel Richardson, *Correspondence*, ed. Anna Laetitia Barbauld, in six volumes (London, 1804), II, 216-218 and 302-306; VI, 128-248.

8. *Ibid.*, VI, 130.

9. Gouge, *Christian Directions*, 107.

10. *The Whole Duty of Man*, 292.

11. Richardson, *Correspondence*, ed. Barbauld, II, 217.

12. Gouge, *Christian Directions*, 120.

13. Richardson, *Correspondence*, ed. Barbauld, V, 263.

14. No summary of Miss Howe's description of Clarissa can be as illuminating as a full perusal of the pertinent letter (VIII, 217-247); however, perhaps a brief list of some of her observations can give the reader an idea of how completely Richardson's realization of his heroine coincides with the notion of Puritan character which we described earlier. Miss Howe quotes Clarissa as saying that " 'The darkest and most contemptible ignorance is that of not knowing one's self; and that all we have, and all we excel in, is the gift of God' " (VIII, 219). Clarissa criticizes an elaborate literary style and authors who "spangle over their production with *metaphors* . . . tumble into *bombast*; The sublime, with them, lying in *words* and not in *sentiment*" (VIII, 224); and she contrasts to this the plain style of learned divines. She disapproves of gaming and never plays at cards. "She was extremely moderate in her diet. '*Quantity* in food,' she used to say, 'was more to be regarded than *quality*: That a full meal was the great enemy both to study and industry: That a well-built house required but little repairs.' " (VIII, 236). Indeed, the needs of the body were seemingly always under control; "For REST she alloted SIX hours only" (VIII, 240). And "she was of opinion 'that no one could spend their time properly, who did not live by some Rule: Who did not appropriate the hours, as near as might be, to particular purposes and employments' " (VIII, 240). Accordingly, she adhered to a rigorous schedule

which governed all activities during her waking hours. And finally, in the manner of a truly devout Puritan, she kept a diary or account book of her life. "For she used indulgently to say, 'I do not think ALL I do necessary for another to do: Not even for myself: But when it is more pleasant to me to keep such an account, than to let it alone; why may I not proceed in my superogatories?—There can be no harm in it. It keeps up my attention to accounts. . . . Those who will not keep a *strict* account, seldom long keep *any*. . . . It teaches me to be covetous of Time; the only thing of which we can be allowably covetous; since we live but once in this world; and when gone, are gone from it for ever' " (VIII, 244-245).

15. *The Whole Duty of Man*, 279.

16. Christopher Hill, "Clarissa Harlowe and her Times," *Essays in Criticism*, V (1955), 315-340.

17. *Ibid.*, 321.

18. The violence of the reaction against the popular masquerade in all serious writing of this period might well be seen as a natural outgrowth of the increased problem of gaining knowledge and insight into the true nature of a man. In the first place, the masquerade deliberately mingled many classes and many types of people, without regard for differences of upbringing or belief (Sally Martin, the mercer's daughter who ends a sad harlot at Mrs. Sinclair's met Lovelace, her first seducer, at a masquerade). Furthermore, the very object of the masquerade is to *disguise*, not reveal, true identity. A generation whose moral concerns were intimately bound up with problems of self-definition and definition of others would scarcely approve of such a procedure.

19. H. J. Habakkuk, "Marriage Settlements in the 18th Century," *Transactions of Royal Historical Society*, XXXII (1950), 15-31.

20. *Ibid.*, 18.

21. Hill, "Clarissa Harlowe and her Times," 315.

NOTES TO CHAPTER V

1. Richardson, *Selected Letters*, ed. Carroll, 94.

2. *Ibid.*, 122.

3. John Bunyan, *Grace Abounding* and *The Life and Death of Mr. Badman* (London, 1956), Preface to *Mr. Badman*.

4. Gilbert Burnet, *Life and Death of the Right Honourable John, Earl of Rochester* (London, 1680), Preface.

5. In *Mr. Badman* this inability to bear governing takes many forms: as a child Badman is compulsively disobedient; his good-hearted parent bewails the son's sinfulness, "but all was one to his graceless son, neither wholesome counsel, nor fatherly sorrow, would make him mend his manners" (*Mr. Badman*, 172). When he is old enough to be apprenticed, he runs away; when he is finally married, he cannot adhere to the marriage contract; indeed, his life is a model of misrule.

6. Burnet notes much the same love of word-wit in Rochester (who was, after all, famous for it), and links it to depravity. See *Life*, 15-16.

7. Again in Burnet's *Life of Rochester:* "He took pleasure to disguise himself, as a *Porter*, or as a *Beggar*; sometimes to follow some mean Amours, which, for the variety of them, he affected. At other times, merely for diversion, he would go about in odd shapes, in which he acted his part so naturally, that even those who were on the secret, and saw him in these shapes, could perceive nothing by which he might be discovered" (*Life of Rochester*, 27-28).

8. We would not wish to give undue stress to the similarities between Richardson's characterization of Lovelace and Milton's of Satan; however, it is undeniable that the two do have a great deal in common. This speech of Lovelace's, for instance, cannot fail to remind one of Milton's description of the fallen angels, swelled with pride and changing shape in a throbbing loss of identity. "For Spirits when they please/ Can either Sex assume, or both; so soft/ And uncompounded is their Essence pure,/ Not ti'd or manacl'd with joynt or limb,/ Nor founded on the brittle strength of bones,/ Like cumbrous flesh; but in what shape they choose/ Dilated or condens't, bright or obscure,/ Can execute their aerie purposes,/ And works of love or enmity fulfill." (*Paradise Lost*, Bk. I, 423-430). The pride of Satan, too may be compared with Richardson's insistence on Lovelace's pride—as may be the splendor of his strength and the cunning of his stratagems. Richardson was quite familiar with Milton's work; he frequently mentions it in his correspondence—always with great admiration. After all, what better source for an example of great religious conflict could he have found than this Puritan rendition of the struggle between good and evil?

A number of commentators have pointed out Richardson's debt to Milton. See F. W. Hilles, "The Plan of Clarissa," *PQ* XLV (1966), 244; Gillian Beer, "Richardson, Milton, and the Status of Evil," *RES*, new ser., XIX (1968), 261-270; and Allan Wendt, "Clarissa's Coffin," *PQ*, XXXIX (1960), 493. Of these, Gillian Beer specifically remarks Lovelace's love of disguise, although she does not go on to draw a psychological conclusion.

9. In *Mr. Badman* we get a poignant picture of what happens to the unfortunate woman who does attempt to enter into marriage contract with such a lost soul. "Her harms may be an advantage to others that will learn to take heed thereby, but for herself, she must take what follows, even such a life now as Mr. Badman her husband will lead her . . . evils came on apace . . . it was but a little while after he was married, but he hangs his religion upon the hedge . . . he would be religious no longer. . . . [He] began to show himself in his old shape, a base, wicked, debauched fellow. . . . Sometimes also he would bring his punks home to his house, and woe be to his wife when they were gone if she did not entertain them with all varieties possible, and also carry it lovingly to them. . . . Now she scarce durst go to an honest neighbour's house, or have a good book in her hand" (*Mr. Badman*, 204-206). Such marriages are, finally, unlawful and unnatural. "Will the sheep couple with a dog, the partridge with a crow, or the pheasant with an owl? No. . . . Man only is most subject to wink at, and allow of these unlawful mixtures of men and women. . . . What fellowship? what concord? what agreement? what communion can there be in such marriages?" (*Mr. Badman*, 209-210). In the final analysis, Badman's wife must reject him if she is to save her own soul, and the speech in which she does so is not unlike Clarissa's rejection of Lovelace. " 'I have a husband, but also a soul, and my soul ought to be more unto me than all the world besides. This soul of mine I will look after, care for, and, if I can, provide it a heaven for its habitation. You are commanded to love me, as you love your own body, and so do I love you; but I tell you true, I prefer my soul before all the world, and its salvation I will seek' (Eph. v. 28)" (*Mr. Badman*, 214).

10. Clearly this picture of jailhouse glory is drawn from the rogue biographies and earlier characterizations of such "worthies" as Jonathan Wild. The moral disorder of such a notion of heroism is explicit in Gay's satire, *The Beggar's Opera*, and later in Fielding's *Jonathan Wild*. Certainly Richardson is attempting to underline the moral chaos here in Lovelace's fantasy. Indeed, the deliberate debasement of the demonic hero-villain is typical of bourgeois standards in the mid-eighteenth century, and the treatment of Rowe's Lothario might serve as a model of the middle-class attitude toward the selfish noble villain. Despite Richardson's conscious efforts to make his villain despicable in the eyes of his readers, however, Lovelace remained a figure of fascination even to those whose publicly avowed moral beliefs would have seemed to militate against such an attitude. Thus the reading audience was virtually unanimous in calling for an eventual marriage between Clarissa and her seducer.

11. Again, anyone familiar with Puritan notions of disorder and of the perverted nature of the fallen angels will see their resemblances to

the characteristics of Lovelace's nature. Milton's Satan was mistakenly seen as magnificent and heroic in the daring of his rebellion; in the same way, Richardson's portrayal of Lovelace is frequently interpreted as flattering. Yet both figures exhibit the same self-deluding pride and swollen conceit, and both ultimately fall because of their inability to understand either themselves or the world around them.

12. The only critic to give any extended examination of Richardson's notion of punctilio is Morris Golden, *Richardson's Characters* (Michigan, 1963); and he sees this break down as part of a more direct form of emotional communication.

13. In *Pamela* we were never sure of the accuracy of the heroine's anxious anticipations concerning Mr. B.; her behavior is provocative, and it is at least possible that Mr. B. is responding to this subtle enticement rather than initiating evil. Here the division of moral responsbility is beautifully articulated: Lovelace's inherent lack of moral structure makes it improbable that he could ever respond appropriately; Clarissa's failure to perceive this anarchy of the soul is a sign of her own moral blindness; her prideful habits prove the final blow to any hope of capitulation, serving instead merely to irritate Lovelace's unstable moral balance.

14. Even here, after the flight has become an irrevocable fact, Clarissa continues to refer her behavior to her father's judgment—seeing him still as the seat of authority. Her obsession with the father can, of course, be seen in the religious terms in which Richardson certainly intended it. However, the psychological impropriety of such an obsession might well reflect the limitations of this religious system. Goodness and order are always seen by Clarissa in terms of being under or having remained under her father's roof and her father's control. Significantly, even in her last deceptive note to Lovelace, she speaks of going to heaven as "returning to my Father's house." Perhaps this clearly sexual fixation may be explained as a return to an earlier and more successful relationship after the alliance with Lovelace proved unsatisfactory. However, it seems more probable that Clarissa's ties with her father were sufficiently close to prevent her from ever (under any circumstances) moving on to an intimate relationship with a man her own age, and her consistent resolutions to remain single would support this assumption. Insofar as the moral system fostered this *continuing* domination by the father, it would prevent any normal rebellion and any normal sexual relationship with another man; and the only viable response to such a system would be the repression of the healthy sexual drive (which was, of course, the Puritan answer). Clarissa's final reward—going to her father's (i.e. God's house)—rather than remaining in the world to make do with human, contemporary substitutes, might suggest

that she never did completely resolve the problem of her own sexuality and that her 'triumph', if viewed in strictly psychological terms, is less than complete.

15. Richardson, *Correspondence*, ed. Barbauld, III, 181.

16. *Ibid.*, 183-184.

17. *Ibid.*

18. Perhaps the simplest explanation for this transformation might be the following. We know from Anna Howe's biography that Clarissa normally kept a religious diary. During the period of these trials with Lovelace, it is clear that the practice was suspended; and it is during this interim that the letters serve the functions of a diary. After the rape has been accomplished and Clarissa has made her final escape, she resumes the practice of keeping a diary, and the correspondence with Anna Howe virtually ceases.

19. There are a number of image clusters that run throughout the novel, illustrating the thematic link among various incidents and pacing the course of the action. One of the most obvious is the group of images concerning sexuality, particularly the recurrent phallic symbols (scissors, knives, pens and the like) which relate obviously to Lovelace's violent intentions. Another series of images has to do with seeing; thus we find mirrors, windows, peep-holes, key-holes. This second series of images has more complex significance. In the first instance it may relate to Clarissa's task of self-discovery, her moral duty to perceive herself clearly; and it may consciously echo the injunctions of those theologians who advised the pious Christian to keep a diary so that he might see himself "as in a mirror." In the second place, it probably relates to Lovelace's incessant spying. Both of these image-patterns have been observed by Richardson's critics (Dorothy Van Ghent, for example, has commented on both of them); however, there is a third series of images which serves to tie the first two together. We might designate these as images of penetration. On the one hand there is intrusion: eaves-dropping, bursting open of doors or strong-boxes; sexual violation; and the attempt to manipulate or control another's identity. On the other hand there is a closing in—the defense *against* intrusion:hidden communication, secrets; locking of doors, various modalities of closing; 'technical' chastity, which might be seen as a fear of acknowledging one's own sexual desires; and all those images which relate to maintaining integrity (of self, of moral standards). At the beginning of the novel Clarissa has a coherent and workable pattern of life; it is, however, a pattern which permits the existence of certain serious character deficiencies—pride and unacknowledged sexuality are the most notable. Clarissa's moral/psychological task is the rectifying of

her life so that she can acknowledge and correct these hidden flaws. The progress of her journey may be traced in terms of a series of intrusions. Clarissa resists these, even as she instinctively resists self-knowledge in the very act of seeking it; they are always painful and frequently traumatic. Yet without these intrusions, Clarissa could not grow as a moral being; virtually every insight she has is preceded by an act of intrusion—her over-hearing the conversation between her father and brother, Lovelace's stealing her letters, the fire scene, the rape. We might conclude that the two more obvious patterns, the images of sexuality and those of seeing, are related to each other insofar as both can become images of intrusion and defense against intrusion.

20. We might remember the importance that Pamela's letters had in her reward, for it is only after Mr. B. has read all of them—seen her completely and artlessly revealed (so, at least, he says)—that he is moved to acknowledge his love for her.

21. It is in this way that Miss Howe and the reader see Clarissa; and this is also the way in which Clarissa comes to know herself. However, it is true that Lovelace's and Belford's knowledge of Clarissa proceeds from a quite different source.

22. In our earlier discussion of Pamela we noted that the form of the novel was more like the autobiography than the diary, for it consciously aimed at demonstrating a moral lesson in its account of personal experience and temptation. We might note here that the narrative differences between Pamela and Clarissa are precisely those which distinguish the Puritan diary from the autobiography.

NOTES TO CHAPTER VI

1. Emile Durkheim, Suicide, trans. by John A. Spaulding and George Simpson (Chicago, 1958), 209.

2. Ibid., 213.

3. Isaac Watts, A Defense Against the Temptation to Self-Murther (London, 1726), 69-70.

4. Durkheim, Suicide, 158.

5. Ibid., 159.

6. Op. Cit.

7. Ibid., 209.

8. Arthur Dent, *The Plaine Man's Pathway to Heaven* (London, 1610), 288-289.

9. Richard Baxter, *Christian Directions*, III, 217.

10. Lewis Bayly, *The Practice of Piety* (London, 1792), 75.

11. Richardson, *Correspondence*, ed. Barbauld, IH, 181.

12. The modern reader may well be inclined to view such repression as a failure rather than a genuine triumph over sin; however, we must not let the differences between our world and Clarissa's obscure the fact that this was the religiously approved method for dealing with the sinful body.

13. The importance of this problem at the particular time when Richardson wrote may be attested to by the fact that the very different attempt to solve the same dilemma is the central concern of all of Fielding's novels as well.

14. The notion of a society of the righteous is based on an analogy between a Heavenly society and an earthly one. However, the analogy is an incomplete or inaccurate one, for in a worldly community any single individual will play many meaningful roles, and it is the unique combination and realization of them which defines his identity. In a Heavenly community, however, there exists only the relationship between the Saints and God. Indeed, one important characteristic of Puritan theology was the sharp distinction it drew between the damned and the saved and the accompanying assertion that the Saints were united and made one only by virtue of their election; the Saints in Heaven would have no relationship with each other, since each man is saved by God's grace and not by his own efforts, and it therefore makes no sense to talk about degree of goodness. All Saints would be like all other Saints, and all would be equally distinguished from the damned. And even when "communities of the Saints" were established on earth—as they were in New England, for example—the relationships within those communities were based on *earthly* roles that had no heavenly counterparts.

NOTES TO CHAPTER VII

1. Richardson, *Correspondence*, ed. Barbauld, III, 168.

2. *Ibid.*, III, 169-170.

3. *Op. Cit.*

4. *Ibid.,* III, 178.

5. Samuel Richardson, *Works* in twelve volumes, ed. Sir Leslie Stephen (London, 1883), Introduction, xxxix.

6. *Ibid.,* xxxix-xi.

7. Such a notion of morality is closely tied to the discoveries about self-lessness that marked the end of Clarissa's personal struggles.

8. Haller, *The Rise of Puritanism,* 116-117.

9. Just as Richardson has adapted the image of character inherent in the Puritan Saint, so he has taken up the literary methods used to describe such characters. This use of a list of public (and private) roles is a notable example. After all, as Clarke says in the *Life of Elizabeth Wilkinson* (quoted earlier): "Such as are real saints show it in their several capacities."

10. See *Clarissa,* I, 18.

11. *Ibid.,* I, 21.

12. Richardson's most direct literary descendant is, of course, Jane Austen, whose novels of manners echo *Sir Charles Grandison* at numerous points. Because Austen chooses to portray character almost entirely in a social setting, relying on the external evidences of self as accurate indices to the inner man, we can find many of the same elements in her characterization of people that we have noted in *Grandison*. There is, for instance, the same insistence on the importance of social roles as a way of defining the complete personality, and Elizabeth Bennet's reflection upon learning of Darcy's true nature is a clear repetition of the kind of statement about character that we find throughout *Grandison*. "As a brother, a landlord, a master, she considered how many people's happiness were in his guardianship!—How much of pleasure or pain it was in his power to bestow!—How much of good or evil must be done by him" (Jane Austen, *Novels,* ed. R. W. Chapman, Vol. II [London, 1952], 250-251). Moreover, in almost all of Austen's novels we find an insistence on the normative value of public opinion as an indispensible aid to discovering the reality of individual personality. Thus when Catherine Morland allows her romantic fantasies to distort her judgment of General Tilney, Henry remonstrates by pointing out her willful disregard for the social mores which should have served as a guide to her opinions. "What have you been judging from? Remember the country and the age in which we live. Remember that we are English, that we are Christians. Consult your own understanding, your own sense of the probable, your own observation of what is passing around you—Does our education prepare us for such atrocities? Do our laws connive at

them? Could they be perpetrated without being known, in a country like this, where social and literary intercourse is on such a footing; where every man is surrounded by a neighborhood of voluntary spies, and where roads and newspapers lay every thing open?" (*Ibid.*, Vol, 197-198). To a certain extent these parallels are the product of direct indebtedness, for Austen read and re-read *Grandison*; however, the basic similarity in technique and assumption is even more closely related to the fact that both Austen and Richardson (in *Grandison*) were writing novels of social realism. Both the belief that a man's public roles will correspond to his inner personality and the faith that in a well-run society public norms and general consensus will provide a reliable guide to reality are necessary to the novel which would make meaningful observations about a man seen only in his public roles.

13. There is a curious split in the novel about this matter. Sir Charles frequently derives satisfaction from doing good (who among us doesn't); yet his moral life is most often described in terms of his doing his "duty." Frequently that duty conflicts with personal preference; he would rather marry Harriet, but will marry Clementina if he "ought." But even when it does, we feel that his talent for virtue is partly an ability to accomodate himself to, indeed to enjoy, what he must do. Thus if he had been obliged to marry Clementina, he would doubtless have derived satisfaction from the marriage. Other characters in the novel are portrayed in a more typically sentimental way: to be specific, the example of Sir Charles seems to reveal the inherent pleasure in doing good. And although virtue and duty are never divorced in the novel, the emphasis on duty is much diminished in those moral problems which do not relate directly to Sir Charles.

14. Although the various letters within the novel have been written by a wide variety of characters, Richardson does something quite new in his handling of the epistolary style—that is, he makes all of the letters available to Harriet Byron, and each letter that we see as readers of the novel is seen by her too. Some are written to her, some by her; others are transcribed in order that she might see them, and some (such as those written by Sir Charles) are collected and kept for her perusal. The reader sees the action described from many different points of view (the vantages of all the different correspondents), and Harriet Byron within the context of the novel has this same multiple insight into the action. Thus the reader's view exactly corresponds to hers, and the tendency to identify with her is correspondingly intensified.

15. Richardson, *Correspondence*, ed. Barbauld, VI, 57-59.

16. Much the same tendency may be observed in *Pamela II*, where Richardson also conceived himself to be presenting the reader with a series of practicable solutions to the problems of *Pamela* I.

17. This device had been used in the earlier novels, but never with anything approaching its frequency in *Grandison*.

NOTES TO CHAPTER VIII

1. Any number of characters in the novel experience moral crises which aptly illustrate this concern. None, however, is so striking as Clementina. In many ways her predicament is not unlike Clarissa's (though, of course, Grandison is unacceptable for entirely different reasons than Lovelace). Now the episodes having to do with Clementina take up a sizable portion of the novel and the reader is treated to a fairly sustained series of emotional scenes. Unlike Richardson's treatment of Clarissa, however, his handling of Clementina scarcely touches upon a reason for these hysterics. We are concerned principally to know two things: that she is mistaken in her behavior (never mind why or how much); and she can rectify it in the fulness of time.

2. The exception to this rule, of course, would be a satire or novel of protest designed specifically to demonstrate that accepted definitions of existing social roles are *not* sufficient.

3. J. M. S. Tompkins, *The Popular Novel in England 1770-1800* (London, 1932) gives a fuller description of this literature.

Index

animal imagery, 150-51
Apprentice's Vade Mecum, The,
7, 167, 207
Austen, Jane: her work and
Grandison, x, 187, 233, 234,
252-3; favored *Grandison,* 177
Bayly, Lewis, *The Practice of
Piety,* 18-19
Behn, Aphra, 2
Belford: affirmation of Clarissa's
goodness, 163-164; conversion
of, 172
Benevolence: as virtue, 171-72,
179-80; doctrine of, 205-06; in
Richardson's novels, 207, 210
brothel, 149-50
Bunyan, John, 18; *Grace Abounding,* ix, 42-43; *Pilgrim's Progress,* 47; Richardson's admiration for, 54
Catholics and suicide, 155
character development, Erickson's theory of, 7-9
Clarissa: as Self-Examiner, 19-20,
127-28, 132; expression of

moral superiority, 27-28, 82-
83, 113-16, 137-38; as Puritan
Saint, 29, 52-53, 162-64, 169-
70, 171-72; letters as diary,
37, 38-40, 128, 131, 133; Miss
Howe's letter to Belford as
funeral oration, 52-53; obedience and passivity, 77-79, 79-
82, 86; passion for Lovelace,
80, 95-99, 141, 143-44, 145-46;
as Virtuous Example, 85-86;
struggle for identity, 86-87,
123-34, 127, 150, 171; and family, 87-88, 93-95, 249; irony of
flight from father to Lovelace,
111-14, 121; desire for social
order, 117, 126-27; rape of,
125-26, 152, 159; protection of
writing materials and letters,
128-29, 129-31; relationship
with Anna Howe, 131-34; role
of pride, 135-36, 139-40, 159,
165-67; scorn of Lovelace, 114,
116-17, 140-41, 146, 160; sexuality, 141, 149, 153, 249-50;

PR3667
.W6   1439